A NOTE FROM RICHARD BRANSON

The biggest challenges of our time may also present the biggest opportunities. It's why we started our foundation, Virgin Unite, to bring together people and entrepreneurial ideas to create opportunities for a better world. *I Am a Girl from Africa* stands as a reminder to see large-scale injustices not as impassable, but as opportunities for action. Elizabeth Nyamayaro recounts her path from Zimbabwe to the UN, sharing powerful insights on female empowerment and the importance of education. In writing about the root of her humanitarianism, her fervent dedication to uplifting women and girls, Nyamayaro inspires an ethos I hope you will take with you after reading this incredible book—one where persistence and determination are rewarded with the promise of progress.

I AM
A GIRL
FROM
AFRICA

A Memoir

Elizabeth Nyamayaro

SCRIBNER

New York   London   Toronto   Sydney   New Delhi

Scribner

An Imprint of Simon & Schuster, Inc.

1230 Avenue of the Americas

New York, NY 10020

This Scribner hardcover edition May 2021

SCRIBNER and design are registered trademarks of The Gale Group, Inc., used under license by Simon & Schuster, Inc., the publisher of this work.

For information about special discounts for bulk purchases, please contact Simon & Schuster Special Sales at 1-866-506-1949 or business@simonandschuster.com.

The Simon & Schuster Speakers Bureau can bring authors to your live event. For more information or to book an event, contact the Simon & Schuster Speakers Bureau at 1-866-248-3049 or visit our website at www.simonspeakers.com.

Interior design by Wendy Blum

Manufactured in the United States of America

1   3   5   7   9   10   8   6   4   2

Library of Congress Cataloging-in-Publication Data has been applied for.

ISBN 978-1-9821-8687-6

For my dearest Gogo, whose indomitable spirit, love, and wisdom formed
the core of who I am.

To my beloved continent, this is my love letter to you.

I cannot imagine any greater gift than being a child of the African soil.

You cannot tell a hungry child that you gave
them food yesterday.

❨❩

—Zimbabwean proverb

1

Deep in the African wilderness, rolling hills open onto a barren maize field. In the middle of that field stands a huge, useless tree. I lie underneath that useless tree unable to move. I am eight years old. I am all alone.

Stand, I tell myself, but I cannot. I lie on my stomach, my legs stretched out, my arms limp at my sides, my palms turned toward the heavens, begging for mercy. I burrow my face deeper into the ground, seeking shelter from the scorching sun, yet the earth feels as hot as fire, practically sizzling beneath me. There is no cool or comfortable place to hide. The leaves of the tree are long gone, and with it the shade, burned away by the punishing drought that has descended on our small village in Zimbabwe.

Rise, I think, but I cannot. I am simply too weak to move. I am starving. I have had nothing to drink or eat for three days. My shrinking stomach growls like two hungry hyenas fighting over a goat. I am so thirsty it's as if tiny, sharp razors slice the inside of my throat with each breath or attempt to swallow. I have never felt so hollow and wasted from hunger. I worry that the drought may never end, and I will never leave this tree. *I will die here,* I think, but I am too tired to be truly frightened.

My world has changed from one of abundance and joy to one of fear and emptiness. It seems a long time ago that I cooked *sadza* (maize meal) with goat stew alongside my *gogo* (grandmother), whom I live with inside our round, grass-thatched hut that is small-small, but big enough for the two of us to cook and eat and sleep and pray. Our warm, cozy hut, just like all the other huts in our small village of Goromonzi, stands at the top of a hill surrounded by cow pastures and farmland. Goromonzi is the only home I have ever known, but through the haze of hunger I struggle to remember the faces and voices of my village: Gogo's three sons and all her other relatives, who are my *ambuyas* (aunts) and *sekurus* (uncles), and their children, whom I call *sisis* (sisters) and *hanzwadzis* (brothers).

Long before the drought, all of us gathered in Gogo's yard on special days, eating and laughing and feasting. Each family brought baskets full of food picked from our fields at the bottom of the hill and the gardens tucked behind our round huts: fresh maize, sweet potatoes, watermelons, groundnuts, pumpkins, mangoes, and guavas. The *sekurus* slaughtered a cow gifted by one of the families, providing plenty-plenty cow stew, which we washed down with soured milk from our stubborn goats until our bellies rejoiced and our hearts felt satisfied. We wanted for nothing because the food belonged to everyone; we shared it all, bartering and trading with each other for things we didn't grow. Gogo traded her large orange pumpkins, which tasted almost as sweet as honey, for small packets of black-eyed beans and groundnuts from the *ambuyas*. If you needed anything, you only had to ask, and often somebody offered what they knew you needed before you did. After supper, on our feast days, we sat around a huge fire under the dark African sky perforated with tiny shiny stars, singing songs of praise to God, calling for the rain to return.

God always answered our prayers, and each year the rain returned, filling our days with purpose. Ox-drawn plows worked the fields; wooden and metal hoes tilled the land; family stood by family, helping to tend the crops until they sprouted from the ground. Our fields were lush and green; our harvest was bountiful. Gogo and the *sekurus* sold our maize, sunflower seeds, and other crops at the Township Center in the next village, to buy any food we couldn't grow ourselves. We found meaning in our work, making sure that we all did our part to take care of our families and of each other. It was a happy life.

That was then, and this is now. For two years, God has refused to answer our prayers. He has left us with Satan's punishing heat, which is killing everything in its path. He has left us with only the little food from the previous harvest, which is not enough. Even though we share whatever we can, even though we count our maize and beans each day before cooking, even though we skip meals, ignoring our hunger pangs, the little food we have left is slowly running out.

At first, when the rain failed to come, Gogo spoke directly to God. "I will not stop until you bring back the rain. I will not rest. Do you hear me, God?" Her prayers went unanswered, but she refused to give up. Gogo gathered all the *ambuyas* and *sekurus*, and together we all prayed for rain again—this time without the feast—as our food began to diminish. We prayed for so many days and nights and so loudly and faithfully that our knees were bruised and our voices were hoarse. Still, God did not respond. Now I wonder if the world is ending, but this thought moves slowly through my mind, as if through mud.

When Gogo left the village a few days ago, she told me, "An illness has visited a *sekuru* from the *mujuru* village," which is far from our village. Sunlight fell across the hut, casting light across the walls and floor. Gogo wrapped her few belongings in a faded brown cloth: a pair of underwear; two maroon dresses, both with tiny holes from termites; a half-used jar of Vaseline; and, of course, her Bible.

"I can help," I said, offering to carry Gogo's Bible as I always do on Sundays when we go to church wearing our nice-nice clothes and special church hats.

"No. I am going with the *ambuyas* and will be back soon-soon. Eat the boiled maize when you get hungry." She pointed to the black clay pot. She tapped the water container. "Yes. There is enough for two days."

I nodded, "Okay, let's pray." Kneeling with Gogo on the floor, I prayed for God to protect my family on their journey. I waved goodbye and watched Gogo disappear behind the guava and mango trees behind our hut, descending the hills with her belongings bundled on top of her head to join the *ambuyas*.

That was five days ago. The water container is empty, and the food is long gone. With no food or water for three days, I feel as though I am slipping out of my body. I manage to lift my face by pushing slowly-slowly into the dry ground with arms that feel as heavy as the thickest tree branches. I sit up, wipe the dirt from my face, and open my eyes.

The light burns my tired eyes as if I'm staring at the sun. Sitting alone in Gogo's devastated field, I am no longer surrounded by *all things bright and beautiful*, as the church hymn goes. Before me is an unrecognizable landscape, strange and scary. All that remains is scorched baby maize shoots that stood no chance against Satan's punishing heat, the heat that dried up our river, leaving us with no water to drink; destroyed our crops; and killed our animals, leaving *ambuyas* wailing inside empty cow kraals and goat sheds.

When Gogo didn't come back home three days ago as she had promised, I felt sad because I missed her, but I didn't feel scared. Gogo always goes away to pray for sick *ambuyas* and *sekurus* in faraway villages. Sometimes she takes me with her. Sometimes when the sick *ambuya* or *sekuru* refuses to recover and their soul is called back to the heavenly father, Gogo stays longer for the funeral. I tell Gogo not to worry about me, because she taught me how to take care of myself for a time when she is no longer here. I cook and fetch water; I noodle-out flying termites with a single straw of grass; I make a catapult and shoot down birds; I catch fish with a sharp stick and roast them. I create fire and cross rivers.

Yesterday I went to the bush above our village, on the other side of the hill, to search for small birds to shoot with my catapult and flying termites to catch. I found nothing. This morning I went to the Good Forest, which sits just below Gogo's field, past the family cemetery but before the river, to search for berries. Gogo and all the *ambuyas* call this forest the River Forest, because we fetch our drinking water here from the crisp, cool river. I call it the Good Forest, because there are no hyenas that might try to eat me, unlike the Hyena Forest on the other side of the river. *I know just the tree! The one by the river with the sweetest black water berries.*

As I descended the hill to the Good Forest, the village felt strangely quiet: no loud children playing in the yards, filling the air with laughter; no busy-busy *ambuyas* running around cooking and cleaning and attending to the children; no *sekurus* mending their goat sheds and chicken coops. Now that we had been left with Satan's punishing sun, *ambuyas* and *sekurus* hid their small-small children inside their huts, away from the heat, while they and their older children searched for food, going deeper into the forest and visiting neighboring villages. I stared at the empty goat sheds and felt my heart ache, thinking about my favorite goat, Little-One.

A few days after Little-One was born, her mother disappeared from the goat shed during the night. When we discovered this the following morning, Gogo placed her hands on her hips, shook her head from side to side, and said, "Eeee, the hyenas." I looked up at Gogo, tugged at her dress, and without being asked, said, "I can help." Gogo nodded in agreement, and that's how the little brown goat became mine. I named her Little-One and became in charge of feeding her and playing with her so that she wouldn't feel too sad about her missing mother.

But then the drought came, and one morning I found Little-One motionless in the shed: her legs were completely straight, her face tilted up to the heavens, her eyes rolled back in her head with a soft smile resting on her face. I called out her name, but she didn't move. She had left me. I collapsed on top of her, wailing, "Dear God, please bring back

Little-One." I wept and prayed. But God did not hear my prayer; he did not bring back my best friend; he did not bring back Little-One. I decided then I would not speak to God again. Now I speak only to Jesus.

Dear, sweet Jesus. Please hear my prayer. Please help me find food. I am too-too hungry. Amen. I prayed silently as I walked through the village to the Good Forest. And when I saw an *ambuya* in her yard making packets of dried black beans and groundnuts so the food would last long-long, and she asked if I was hungry, I responded, "No thanks, Ambuya. Me, I am fine-fine," refusing to take her little-little food which must feed all of her children. *Ambuya has eight mouths to feed. I only have one.* Besides, I wanted Gogo to be proud of me for taking care of myself. Also, I had a perfect plan to find my berries in the Good Forest, which always had plenty-plenty fruit to pluck: the red berries that make my eyes water; the black water berries that turn my tongue black; the brown *mazhanje* fruit that tastes as sweet as honey. The Good Forest is my magical place, filled with beautiful birds—some with sparkling blue wings and red-and-yellow coats, others with bright orange beaks, and very tiny ones with black and white spots.

But when I reached the Good Forest there was nothing. The berries were gone, and the tree was completely bare, the bark and branches dry and brittle in the hot, motionless air. Hopelessness fell over me like a long shadow.

I will go back to the village and ask an ambuya *for food*, I thought. But then I grew too tired and I collapsed in Gogo's field. Now, here I am, so weak from hunger I cannot stand, the sun punishing me for a sin I don't remember committing. I say another silent prayer to Jesus, pleading with him for the strength to move before the darkness comes and brings out the hungry hyenas from the Hyena Forest.

Move, I remind myself. I will try crawling back to the hut. Gogo always says, "You must never ever give up." I plant my palms on the ground, steady my knees, then slowly move my right arm and then my left. The effort is too much. I fall to my stomach and everything goes dark.

I dream that I am spinning, surrounded by butterflies that circle slowly around me; the yellow ones remind me of Gogo's beautiful sunflowers. I am so dizzy, so happy and warm, and when I lie on the ground the butterflies cover me. For a moment, everything is perfect.

I am drifting in and out of consciousness, between darkness and light, between pain and happiness, when I feel a shadow, shielding me from the sun. *It must be Gogo!* I feel a rush of relief in my aching body. I'm also ashamed to be found like this, helpless, when she has worked so hard to teach me to take care of myself.

The person standing in front of me is not Gogo. I notice she has shiny-shiny legs like none I have ever seen, and shiny shoes that match. Sometimes Gogo and I use Vaseline on our legs when we go to church, but only on the exposed parts between our hemlines and ankles, so we don't waste it.

This person kneels down next to me; she is a much older *sisi*. I have never seen her before, she is not from our village, and when she smiles, I see her white-white teeth. She is so beautiful! She places a blue plastic bowl of porridge next to me, and without waiting for an invitation or even sitting up, I dig my dirty fingers into the warm porridge and scoop it into my mouth as quickly as I can. Gradually the sounds in my stomach diminish and disappear. The girl lifts my head gently and rests it on her chest, placing a plastic bottle in my mouth. I close my eyes and guzzle the fresh water that tastes so cool and wonderful it sends shivers down my back. I feel life returning, filling me up. I lift my head from the *sisi*'s chest and sit up on my own. I am back in my body. I am alive.

I take in this *sisi* more carefully. I see that she is wearing a uniform as blue and as pretty as the brilliant sky. Now that my hunger is gone, I can see without wincing or squinting. I see words written on the front of her shirt. I cannot read, and I wonder what they mean. *Where is she from?* It's as if she is an angel, dropped from heaven. *Thank you, God*, I pray silently, speaking directly to him. The *sisi* keeps smiling at me, and I finally have the energy to smile back, which feels like a miracle.

"Thank you, Sisi." My voice is weak and scratchy.

She nods. "What is your name?"

"Elizabeth."

"What are you are doing here all by yourself?"

"I am not alone. I am with my butterflies," I say, and she looks confused. I don't want her to ask me any more difficult questions, so I ask, "Why are you here?"

She squeezes my hand and smiles. "I am here to feed hungry children in the village, because as Africans we must uplift each other."

I don't understand what it means to uplift others, but I nod.

I know that I can finally stand up. I will search for food. I will live.

I will never forget this moment, when I hovered so close to death and was saved just in time. What I don't yet know is that this particular encounter will define the purpose of my life, acting as a beacon that motivates my actions and aspirations; the light that guides me through every darkness.

We desire to bequeath two things to our children:
the first one is roots, the other one is wings.

❨❩

—Sudanese proverb

2

A surge of excitement courses through me as the plane begins its final, bumpy descent into London. As we drop below the clouds, I press my face against the window and look closely, trying to take in everything at once. The River Thames is a shiny ribbon, snaking through buildings I have only ever seen in books: clock towers that I imagine strike at the top of each hour and row after row of tall, glass buildings reflecting the early morning light. The whole city shimmers, and I have to blink several times as I have never seen so many lights before. They flicker and glimmer all the way to the horizon, merging with the sunrise as London wakes up and the plane descends. The year is 2000; I am twenty-five years old. I can hardly believe that I have finally made it to the United Kingdom.

I couldn't sleep for the length of the flight. Leaving the African continent for the first time and literally flying into the unknown, I peered through the window into the darkness and listened to the whirring engines. I was thrilled. *I'm finally doing it!* I was finally taking the first big step to fulfill my dream, after so much struggle and hard work. But then I immediately felt anxious, remembering that I had no friends or family in the UK, and only two hundred and fifty pounds to last me until I got a job.

A few years after my encounter with the girl in the blue uniform, who gave me a bowl of porridge and saved my life, I learned that she worked for UNICEF, which is part of the world's largest humanitarian organization: the United Nations. The mission of UNICEF is to protect the rights of children across the globe, providing food and resources to communities in times of acute need. This explained the *sisi's* blue uniform and the lettering across her chest. The encounter stayed with me throughout my childhood; inspired by her, I dreamt of one day working for the United Nations, where I too would be able to uplift the lives of others, just as my life had once been uplifted. And after much research and planning and support from my family, I am confident that coming to London is the first step to pursuing this singular dream. I have a plan, a clear purpose, and all the motivation in the world.

Through the window, the sky is overcast. I immediately miss the bright, clear African sky, which to me has always felt as big as the world, stretching across villages and fields and people walking along footpaths, headed to work or to bring food to a neighbor. I think of Gogo and how much she has sacrificed for me to be here, selling her cows and goats to raise money for my plane ticket. Yesterday, when I left Zimbabwe, Gogo's face was transformed by sadness. She did not want to see me go and refused to say goodbye. Instead, she threw her arms around me and we knelt on the dusty airport floor in Harare and prayed for my journey ahead.

Now, as the plane comes to a halt at the gate and the flight attendants crack open the doors, I suddenly feel how far away from home I truly am. I feel lonely and panicked—even fearful. *Can I do this?* I am thousands of miles away from everyone and everything I have ever known, here on British soil with a single intention. My dream is to become the girl in the blue uniform. *But what if I can't? What if I fail?* I stand to file out of the plane with the other passengers, my heart on fire in my chest. As I prepare to make my way in a new country, I feel a hollow pit of anxiety in my stomach. I have read about Britain in books, but the very first time I learned about the existence of the nation in which I'm about to set foot was when Gogo told me the story of *Chimurenga*.

I am six years old, sitting on the small stoop at the entrance of Gogo's hut in Goromonzi. I am busy-busy, shelling the maize harvested from Gogo's field. The wooden door of the hut is a bit rickety, so I lean against it gently, slowly stretching out my ashy shins to soak up the sun, while the hut's small roof shields my face from the scorching heat. In the distance I can hear the clucking of chickens in the neighbor's yard. I smile, fill my lungs with warm, earthy air and cluck back. I pick up a cob of dried maize from the ground and shell its seeds into the clay pot balanced between my thighs, which Gogo cleans with a palmful of dry sand every morning. I place the seedless cob on the ground to my right, then reach to my left for another cob. It is the middle of the day; I am all alone and entirely in charge of Gogo's house and goats, and I know just what to do.

This morning, like most mornings, Gogo left to work in the field, leaving me with plenty-plenty things to do. First, I must tie up the goats in the bush, then sweep the yard, wash the dirty dishes from last night's supper, and finally shell enough maize for tonight's meal. Once all of this is done, I will join Gogo in the field. I am nearly finished with my last task; I shell another maize cob into the clay pot, then another one, and another one.

I am happily lost in my thoughts. I'm thinking about how tonight I will pile the cobs in the fire pit in the center of our clean hut; how I will light the match and create fire; how I will place the clay pot full of seeds over the fire and then add water, salt, okra, and sliced tomatoes from our large garden, making a nice-nice supper for Gogo and me. As always, the thick, fragrant smoke will fill the hut, making me cough and my eyes water, and I'll say, "Eeee, too much smoke," as I wipe tears from my cheeks, and Gogo will say, "Eeee, open the door," as I blow the dark smoke away from me. "Aaaa, the door is already open," I'll respond, tasting the bitter smoke as it moves down my throat.

My wandering thoughts are interrupted by a scream. I stop and listen. Nothing. I return to shelling maize. I hear the scream again. I can't make out the words, but I can tell it's a woman's voice. My heart pounds in my chest. "Who is it?" I ask quietly, as if I'm speaking to myself and not to the person screaming.

The woman screams again, much louder this time. I'm startled, because it is Gogo's voice. *What is wrong?* I jump off the stoop and send the clay pot flying through the air; it crashes to the ground and shatters into tiny pieces, scattering our dinner everywhere. Panicking, I drop to my knees and scoop up as much maize as I can into my tiny palms. I feel frantic as I look around the yard, searching for an empty container.

Gogo screams again, and this time she sounds even more distressed. I abandon the maize to the ground and take off running as fast as I can. I run behind the hut, past the maize bin set up on wooden stilts to protect the food from mice, even though the mice always find a way in. I run harder, my breath coming fast and quick, past the colorful guava and mango trees and past the neighbors' yards. I run and run until I reach the edge of the village. I see Gogo charging toward me through the open cow pastures. It's as if the wind is pushing her forward, her feet practically flying off the ground, dust trailing behind her on the narrow dirt path. I don't know what is happening, but Gogo is clearly upset. Her sarong is barely hanging around her waist. I have never seen Gogo outside without a head scarf, and now it is bunched up in one hand, the sun bouncing off her white hair.

Everything is happening so fast. I forget about the stabbing pain from the sharp stones underneath my bare feet. My heart is beating hard, as if trying to break free of my body. Arms spread wide, I reach out for Gogo and throw myself into her embrace. She wraps me in her arms and lifts me off the ground. My face is pressed to her sweat-drenched cheek. Now that Gogo is holding me, I can see that she is crying. Sobbing, actually; her eyes overflow with tears that blend with her sweat; it's as if a river of water is running down her face. I'm so confused. My Gogo is crying. I have never seen her cry before. Because she is crying, I cry with her.

"*Tasununguka*," Gogo says, her voice thick with tears. I have no idea what she's talking about, so I cry even harder.

In the middle of the hot day, we stand alone next to the empty cow kraals, the cows having long gone to their pastures with the *sekurus*, and the *ambuyas* now busy working their fields at the bottom of the village while their children help with chores or go to school. It is as if Gogo and I are alone in the world, but Gogo is crying. *I don't know what to do.*

Gogo's knees buckle beneath her. She is gripping me in her arms like a baby, she will not let go, and so we land together on the ground with a thump. My face is pressed against her breasts and my legs stretch out on the ground. I hear Gogo's heartbeat in my ear, da dhum, da dhum, da dhum, faster and faster, trying to catch her breath as it keeps tumbling away from her. I want to say something, but I don't know what to say. Instead I throw my tiny arms across her shoulders, trying to comfort her without words, praying silently to God. I want Gogo to stop crying, but instead she opens her mouth and wails. She is sobbing, freeing herself from her sorrow, wailing like a child. I don't understand what has happened, but I want to take Gogo's pain away, the way she always takes my pain away, protecting me from sickness and hunger and every sadness. I press myself against her and pray: *God, please heal her.*

Gogo says again, more clearly this time, "The radio announced *Tasununguka.*"

I still do not understand her meaning, but she is no longer crying and I want to keep it that way, so I nod and repeat the word into her shoulder, "*Tasununguka.*" This is the word Gogo has heard on her small-small radio, which she takes to the field when there is enough money for batteries. We listen to music and weather and news as we work together.

I pull away from Gogo and smile at her. She smiles back, then lets out a huge laugh, rumbling from deep within her chest, that feels as loud as thunder. Still laughing, she lifts me off her lap, sets me on the ground, and begins to sing and dance like a madwoman. Her bare feet stomp the ground with tremendous force, and her arms flap in the air like the powerful birds that soar over the Good Forest and drop down to steal fish from our river. Gogo's loud laughter calls the light back into her eyes. She is absolutely ecstatic; I think she sounds as hysterical as the hyenas in the Hyena Forest.

Gogo's sudden happiness confuses me as much as her crying did, but I am relieved she is happy, and so I join her madwoman dance, following her feet in their one-two, one-two, one-two pattern. We dance in a wild circle as dust swirls around us, panting as our lungs run out of air. We are laughing with our souls, emptying out all of our pain like water being poured into the ground.

When Gogo abruptly stops singing, I stop with her. Fat beads of sweat mix with dried tears on our faces. I search Gogo's face for answers. *What is happening?* She says nothing. Instead, she bends down, locks her hands under my arms, and lifts me off the ground until my feet are dangling in the air. Looking directly into my eyes, she smiles and proclaims loudly, "*Tasununguka*—We Are Free! We are free, my dear child. We are free."

What does she mean? What has just happened? Why was Gogo crying, then happy, then dancing? *What does it mean?* I wonder. *We are free?* I want to ask questions, but I do not, because Gogo is laughing and I want her to stay happy. Gogo always tells me, *You ask too many questions for a child*, and this does not seem like the time for questions. I smile and nod as she lowers me to the ground.

We walk back home in silence, up the narrow dirt path and through the village, my hand inside Gogo's. She is smiling, but my mind is full of questions. *Tasununguka*, I repeat silently in my head. When we reach Gogo's yard, the shattered clay pot is still in pieces on the ground. I drop down to pick it up, looking at Gogo anxiously, waiting for her to ask me why I thought it was okay to throw food on the ground, because food is never to be wasted, not in our village where we share our bounty with everyone. But she says nothing; she simply swipes the maize off the stoop with her foot and sits down. I pick up the scattered maize, blow off the sand, and place it in her lap. Gogo looks far away, lost in her thoughts.

"Tomorrow," she says finally, "we will celebrate." A smile on her face, the head scarf back on her head, and her sorrow gone, she shells maize without a care.

She is so happy, so I ask, "What is *tasununguka?*"

Gogo's hands are still busy-busy with the maize as she begins, "A long, long time ago, the *vapambepfumi*—white oppressors—came to our country of Zimbabwe. They came from Britain, a country far-far away."

Where is Britain? I wonder. But I know this is an important story, I want to hear all of it.

"We welcomed them," Gogo explains. "We gave them our blackest cows and said, 'This is the meat with which we greet you.'"

Legs folded neatly beneath me, elbows resting on my thighs, face cupped in my palms, I train my eyes on Gogo's face and listen.

"But us, we didn't know. We didn't know that the *vapambepfumi* were not nice people. They were not kind to us. They took our land, then forced us to work on it without pay. They kept all the crops for themselves, giving us very little in return."

Gogo's shelling pace picks up together with the speed of her voice. "They killed our elephants, our buffaloes, our giraffes, and our lions. They stole nice stones from our mines. They made us call them Sir or Madam, demanding our respect. Yet they referred to us as monkeys." She sighs and looks out into the distance, still shelling maize. I watch the sadness return to her eyes, like the shadow of a cloud hiding a patch of sunlight.

"Uuuu, we suffered so much from the way they treated us. We wanted the pain to go away. So one day, we asked them nicely to leave. But the *vapambepfumi* refused."

Gogo closes her eyes and continues. "We prayed to God, but God did not hear our prayers. The *vapambepfumi* did not leave our country. They did not give back our land. So in 1896, we started a war and we called it our *Chimurenga*—the Liberation Struggle. We called ourselves the rebels and we fought the *vapambepfumi*."

I do not know what war is, but Gogo's voice is sad, her eyes still closed.

"We wanted to be free," she says. "Free to have our own country back from the colonizers. Free to grow our own crops, on our own farms, and to feed our own children. Free to own our land."

Gogo stops shelling and talking, and hangs her head, shaking it from side to side as if emptying her mind of troubling memories. She places her palms over her eyes and opens her mouth, but no words come out. Her sorrow consumes her again. I reach out, place my hand on her knee, and squeeze as tightly as I can.

"Huhhh," Gogo finally says. "But the *vapambepfumi* won the war. They killed so many of our people." Gogo has taught me that when good people die, their souls go to a better place called heaven. I say a silent prayer to God to take care of all the souls of our people.

Gogo's hands slowly leave her eyes and I can see her face again. "In 1966," she continues, "we started the second *Chimurenga*. This time we would never give up. Us, we had nowhere else to go and nothing left. The *vapambepfumi* could go back to Britain. They had a choice; a choice we never had. All we had was the land and the pain and the burden that came with fighting for it."

I watch fire return to Gogo's eyes, replacing the sadness, and I want my eyes to look just like hers. She looks focused and determined. She will never give up. She will always fight for what's right. That is exactly what I want to do. This is exactly what she has taught me.

"So this time, we got more serious. We got more rebels and weapons and we fought with everything we had. We fought with our lives. We fought for the lives of our *sisis* and *hanzwadzis* from the first *Chimurenga*. We fought for our freedom."

Finally, I interrupt, because I must know. "Did you fight the *vapambepfumi*, Gogo?" I imagine her fighting—her fierce glare, her absolute determination to win freedom for her people. Who would dare to cross my Gogo?

Gogo is crying again. There is no wailing or sobbing this time, just a waterfall of tears that cleanses her face.

"Eeee, yes, we all did, my dear child. All the women took care of the rebels. Some of us cooked. Some of us carried their weapons. Some of us fought the *vapambepfumi* with our own weapons. We all did our part to help in the second *Chimurenga*."

"Rebels?" I ask softly. "What is a rebel?"

She doesn't answer my question, but continues the story. "And then all my sons, your *sekurus*, joined the other rebels to fight the *vapambepfumi* in the forest in the second *Chimurenga*."

Rebels. I know the word. I think-think and then remember that I once met a rebel. One day he emerged suddenly from the Good Forest unannounced, and found me pulling weeds in Gogo's field. I was hunched over, but I felt his presence behind me. I stood up and took in this tall, serious *sekuru* with no light in his eyes, which were red as if he had been crying. His hair was twisted in knots and needed to be combed. His skin was dark and glistened in the sun. He did not smile. He did not say, *Hello*, or *God bless you*. He stood silently before me in his matching trousers and shirt, wearing big heavy boots on his feet, a brown bag on his back, and a big weapon strapped to his shoulder. He was in a hurry and did not have time to waste. He asked, "*Une mvura?*" I did not have water, so I shook my head. His response was quick: "*Ko, chikafu?*" I did have food. I had boiled sweet potatoes in the clay pot under the tree. "Me, I cooked them myself," I added, as I led him to the tree, happy to help this sad-looking *sekuru*.

Suddenly I felt Gogo's hand yanking me away from the *sekuru*. She shoved me behind her back, still holding her hoe in the other hand. She dropped her hoe and handed the *sekuru* a sweet potato, still gripping me tightly with her other hand. He took the food and walked away. He did not say thank you. He did not ask about Gogo's crops or ask her for God's blessing. This was all so strange. We always asked each other for God's blessings in our village. Gogo explained that this *sekuru* was not from our village. "He's a rebel," she told me before I could even ask the question. The *sekuru* had disappeared back into the forest, but there was still terror in Gogo's eyes.

"The rebels are looking for useful young children to cook for them and carry their guns," she added.

I was useful. I could cook and carry heavy things. "I can help!" I announced to Gogo, lifting the big pot of sweet potatoes over my head.

My words visibly startled her. Gogo yanked the pot out of my hands and threw it to the ground, sending sweet potatoes flying.

"The rebels are dangerous. Do you hear me?" She shook my shoulders hard. "They take our children and never bring them back!" She was fuming. Up to this point, the rebel had not frightened me. To me, he was just another *sekuru*: a sad one, perhaps, lost in the forest, searching for food. But now I was terrified; a *sekuru* that could take me away from my Gogo? I never saw the rebel again.

Now I look up at Gogo on the stoop and say, "But you said rebels were dangerous."

She does not answer.

"Gogo, you said the rebels were dangerous, remember?"

Gogo ignores my question as if she hasn't heard it and continues, as if reliving the story for the first time. "Eeee, God knows how much I prayed. Me, I prayed every day and every night for your *sekurus*, worried I would never see my sons again. I worried they would never return to me, that they would die in the bush without a good burial. But God answered my prayers. He brought all your *sekurus* home to me." Now I remember that Gogo's three sons who live in Goromonzi were always gone for long periods of time when I was young-young. But now they have all been back home since Christmas, back from the second *Chimurenga*. I have so many questions, but I let Gogo continue.

She lets out a sigh of relief and says, "Aaaa, your *sekurus* and all the other rebels defeated the *vapambepfumi*." She pauses, smiles, and says, "And now, us, we are free. Free to take back our land. Free to call our country Zimbabwe, instead of the colonizer's Rhodesia. Today is an important day. Today is our Independence Day. Never forget that, my dear child. Never forget." Her face is glowing and light returns to her eyes, the burden of *Chimurenga* finally lifted from her shoulders. She is proud of herself and her sons for demanding respect for our people, proud of the rebels for winning back our land, and because she is proud, I am proud too.

I am still sitting with my legs crossed, my body soaking up the sun, my hand still squeezing Gogo's knee, when she finishes her *Chimurenga* story. We are both crying, but we are not sad.

"*Tasununguka*," I say, feeling proud of the things I still do not yet fully understand.

"Yes, we are free," Gogo says, a big smile on her face. She pauses, looks into my eyes, reaches for my hand, and says, "And you, my dear child, you are now *Mwana Wevhu*."

I smile and say, "I am *Mwana Wevhu*." What this means, I am not certain, but deep down I feel—I know—that everything has changed.

If there is cause to hate someone,
the cause to love has just begun.

◐

—Senegalese proverb

3

I climb up the steep stairs out of the hot and stuffy London Underground, emerging onto a busy street in Bayswater. Commuters flow in and out of the Tube station's entrance like ants rushing in and out of a hive. Cyclists weave carefully through the chaos, while clusters of people wait at stoplights. I am surrounded by noise: horns honk nonstop, and traffic moves so quickly it makes a rushing sound like water in a river, making me feel dizzy. For just a moment, I forget that my fingers have gone numb after clutching the plastic handle of my small green suitcase so tightly for so long. I forget about the throbbing blisters inside my tight new shoes, and about my damp yellow dress clinging to my back beneath a heavy satchel strapped to my aching shoulders.

I look up to the heavens and fill my lungs with brisk air. The sky is gloomy, and certainly not the springtime weather I was expecting. Still, I let the misty drizzle falling from the gray sky cool my face, ignoring the strange looks cast in my direction. *Let them look*, I think. *I have arrived*, and I will take the time to revel in this moment.

I weave my way through the crowded sidewalk, which heaves with people walking as if headed somewhere in a great hurry. People rush around me as if I am a stone in a river, so busy and lost in their own thoughts that their umbrellas occasionally crash together over their heads. I try to take it all in, noticing everything. Nobody stops to greet another person; nobody makes eye contact with me or with anyone else; everyone seems to be moving in their own private bubble, afraid to touch or speak to anyone else for fear it might pop. This is strange to me. On the foot paths of Goromonzi, in the fields and at the river, we always greet each other, a stranger or a friend, with blessings and inquiries about each other's health and family. Not doing so would be considered deeply impolite, even a sign of disrespect.

I quickly learn how to move through the flow of fast-moving people and begin to take in all the sights I have been so curious to see for so long. And there is much to see. As I make my way toward the youth hostel where I will be staying, I stare at the perfectly manicured garden squares surrounded by Victorian stucco terrace homes, the likes of which I have only ever seen on television, in British sitcoms and news stories. I almost pinch myself—*yes, you are actually here!*—when the red double-decker buses and black cabs roar past me, so quickly that I cannot even get a good look at the passengers inside. Through the spotless windows of fancy-looking shops I see mannequins in nicely tailored gray suits and black dresses. I stop and look for a few long moments at the breathtaking Kensington Gardens blooming with flowers in pink, yellow, and blue—colors as vivid as the African prints we wear in Goromonzi.

How I wish my Gogo could experience everything alongside me. When I pass a red phone booth, I wish she had a phone and that I had the money to call her. *Gogo, I made it! Gogo, I'm here!* I imagine saying to her. When I think about how proud she would be, seeing me here, I feel as joyous as a child. Then I realize I am lost, and not for the first time today. On the Tube from Heathrow Airport, I missed my exchange stop at Gloucester Road Station, and then I took the train in the wrong direction from the South Kensington Tube station, forcing me to backtrack. Now I can't find the street I'm looking for. *No problem*, I think. *I'll just ask for directions.*

"Good morning, sir," I say as cheerfully as possible and in my most polished British accent as I approach a well-dressed British man walking toward me. "Might you please—" He avoids making eye contact, steps out of the way, and says, "Sorry," zooming past me. I try again when I see a woman walking in my direction: "Excuse me, madam." I'm grinning from ear to ear. "I am trying to find—" The British woman cuts me off. "I am terribly sorry," she says, and walks briskly away.

I am as stunned by these encounters as if I've been slapped. I start to feel self-conscious and even a touch frightened. What did I do to prompt such a dismissive reaction? Why wouldn't they try to help me or even let me finish asking a question? I am mystified, and my confusion triggers insecurity. Maybe it's the way I look, or sound. Is it because I'm wearing a sundress in the rain? Can they not understand my African accent? My yellow dress is now soaking wet and I still can't find the street I'm looking for. Suddenly, tears sting my eyes.

Seconds ago, I was full of curiosity and excitement, but now I am in a mood as grim as the weather. The rain, no longer a light mist, falls relentlessly from a sky the color of concrete. This greatly anticipated moment of arrival is beginning to lose its magic. Each step in my tight shoes is painful; the cold clings to me like Velcro.

As my excitement fades, doubt and fatigue fall on me as heavily as the rain. How will I survive in London long enough to work for the United Nations if nobody will even stop for three seconds to help me find my way? *I miss home.* I miss being surrounded by friendly people who are always willing to stop and help, even if they are busy or have somewhere important to be. I feel a fierce longing for my community. I also know that Gogo would tell me to never give up, to try again, and so when I see a friendly woman approaching and she meets my gaze, I force a smile on my face and try again. "Excuse me, madam, might you help me with directions?" I say, showing her the hostel's address scribbled on a piece of paper that is now damp and crumpled in my hand.

"Right," the woman says, and holds her umbrella over the two of us as I repeat the address of the hostel. "You're about five blocks away," she says, and gives me detailed directions. I thank her again and again; at first, she seems put off by my effusiveness, but she finally smiles and says, "Good luck to you," before walking quickly away in her high-heeled shoes. Perhaps, I think, this city will be friendlier than I thought.

I weave through the streets in the direction I've been pointed, and now I feel the exhaustion setting in: the travel, the adrenaline, the fear, all the walking in the rain, and feeling lost and out of place. When I finally reach the youth hostel, I am overcome with relief. I set down my green suitcase on the squeaky wooden floors, look around the tiny lobby, and feel my heart sink. The room is crummy and as narrow as a corridor, bearing absolutely no resemblance to the glossy images I saw in the travel agency brochure. The entire eleven-room hostel looks much smaller and dirtier than it did in the pictures. The walls in the lobby are bare save for a broken black-and-white clock that hangs above the reception counter. A freckled girl with a tiny nose and bright orange hair sits at the desk.

As I approach her, trying to look friendly and upbeat, I see her lips moving and hear sounds emerge, but I do not understand a single word, so I stay silent. She shakes her head and speaks louder, but her words still sound like gibberish, no matter how loudly she speaks or how often she repeats herself. I can see by the look on her face that she thinks I am stupid. This makes me nervous. I assume that she is asking me where I am from, so I panic and blurt out, "I am from Africa!"

The girl laughs at my response and says, "Aye, so do you speak English, huh?" She speaks very slowly this time, and the words do not roll over each other so much, and I understand her. This is a great relief, because I worry that if I close my eyes, I might fall asleep on my aching feet.

As I hand the girl my passport, I say, "Sorry. I didn't understand your accent."

"Aye, something wrong with my Irish accent?" she asks with a cheeky smile.

I know where Ireland is on the world map, but I have never met an

Irish person before, and the accent is totally new to me; the vowels are very round, and she speaks very quickly. She has not told me her name, so I decide to call her Tiny Nose in my mind.

Tiny Nose returns my passport and runs her finger down a list of rooms in a book. "Right. You're staying with us for . . . ?"

"One month," I say, and as I hand over ninety pounds, I feel a jolt of panic. I have just one month to find a job.

"You know the rent is nonrefundable once you hand it over, yeah?"

I nod.

"Well then. Welcome to London, girl from Africa," she says, and hands me a room key. I understand now that she must have been asking for my name when I walked in. I almost try to tell her, "my name is Elizabeth," but I am worried that I will not be able to understand her again and I quite simply do not have the energy. I've had enough newness today.

Besides, it's fine with me if Tiny Nose calls me "Girl from Africa." I could not want to be anyone or anything else. The fact that I'm African is all that matters, and that is enough. I am after all *Mwana Wevhu*—a child of the African soil.

✛

It's dawn and I am in the middle of the African bush staring at the brightest and prettiest of all yellow skies, a sky more beautiful than yesterday's yellow sky. Our country is finally free, and Gogo has said that I am now *Mwana Wevhu*. I assume this must be an important and special distinction. Gogo has said so! And so, as *Mwana Wevhu*, I decide I will do everything that I think *Mwana Wevhu*, a child of the soil, should do. I think about this latest development as I tie up Gogo's goats in the bush. The tall meadow grass cuts into my skinny legs. It is wet and itchy, and I don't like it. Now that I am *Mwana Wevhu*, I decide I will be able to do something about that. Now that I am *Mwana Wevhu*, I decide that I will be able to do something about so many things.

Gogo always says that "to be African is to be blessed," and that we should always share our blessings with others. I pray with Gogo every day, and I decide that I will pray for everyone, giving them my special blessings, as part of my important *Mwana Wevhu* duties. But first, I must tell Gogo's goats. "I am now *Mwana Wevhu*, you know!" I shout, startling them.

I chase after the goats as they scatter, weaving under and around the trees and shrubs and pointy termite hills full of biting ants, following the blue ropes around their necks that slither like small, happy snakes through the grass. I run and run, wrangling each stubborn animal, one at a time, until my nose refuses my lungs the gift of air, and until they are all tied to a tree. Finally, when I am done, I breathe in the crisp morning air and look up to the heavens, pleased with myself. My eyes wander past cheerful little yellow and red birds sitting on the tree branches, then up again to the bright yellow sky. Its color fills me with so much happiness, and I suddenly realize—now that I am *Mwana Wevhu*, I have the answer to a confusing situation that has troubled me for so long. Now that I am *Mwana Wevhu*, I am no longer a sin.

When I was five years old, busy-busy tying up Gogo's goats, I saw a skinny boy with a big head from the next village walking through the bush with a catapult in his hand. I ran to him, happy to see another child to talk to.

He pointed at me, laughed, and said, "What's up, *nherera*—orphan," and kept walking. *He is wrong*, I thought. I had my mother, whom everyone in the village called Gogo.

That night I told Gogo what happened. She was so upset that she said a prayer and went to sleep without eating her supper, which Gogo never did. I asked again in the morning what the boy meant by calling me *nherera*, and I asked the next day and the next. I kept asking until she finally said, "The boy is wrong."

We were in the middle of Gogo's field, taking a short break from plowing and plucking weeds from our maize, sitting under the big useless tree. Unlike the guava and mango trees in our yard, this tree never bore any fruit. In that moment, I conclusively decided that it was a useless tree and I would call it by that name in my head.

"So why did he lie?" I asked, leaning my tired back against the tree's thick trunk. I knew that lying was bad.

Gogo looked down, refusing to meet my gaze. "Eeee, he didn't fully lie." This did not make sense, as Gogo had taught me that people either lie or tell the truth. A half lie is not a thing.

"What does that mean-mean?"

"Eeee, my dear child, I am not really your mother."

I was shocked. Gogo had been my mother since I was a baby. I had called her Mother all my life, and she called me her dear child. Maybe her old mind was starting to forget things. I gently placed my hand on her knee and said, "Of course you are my mother, remember?"

"I raised you since you were a baby, my dear child," Gogo began as I listened intently, "but I am your *gogo*." I did not understand her, and this time, I did not nod. I needed more answers. I kept staring at her, willing her to say more.

"Huhhh, your mother brought too-much-too-much shame to our family. We are never to talk about her again." But I kept pushing, asking my many-many questions, searching for plenty-plenty answers.

It was too painful to hear what Gogo said, but I finally understood that my real mother was Gogo's middle daughter, and that years ago, when she was a teenager, she fell pregnant and ran off to have a child with an irresponsible *rombe*—useless boy from another village—and that boy was my father. I understood that having a child before marriage was a sin in God's eyes. I was that child, born a sin.

I thought a sin was something a person *did*, a sin was an act you *committed*, and I had done nothing wrong. *But if I am a sin myself, can God forgive me? Can my mother ever love me? Is that why she left me, because I am a sin?* I needed to see her. I longed to know her, to hear her voice, to touch her face, to be held in her arms.

But this father person confused me the most; I had no idea what to do with him. What was his purpose? A mother had a purpose, I knew that all too well. When I was sick, a mother boiled chicken feet and fresh leaves from the Good Forest to chase away my fever. When there was not enough food in the house, a mother pretended not to be hungry so there was more for me to eat. She didn't think I noticed, but I did. A mother taught me how to pray and look after myself and the goats. A mother had a purpose and I needed her. But this father person—where would he sleep? There was only room for me and Gogo in our tiny hut. We could squeeze in an extra mother if we tried, and I really-really wanted to, but the thought of this father person made me very sad. Like Gogo, I decided to forget about this *rombe* father person.

I stopped asking Gogo questions, but I never stopped praying. I never stopped waiting for God to bring my mother back to me. When God did not bring her back, I decided to pray for God's will to be done, and now my prayers had been answered. God's will had been done, I was *Mwana Wevhu*, which meant I was special: I was no longer a sin.

"God's will has been done!" I shout to the goats.

Suddenly, I burst into tears. I turn my face to the sky once more, eyes wide open, staring right up at God so he can see how grateful I am to be a sin no longer. I say aloud, with passion in my trembling voice: "Dear God: Thank you, thank you for making me *Mwana Wevhu*. I promise to pray every day for Gogo, and for all the *ambuyas* and *sekurus* and their children. I promise, God. Please don't make me a sin again. Please! Amen."

When I finish praying, I keep my eyes on the yellow sky and think, *I am* Mwana Wevhu, *and someday I will have a yellow dress and I will be as pretty as the African sky.* But first I must come up with a short-short *Mwana Wevhu* prayer so I can pray quick-quick for everyone in our village and I will never be a sin again. *Dear God. Please hear my prayer. Please bless* ambuyas, *and* sekurus, *and their children, and their goats, and their cows, and their crops. Thank you, sweet Jesus. Amen.* As *Mwana Wevhu* I now have special duties. I have work to do!

I wave goodbye to the goats and take off running back down the hill to the village, until I reach the wide tarmac road that separates the bush from our village. Gogo calls it the Township Center road, because it goes all the way to a faraway place with lots of shops that sell nice-nice food and where serious men in white coats buy Gogo's maize and crops after each harvest. I call it the Danger-Danger road because it has fast-fast cars that kill wandering small children and their goats if they do not pay attention. I don't want to be like the small children that wander straight to their deaths, so I stop at the edge of the road and carefully look both ways, just as Gogo taught me.

There are no cars coming, only two cows pulling a large cart stacked with white bags of maize. Two *sekurus* sit quietly inside the cart, their faces dark against the bright sky. When they get closer, I recognize Sekuru Widzi, Gogo's second eldest son, whom I call Big Sekuru inside my head; and Sekuru Oweni, Gogo's youngest son, whom I call Baby Sekuru, even though he is not a baby or even young-young. I call him Baby Sekuru inside my head so as not to confuse him with Big Sekuru or Sekuru Henzi, Gogo's middle son. All three of them live with us in the village with their wives and plenty-plenty children. Gogo has another big-big son, her firstborn child, who lives in a faraway place—a city called Harare. I haven't met this big-big Sekuru, so I don't have a name for him inside my head. Gogo's three daughters also live in Harare, and I have never met them either. Gogo says she used to have a husband, whose soul was called back to the heavenly father when I was a baby. I don't remember this man who left Gogo for God, but her face looks very sad anytime he is mentioned.

Big Sekuru and Baby Sekuru both hold whips made from the tails of dead cows, and they use these to keep the living cows drawing the cart forward. I chuckle inside my head at the picture, and shout, "Good morning, *sekurus*. I greet you in God's name."

"Good morning, my niece," Big Sekuru answers. He stops the cows, and the cart grinds to a halt. "Does Gogo need help selling her maize at the Township Center?" he asks, honoring his duties as a son. In our Shona culture, it is sons who are supposed to take care of their parents, which is why Gogo's three sons, my *sekurus*, stay with us in the village so that they can take care of Gogo. Except Gogo is stubborn like her goats and doesn't want anyone fussing over her. She says she is more than capable of looking after herself and prefers to sell her own maize, even though it takes us a whole day to get there, because she says the *sekurus* will drink away her money.

I don't want to upset Big Sekuru. "Me, I don't know, Sekuru. I can ask." I look down, ashamed of my lie, then quickly change the subject. "Can I pray for you, Sekuru?" Here is my chance to begin my *Mwana Wevhu* prayers.

"Eeee, us, we are in a hurry, my niece," Big Sekuru responds.

"Me, I will be quick-quick, Sekuru," I say, leaning against the cart. I try to hold both of their hands as we always do when we pray for each other, but I am too short-short and I can't reach inside the cart.

"Why don't you pray for us next time, my niece. Us, we have a long journey ahead," Baby Sekuru suggests. He does not understand my new status and responsibilities, or that I have just made a big promise to God to pray for everyone.

I must find a way to pray for the *sekurus*. I run to the front of the cart, place my hand on the side of one of the cows, and say, "Dear God. Please hear my prayer . . ." Suddenly, I feel my hand glide along the side of the cow as it begins to walk away. I stumble back, then steady myself and run after the cart, setting my hand back on the cow.

"Eeee, this is dangerous! *Iwe*—You! Let go of the cow!" Big Sekuru screams.

I ignore him. I must finish my prayer. I will not be a sin ever again. I run alongside the cow and, practically breathless, finish my prayer. "Dear

God. Please hear my prayer. Please bless *sekurus*, and *ambuyas*, and their children, and their goats, and their cows, and this cow, and their crops. Thank you, sweet Jesus. Amen." I wave goodbye to the *sekurus*, place my hands on my hips, and feel deeply pleased with myself. "I am *Mwana Wevhu*, you know," I gleefully shout to the sky, then take off running again, this time home to Gogo's hut.

I find Gogo at the bottom of the yard, underneath a big tree that sits beside our round, grass-thatched hut. She is cleaning last night's dirty dishes. Next to her bare feet are two white metal washbasins—one filled with soaking dirty plates and the other filled with clean water for rinsing.

I announce myself. "I am back, Gogo."

"Okay, my dear child."

Gogo picks up a large water container and hands it to me, then places a big black clay pot of cooked pumpkins on her head, balancing it on top of the bright orange head scarf wrapped around her hair. She flings a metal hoe over her perfect, strong shoulders and says, "Aaaa, let's go," signaling it is time to head to the fields and to the river. Gogo leads us out of the yard, walking with purpose, her legs straight, her hips swaying sideways, her heels hitting the ground forcefully, as her toes propel her forward: left, right, left, right. I want to walk with purpose like Gogo. I mimic her feet and her hips, but my legs are small-small. Still, I try, holding on tightly to the empty water container resting on the top of my head.

We walk down the hill through the village to Gogo's field, weaving through the yards of the *ambuyas*, past their grass-thatched huts and tall maize bins, past their large sleeping houses covered with rusty tin roofs. The *ambuyas* rush around like buzzing bees in a hive, sweeping their yards, washing crying babies inside metal washbasins, and cooking white maize porridge with peanut butter over smoky fires. They work quick-quick so they can go to the river to fetch water. Then, like Gogo, they will spend the rest of the day working in their fields.

Even though the *ambuyas* are busy when they see me and Gogo approach, they stop everything and say, "*Mangwanani*—Good morning, Gogo. How are you this morning?"

Gogo responds with our proper Shona greeting, "*Aaaa, tiripo kana makadiyiwo*," which literally means "We are well, as long as you are well."

Gogo says that our Shona greeting is important because it is a daily reminder that we all belong to one community, and that if one of us is unwell, then none of us is well. I don't know what that means-means. All I know is that our Shona greeting is long-long, but I keep my thoughts to myself.

The *ambuyas* respond, telling Gogo plenty-plenty things about their husbands and children, about their crops and goats and cows. One of their children is not well; a cow just had new calves; they found insects on the tomatoes, which they fear will destroy the crops; they had a specific dream last night which they can't figure out.

Gogo listens intently, nodding and shaking her head, saying "Aaaa," when the news is pleasing; and "Eeee," when the news is sad; "Uuuu," when she is shocked; and "Huhhh," when she is shocked for real-real.

I normally get restless during these long greetings. But today I welcome them because of my *Mwana Wevhu* duties. As the *ambuyas* tell Gogo that they are well as long as Gogo and I are well, and then listen as Gogo responds, I grab the hands of each *ambuya*, loudly blessing them with my *Mwana Wevhu* prayer.

When finally, Gogo says, "We wish you a blessed day, full of God's love," I say, "Yes, may God bless you, *ambuyas*," and place the empty water container back on my head. "May God bless you too," the *ambuyas* answer, finishing our goodbyes.

We walk with purpose to Gogo's field. "Okay, me, I will be back soon-soon, Gogo," I say, leaving Gogo to work in her field of maize, as I take the narrow footpath into the Good Forest, headed to the river to fetch water.

At the river I find plenty-plenty *sisis* and *ambuyas*. Some are kneeling, busy-busy washing dirty clothes inside large metal washbasins.

Some stand upstream, collecting water in large plastic containers like mine. I walk along the riverbank and pray for each of them, one by one, placing my hand on their heads like the pastor at church and holding their hands whenever I can. It feels so wonderful to bless all of them with my *Mwana Wevhu* blessings. I am so happy that I am no longer a sin.

I return to the river each day, praying for the *ambuyas* and *sisis* as I fetch water. They pay me no mind and get on with their work. When I drop off the water at home and head back to the field to join Gogo, I pace up and down the cow pastures with my arms neatly folded behind my back, just like the serious-serious *sekurus* do when they want to command attention and respect. One by one, I grab their hands with my hand and pray for the *sekurus* and *hanzwadzis* as they herd the cattle.

I take being *Mwana Wevhu* very seriously and find great joy in praying for others. Then one day at the river, I hear a *sisi* call herself *Mwana Wevhu*. This upsets me, and when I ask Gogo about it and she says, "We are all *Mwana Wevhu*," I feel totally confused. *How can this be?*

It is nightfall, the hut is dimly lit, and Gogo is kneeling next to the fire cooking *sadza*. She scoops out ground maize powder from a small white container, stirring it into warm water inside a black clay pot balanced over the fire.

I am furious and I startle her when I shout, "Gogo, you said I am *Mwana Wevhu*, remember? How can it be that we are all *Mwana Wevhu*!" If everyone is *Mwana Wevhu*, then how can I be special? And if I'm not special, does that mean I am a sin once again? This cannot be true. I cannot bear it. I close my eyes and mutter softly under my breath: "Dear God, please hear my prayer. Please don't make me a sin again, God. Please, God. Please, I can't be a sin."

I open my eyes, feeling my chest get hot and painful as angry, desperate tears gush down my face.

"Shhhh, stop crying, my dear child," Gogo says, placing a hand on my back.

I flinch and slide away from her touch. I don't want Gogo's kindness, all I want is to not be a sin again. I feel as though the small walls of the hut are closing in on me, and my breath comes in quick, shallow bursts, as if I've swallowed too much smoke from the fire. My mind spins with plenty-plenty questions. Why did Gogo tell me that I am *Mwana Wevhu* if it is not true? Why is God breaking our promise? I promised to work hard, praying for all the people in our village, if I could remain *Mwana Wevhu*: special, set apart, no longer a sin. And I had worked hard: never complaining about the blisters on my feet, never complaining when the *ambuyas* and *sekurus* refused to stop for prayers. I burst into a loud cry and sob until my tears run dry.

Gogo sits in silence, letting me empty out my pain. Finally, she says, "*Mwana Wevhu* means you are a child of the African soil." Her voice is patient and kind, and I listen carefully, because I know when she speaks gently and softly that she is telling me something important. "We are all *Mwana Wevhu* because each of us is like a single grain of sand, connected to our land and to each other." Gogo reaches for my hand, looks into my eyes, and says, "You, my dear child, you *are* special. We *all* are. This is who we are as Africans—we are all children of the soil. Never forget that, never forget." I wipe my face and take in Gogo's words.

Gradually my confusion and anger subside. I begin to understand that being *Mwana Wevhu* makes me special because it connects me to my land and to my community, deeply and forever; our connection is rooted in the rich African soil from which we grow our food, where we live our lives, and where our bodies rest when our souls are called back to the heavenly father. I understand that I am not a sin and still special, just in a different way. What makes me special is what makes all of us special. I am part of my community, connected to everyone I know and love, and I belong here, in this place, with all of Gogo's relatives and all the other African people whom I have not yet and may never meet. To be *Mwana Wevhu*, I finally understand, is to be *African*.

✤

Years later, I stand in a hallway of the youth hostel in Britain. When I open the door to my room, I am shocked to find three men sitting on two bunk beds. I realize that I have booked the cheapest room, which is apparently a mixed gender dorm. I am completely stunned. In my culture, young girls don't sleep in a room with a man that they don't know or are not related to. I feel a new panic that knocks away my fatigue for a moment. How can I share a room with three men I have never met before? How is this possible? What is going to happen to me? Will I get raped? Who am I going to tell if one of them tries to hurt me? I know nobody here except Tiny Nose, and I don't even know her real name. Have I come all this way only to be attacked by a strange man?

Tiny Nose made it clear that my payment is nonrefundable, but even if I could get the money back, I don't have a phone or a computer to help me find a new place and I am sick of getting lost. What if I'm not as lucky next time and nobody will stop to help? I don't know anything about this city or how to navigate it apart from buying and using a ticket on the train. I don't know anyone I might call or turn to. I feel trapped and alone, my mouth bitter with emotions. I want to run away back home, or just will myself there, but I know that I cannot and will not. I can't give up—not after all I've been through to get here.

I take in the tiny room again, painted light blue, with two metal bunk beds pushed against opposite walls leaving only a narrow pathway between them. Backpacks clutter the floor, clothes are hanging off the beds, and the whole place smells of dirty feet. It feels like a far cry from home.

One of the guys jumps up and greets me warmly. "Hello, my friend!" This is Val. With broad shoulders and dark hair combed forward, he looks like he could be a wrestler. He takes my suitcase and makes a space for it on the floor. "Welcome, my friend!" he says, his smile exposing a miss-

ELIZABETH NYAMAYARO

ing front tooth. We shake hands, and I nod to the other two guys sitting together on another bed. Val explains they are childhood friends of his visiting from Ukraine. Val seems nice enough, but I am already planning an escape route in my head. I ask for a bottom bunk; it will be easier to flee if necessary.

"No problem, my friend!" Val says warmly, as if we are in fact old friends.

When I sit down and remove my shoes, I see that my feet are covered in blisters that are about to burst. I rub them gently to ease the pain. I am still brimming with anxiety, but at least I am finally sitting down, and at least Val is friendly and does not appear to be dangerous. Instead, he is quite kind.

"Long trip, my friend?" he asks.

"Yes, from Zimbabwe."

"Where is that?" one of Val's friends asks. Both guys have round faces, their thick jet-black hair combed forward like Val's, and both wear red football fan T-shirts. When I say Africa, the guy asks me why I speak English.

"Ignore him," Val says, and asks if I'm on holiday.

"No," I say. "I am here to pursue my dream. I am here to work for the United Nations." As I state this unequivocally, my anxiety subsides just a bit. I know what I'm here to do. I take a deep breath.

"Ah, long shot! My friend, getting a job at United Nations not possible!" Val says.

"I am going to their office tomorrow, and I am going to get a job," I say with a confidence I do not feel, as panic hits me again; this is not helped by the fact that Val and his friends burst out laughing. I feel heat rising in my face.

"Good luck, my friend," Val says, not unkindly, but he keeps laughing.

When night falls, I lie wide awake in my narrow bed, physically and emotionally exhausted. Still, I am afraid of falling asleep in this small room with these strange men. They seem nice enough, but who knows?

I say a silent prayer, reminding myself again who I am: I am *Mwana Wevhu*, a child of the African soil with big ideas and big dreams. I am a girl from Africa. And I am, as of this moment, one step closer to my dream. For now, that is more than enough.

You must act as if it is impossible to fail.

—Ghanaian proverb

4

As soon as I see the logo on the wall, I run toward it, my heart thumping wildly. The last time I was this close to the iconic blue-and-white seal of the United Nations was on the blue uniform of the *sisi* who saved my life in Goromonzi during the terrible drought. That was the moment that sparked my dream; it is the reason I am here. I touch the seal with trembling fingers, the metal frame cool against my skin. *This is really happening.* I am finally here at the United Nations offices in London, so close to achieving my dream that I am actually touching it. I chuckle to myself in utter disbelief when I hear, "Excuse me, might I help you?"

I blush with embarrassment, realizing that my laugh must have been audible and it is likely seen as quite odd to be tracing this seal with my fingers as if it is a priceless artifact. I turn around to see a neatly dressed British woman with eyes that match the color of her short brown hair. Her face is as warm and friendly as her pink-and-green floral dress. *This is it.* This is the moment, the opportunity to achieve my dream so that I can uplift the lives of others, just as my life was once uplifted. My excitement could fill this building and all the others on the block.

"Yes, please. Madam, I am here for a job." I hand her a copy of my CV that lists my previous work experience as a customer service representative—first in a large supermarket, then at a travel agency—

as well as my work as a care assistant at several HIV/AIDS clinics in Zimbabwe. I can feel myself beaming with enthusiasm.

She shakes her head and refuses to accept it. "I am afraid we aren't hiring," she says matter-of-factly, although not unkindly; and with that, she turns around and walks away, returning to the reception desk that I sprinted past when I entered the building.

I follow her, still gleeful and hopeful. I've done the hardest part—I've gotten here. This next step must be easier. "When will you be hiring, madam?"

"You can check our website for listings." She lowers her head and begins typing on her computer. Her voice is no longer warm and friendly but dismissive, clearly inviting me to leave without saying so outright. I cannot leave. This is the job I have longed for since I was a child. *This is my dream.*

I stand, CV in hand, and search for the right words to say. "Please, madam! Please! How might I be considered for a job?"

The woman stops typing, sighs, and says sharply, "Tell you what, we will gladly keep your CV on file."

I hand her my CV and watch her scan it quickly. "I see that you don't have a university degree," she says without looking up. I knew that I would need a degree, but I was still hoping to get a junior position. When I explain this to the woman, her response is curt. "I'm afraid you still need a degree. The same is true for our unpaid internship program; one must be enrolled in university."

When she hands my CV back, I feel deeply ashamed, as if it is a truly worthless piece of paper. But I cannot miss this opportunity. I need to make her understand why I am here, and how important it is, and so I tell her how far I have traveled, the long journey I have taken, "just so I can work for the United Nations. I am . . ." I am practically breathless, trying so hard to make her see me, hear me, to give me a chance.

"Did you say the United Nations?" She cuts me off. I nod yes.

She explains to me that this is not the United Nations, but an entirely separate organization. I look at the UN seal on the wall, then at the woman, then back at the logo. "Yes, this is rather confusing to most people, our logo is the United Nations seal and our name is quite similar, but we are in fact a different nonprofit organization—the United Nations Association—and we simply work to promote the work of the UN, that's all. I can help you with the UN address if you like," she offers, softening a bit when she registers my distress.

She scribbles on a piece of paper and hands it to me. I feel a rush of relief. *I am still on track.* I ask for help with directions, and a look of confusion crosses the woman's face once again.

"The address is in Geneva, in Switzerland. That's the nearest UN office."

I ask for the *local* address of the United Nations—surely there must be one!

"The United Nations doesn't have an office in London," she says.

"Are you sure?"

"Absolutely. You must either go to Geneva in Switzerland or New York City in the United States."

I feel my heart drop into my feet. *How is this possible? How have I made such a huge mistake coming to London?* I feel incredibly stupid for having taken such a massive misstep. I was not aware of the distinction between the real United Nations and the United Nations Association, given the exact same logo and similar name. I spent hours at the library researching the United Nations before leaving Zimbabwe. I knew that the UN had more than sixty different entities, with different names like UNICEF, UNESCO and WHO, each focused on different issues. I assumed that UNA-UK, which is how the United Nations Association was typically referenced, must be one of them. Besides, how could they call themselves the United Nations *anything* and not be a part of the actual UN? Not only do I lack the financial resources to travel to Switzerland or the

United States, but neither country is part of the Commonwealth, making it nearly impossible for me to obtain a visa.

I am devastated, utterly defeated, as if my dream is dying around me, right here in the office that I thought was the right one, but is in fact the wrong one. *What I am going to do now?* I tear out of the office and run onto the busy street. Rain is pouring from the sky, and the loud noise of black cabs and red buses rumbling past is unbearable and disorienting. *I have to get as far from here as possible.* I keep running, and when I finally run out of breath, I realize I'm in a small, dark alley, lost again, with my clothes soaking wet from the rain that falls all around me.

Everything begins to spin: the ground, my mind, my thoughts. I have left everyone behind, Gogo and my family, my home and everything that I have ever known—to come here to this country that once ruled my own, only so that I could work for the United Nations. But now that is never going to happen. Water tumbles around my body, drenching me completely, as I feel myself begin to unravel. I am shattered. *What I am going to do now that I have lost my dream, now that I have lost everything?*

✛

I am ten years old, and Gogo and I are making food packets inside our hut. We are in the middle of a second terrible drought just as powerful as the first. During the first drought two years ago, death took so many lives—just as it nearly did my own. It took the souls of many young children and sick *ambuyas* and *sekurus*. And now it is coming for us again. Once again, God has forgotten us. Once again, the rain has refused to come, leaving us with Satan's punishing heat, which dries up our river and kills our animals, trees, and crops. Once again, there will be no harvest this year. So we ration our food, counting our maize and beans before cooking, skipping as many meals as possible, ignoring our hunger pangs, as we brace ourselves for the worst that we know is coming.

"We must make our food last-last," Gogo warns. We measure and pour the beans we just received from one of the *ambuyas* into small bags, leaving the door slightly open to let in "God's light," but not wide enough to let in "Satan's punishing heat."

Suddenly, I hear an unfamiliar woman's voice outside the hut say, "I come in God's name."

Still busy-busy with the beans, I say, "We welcome you," as I greet every visitor, known or unknown. The woman asks if she may enter, and I say again that she is welcome.

When the woman opens the door, the hut is instantly flooded with a shimmering light. As this stranger steps inside, the sun's rays surround her with a radiant glow, as if she is one of God's angels from the Bible. She sets a large bag on the floor, straightens her dress—red, with white buttons down the front—wipes dust from her brown canvas shoes, and sits down next to Gogo, who does not greet her. This is very strange, as Gogo smiles at everyone and is always quick to offer God's blessings. But now Gogo does not even look up.

The woman smiles at me, and I notice a big gap in her front teeth. I smile back, trying to remember if I have seen her before. She studies me carefully, and without looking at Gogo, the woman says, "How are you, Gogo?" clapping her hands together in greeting.

"Eeee, things are hard," Gogo responds, but still does not look at the smiling woman. I am stunned by Gogo's reaction. She seems upset with the smiling woman. *Why?*

"Are you okay?" the woman asks me, and because I am fine-fine, I nod. She reaches inside her bag and pulls out two loaves of bread, a big box of Tanganda tea bags, a bag of brown sugar, a small packet of salt, a small sack of rice, and several tins of beans.

The sight of the food thrills me, and I thank God for sending this

45

angel-woman to Gogo and me, just like he sent the girl in the blue uniform who found me and gave me porridge during the last drought, saving my life. This angel has not only brought us food, but also special gifts for me. She holds up a pretty dress patterned with yellow, red, and orange flowers, and then a pair of black canvas shoes that look brand-new. Gogo nods her approval, and so I accept the gifts, saying, "Thank you, Ambuya," because I assume this is what she is.

"Let's see if it fits," the woman says, and although the shoes are too tight and pinch my feet, I put them on, together with the new dress, and smile.

"Aaaa, now you look smart-smart," the angel-woman says. She turns to Gogo and says, "We must go."

Gogo sighs and says to me, "Come here, my dear child." Her eyes fill with tears. "I must tell you something." She explains that our situation is getting worse, and if the rain doesn't come soon, things will worsen still. "I can no longer take care of you, my dear child," she says, but she cannot look at me as she says this. "This is your *amai*—mother—and she has come for you."

My mother? The amai *I have never met before? The* amai *who abandoned me when I was only a year old?* Suddenly Gogo's anger and refusal to address the woman make sense. Gogo said this woman, my *amai*, brought too-much-too-much shame to our family.

I have prayed and longed for my *amai* for so many years. And now here she is, sitting in the hut I share with Gogo, her braided hair gathered stylishly on top of her head, her gap-toothed smile wide and friendly, her long, slender face a mirror of Gogo's. I have imagined meeting her so many times; I imagined running into her arms, crying with joy. Instead, I feel nothing. It's as if the light around her disappears and a dark shadow blankets her face, making her look like a dark angel, one that comes bearing terrible news. She is a stranger, and I do not want to go with her. I cannot imagine living anywhere but Goromonzi, or with anyone but Gogo.

I throw my arms around Gogo's waist and beg her to let me stay.

"Please, please don't let this woman take me!" I beg. "I promise I will find more food. I promise I will eat less, Gogo."

Gogo strokes my head, and her voice is thick with emotion when she says, "It is better this way, my dear child."

"We can't miss the bus," the *amai* person says in a tight voice.

"Why didn't you tell me you didn't want me anymore!" I wail at Gogo. I am so hurt, it's as if a pain has lodged deep in my chest, heavy and spiked. *How can she send me away? What did I do wrong?*

"Eeee, it is very difficult for me too, my dear child." Gogo's voice catches in her throat.

"Gogo, please! I need you. I need you so much!" I can feel my chest crack wide open at the thought of leaving her.

"Eeee, my dear child. Listen to me." Tears flow from her eyes. "You have a special *shinga*—strength—that will always protect you. Me, I think that when God created us Africans, he knew that life wasn't always going to be easy, so he gave us all this special *shinga*."

I keep sobbing.

"*Shinga* is your inner strength, but it also means so much more— *shinga* means courage and to 'be strong,' and it also means to 'persevere' and to be 'resilient.' You, my dear child, you can always draw on your *shinga*, no matter the challenges you may face."

This does not soothe me; Gogo is my strength. "But I can't live without you, Gogo." I bury my head in her chest and wail loudly.

Gogo takes my hand and places it on my heart, and holds it there. "Whenever you need me, I will always be right here with you inside your heart. Never forget that, my dear child. Never forget." My sad heart beats wildly against my hand.

Now I am terrified. *Where will this* amai *person take me? Will I ever see Gogo again?* "We have to go now," Amai says. She pulls me away from my beloved Gogo, and practically drags me out of the hut. And in that moment, my world falls apart.

"Where are we going?" I ask, and this *amai* person tells me in a quick-quick way that we are going to the big city of Harare and then to Epworth, which is a township where she lives, near Harare. I know that Harare is the capital city of Zimbabwe, so I listen carefully and try to remember everything so that I will know how to get back to Goromonzi, back to my true home with Gogo.

We will take two buses. I have never been on a bus before. I am so scared that I force myself to grab this *amai* person's hand, but I let go immediately once we've climbed inside the first bus. A frightened chicken clucks loudly, running up and down the center aisle, disturbing the serious *sekurus* sitting in the front seats lost in their thoughts. A few solemn *ambuyas* at the back of the bus chat softly, holding woven baskets and skinny chickens on their laps to sell in Harare.

When we sit down, this *amai* person takes out her yarn and knitting needles and begins to knit. Clearly, she is not going to give me any more information about what is happening. I press my face to the window and watch the women and girls selling clay pots and woven baskets by the side of the road. In the distance are forests of dead trees and brown grass, as well as field after field littered with rows and rows of dead crops.

Eventually I fall asleep, and when I wake up, Amai says, "We are in Harare." I know Harare as the place where most *sekurus* in the village go to look for work so they can buy the *ambuyas* and their children nice-nice things. Harare is also where Gogo's big-big son and her other two daughters live. Through the smudged glass I see only strangers and chaos. Plenty-plenty cars move fast-fast in all directions over wide roads. People look busy-busy rushing everywhere, and men weave between the cars on their bicycles. There are buildings of a kind I've never seen before, made entirely of glass, and I fear that a fast car might drive straight into one of the glass buildings, shattering it into tiny pieces. I shudder with fear.

We alight at Mbare, which Amai tells me is the main station for the buses to the villages. Now that I am not with Gogo, I feel more alone in the world, and I observe everything with careful eyes. The world itself feels suffocating and much less friendly. Women wearing colorful dresses with crying babies tied on their backs sell beautiful beads at the side of the road. Men shout at the top of their voices for people to board buses to places I have never heard of and cannot even imagine. Two policemen chase a young boy, screaming, "*Tsotsi, tsotsi!*—Thief, thief!" It couldn't be more different from the peace of life in Goromonzi; here it is all shouting and honking and crowds. The air is no longer crisp and fresh as it is in our village, but clogged and smelly from bus and car fumes.

We take another bus to Epworth, and when we stop at a small township center, music blares from a radio in a store while men pound their feet to the beats and rhythm. Girls almost as young as I am, with bright red lips and dressed in tight-tight clothing, dance with the men in a way I have never seen before. I look away with embarrassment. "Eeee, those ones are trouble!" Amai says, nodding in the girls' direction. I get nervous, so I hold tightly to Amai's hand, even though I desperately want to run back to Gogo. We march in silence, winding between small houses made of rusty metal and colorful plastic; past piles of decaying rubbish covered in flies; past young girls cooking supper on small fires in their tiny yards.

Amai's house is made of brick; it is dark when we arrive, but there is a man sitting on a small sofa, and a paraffin lamp on top of a cabinet casting weak light across the room. Sitting at a short, round table covered in a white cloth are a young boy, a young girl, and a baby. They scream "AMAI!!" and rush to the door.

"Children, say hello to your sister, Lizzy," Amai says, gently pushing me forward, and the children throw their arms around my legs and smile up at me. I learn that Osi is the boy, Memo is the girl, and the baby girl is called Chio. I am so overwhelmed that I cannot speak or move. This is too-much-too-much of too many things. Too much that is new and different. *Who are these children? Where are we? I do not want to be here. I want my Gogo. I want to go home.*

"And this is your *baba*, your father," Amai tells me.

"Hello. Welcome home, Lizzy," the *baba* person says with a wide, beaming smile as he extends his hand to me. I never knew how to think of him in my head, so when faced with the actual person, I cannot say a word or even offer a greeting. Didn't Gogo say he was irresponsible and useless? He pats me on the head and returns to the sofa. I am practically trembling with confusion; I am so disoriented and sad. Amai offers me food, but I do not respond, even when she places a small bowl of *sadza* and vegetables on the table. She asks me if I am hungry, or if I am tired, and I remain still and silent.

"Okay, come," she says abruptly, clearly irritated, and leads me to a small, dark room behind a curtain. Some light from the paraffin lamp filters into the room, where Amai arranges a small pile of blankets in the corner. I wait for this stranger, my *amai*, to leave, and then I take off my dress, roll it into a pillow, and slide between the blankets. I burst into tears. *I want to go back to Goromonzi. I want my Gogo.* I place my hand on my heart and try to speak to Gogo, trying to feel her familiar presence, wanting nothing more than to run away. I fall asleep still sobbing, praying to God to send me back home.

✛

Without my dream to keep me going, I struggle for weeks to find purpose and meaning. My days in London are as gloomy and depressing as the weather, spent pounding the pavement in the continuous drizzling rain, looking for work. I go door to door, asking for jobs at supermarkets and clothing stores; I inquire at restaurants and travel agents, explaining to the managers that I have previous retail experience. I decide that if I'm already in London, I will need to make the most of it. I will find another job—any job. I will save money, go to university, and then apply for a job with the United Nations in Geneva or New York City.

"Sorry, love; we're not hiring," I hear over and over again, followed by a long glance up and down my body, making me feel self-conscious of my appearance and my inexpensive clothes. "I am a hard worker and I learn quickly," I always reply. Still I fail to find a job. I cling to Gogo's *shinga* mantra. "*Shinga*," I whisper to myself each time they turn me down. "*Shinga*," I chant out loud before I knock on every door. I call on that inner strength as if it is water in a well that I might drink from to sustain me. I try to let it fill me up.

Just as Gogo and I rationed our food during the drought in Goromonzi, I keep careful track of my food so it lasts as long as possible, rationing three slices of bread per day thinly covered with peanut butter and marmalade jam. Just like in Goromonzi, I barter and share food with Val and the other guests at the hostel, roughly forty fellow immigrants from more than thirteen different countries, including an aspiring nurse from South Africa called Bronwyn, and Iman, a recent law school graduate from the Middle East. In this filthy place we create a small and supportive community as we attempt to adapt to this new home. We connect with one another over our desires and dreams to uplift our families and communities out of extreme poverty and build a better life for them and for ourselves. At night we sit on mismatched plastic chairs around the grimy blue plastic kitchen table, sharing our stories from home.

"I am gutted. The UK won't recognize my qualifications, so now I have to retrain, which is very expensive," Bronwyn says. The frustration is palpable in her voice as she talks about all the rejections she's received from local hospitals and clinics. We discuss our shared experiences, exchanging tips for finding work and laughing at our failures. This is how we briefly forget about our own individual struggles: being seen by hiring managers as suspicious, sometimes simply based on the "strange" sounds of our foreign last names; being judged as "less than" due to our nationalities and the misperceptions or stereo-types that come with them; being thought of as "other" because of the color of our skin, or the texture of our hair, or the thickness of our accents, or the "odd" style of our clothing. Iman chimes in with her own story. "Can you believe that the hiring manager asked if I would be okay with not wearing my hijab to work if offered the job, so as to not offend the clients? How culturally insensitive is that?" she says. We all nod, sharing in her pain. These conversations stave off loneliness and give me a sense of belonging somewhere in this huge gray city.

Our status as outsiders binds us together; and yet we are still out-siders. I know that when some managers hear that I am from Africa, they don't see the beauty of my village, or the generous and kind nature of the people who raised me. Instead, they see images like the ones featured in fundraising commercials that play constantly on the tiny television suspended in the corner of the hostel's greasy kitchen: images of naked, severely malnourished African children with their mouths agape and their faces covered in flies; images of destitute women in tattered clothing, wandering aimlessly in refugee camps; images of skeletal-looking people dying of AIDS in crowded hospi-tals.

"My friend, is it really that bad in Africa?" Val asks. I share with him my own experience with poverty when the drought hit my village, but I also tell him that life on either side of that crisis was defined by richness and abundance and joy. I tell him that Harare is a developed, modern, and bustling city with skyscrapers and wide paved roads, lined with busy cafés and trendy shops. I explain that the images flashing across the screen are completely skewed and one-sided, reinforcing a single, negative narrative—one very different from the Africa I know and love. The images I see in the UK depict Africa as a country, rather than a culturally rich, socially and linguistically diverse continent of more than fifty vibrant, independently governed countries. In short, what Val has seen and what I see and what, no doubt, the hiring managers see are images that do not show the full African story. I tell Val that our people are proud and hardworking, and our cultures colorful and joyous. I tell him that we define ourselves not by the enormity of our struggles, but by our resilience and strength in facing them, working together as children of the African soil.

"Okay, I see," Val says, and smiles at me. "I understand."

When I count my money after paying for my second month of rent, I realize that I am down to my last forty pounds, and that I have been searching for a job for over a month. I panic. I can't go back home to Zimbabwe without having accomplished anything. I can't waste the opportunity that Gogo has given me to be here in London to pursue my dream. An opportunity that most of the *sisis* in Goromonzi will never have. I have to do more with my life. I have to find a solution. "*Shinga*," I whisper to myself, and decide that if no manager will hire me, I will create my own work.

I visit African communities in the London neighborhoods of Lambeth and Croydon, offering to braid women's hair in their homes in exchange for a small fee. As I anxiously wait outside supermarkets, colleges, and bus terminals, shivering in the cold rain and scouting for potential clients, I am completely deflated, but I keep a friendly smile stretched across my face. I hold on tightly to Gogo's *shinga* mantra. I hold on to it with everything I have, with my full heart, praying to God. Sometimes, if I am lucky, and if God answers my constant prayers, I get a customer or two, earning just enough to buy a loaf of bread, a box of tea, and a bus ticket. This work—this life—could not be more different from my dream or what I intended to do in London. "*Shinga*," I chant as I walk for hours or ride the bus back to the youth hostel. "*Shinga*," I whisper as I slowly eat my bread and peanut butter in the kitchen, my stomach growling. "*Shinga*," I repeat to myself as I lie in bed at night. Eventually, this mantra becomes a kind of lullaby, and I fall asleep thinking of the strength that Gogo promised would always be within me. I know that I will need to call upon it for whatever tomorrow might bring.

It is not fear but courage that is important.

⊘

—South African proverb

5

"**Your rent is due; no** discussion." The pudgy hostel manager glares at me over the top of his glasses. He has a greasy face, with puffy cheeks, wafer-thin lips, and a wispy comb-over, and he's disheveled—dressed in a dirty-looking grayish shirt, open at the neck, that exposes a silver cross necklace nestled on his hairy chest. I feel rattled.

Although Tiny Nose warned me about the hostel manager's gruff attitude, I had not expected him to be this cold and dismissive. I don't have the rent, although God knows, I wish I did. Even though I have been searching for a job almost nonstop for close to two months, I am still unemployed and have now completely run out of money. I am out of options. "*Shinga*," I whisper to myself, quietly summoning all the confidence I can muster.

"I intend to pay my rent, sir. Perhaps I could work for you so that I may be able to do so. I . . ." I am pleading with him, even though Gogo says we should always maintain our dignity and never beg, except to God.

My words agitate him. "Is this a bloody joke? You either pay your rent or you better bloody well leave first thing tomorrow morning. Am I clear?" His voice is raspy and he shakes a chubby finger at me.

Beads of cold sweat break out on my back. *Where will I go?* This hostel is my only home in London. It is the only place that feels familiar and safe. Even though the dorm smells like feet, the kitchen is always covered in crumbs and dirt and dust, and the moldy communal bathroom is hardly the stuff of dreams, my friends are here. I cannot lose my new community of fellow immigrants; I would feel even more alone without their support and companionship. This is the only place in this gigantic city where I am accepted without judgment. Out of options and out of money, I have no other place to go except the street.

I try again. "Perhaps I could help out at the reception, sir. I used to work at a travel agency back home." I hand him a copy of my CV, which he refuses to accept, shaking his head.

"I am not bloody hiring. I need you out tomorrow. Do you understand me?" Without waiting for an answer, he turns to leave.

I am desperate. My only other choice is to give up on my dream and go back home to Zimbabwe. That is not an option. I will not disappoint Gogo. I have to make this work.

I run after him. "I have no other place to go, sir." I feel diminished, small, as if I'm watching myself from above. Suddenly, I have an idea. "Perhaps I could take care of the rat and cockroach problem for you, sir," I shout to his back, offering a solution to both our problems. Val recently told me that health inspectors have threatened to shut down the hostel if the pest infestation doesn't improve.

The manager stops, turns to me, and says, "Go on." I do not want to do this job at all, of course, but any job is better than no job. Nobody said chasing a dream was easy, and that has certainly been the case for me. I have survived for almost two months; I can do this unappealing work if it means staying in London. *Shinga*, I remind myself, remembering my inner strength. "I would be more than happy to clean the kitchen and communal areas in exchange for rent, sir."

To my surprise, the manager perks up. Although I see the concern in his shifty eyes, and he is still completely unfriendly, he accepts my offer. When we shake hands, I become the hostel's janitor in exchange for my rent.

This could not be more different from the job I was hoping for, but it will keep me off the street, and that is what matters. Now that I am in charge of all the cleaning, I rise at the crack of dawn just like I did in Goromonzi, taking care of all the chores before any of the other guests are up. I clean the kitchen and the bathrooms, scrubbing out all the smells, filth, and mold. I wash up in the kitchen again after dinner, disinfecting all the communal rooms and spraying for pests. The work is disgusting and endless and tiring, but I find meaning in the job: I take pride in creating a healthier and more hospitable environment for myself and the other guests; I find gratification in putting in an honest day's work in exchange for my rent; and I feel clever for finding a solution to a problem that would have ruined my chances to take the next step toward my dream. After I complete my janitorial duties, I go out into London once again, searching for a paying job. I still need to buy food and I must save for university. My dream anchors me—even when I'm tired and hungry, and even when the days are long and unpleasant.

Still, I am feeling solemn and worn down one evening when Val finds me cleaning the kitchen. Without being asked he jumps in to help, washing the crusty dishes and keeping me company.

"Don't worry, my friend, everything works out," he says, his hands covered in soapsuds. "In the beginning, I have no job. Now, I have job. Now, I have job *and* college," Val says proudly, flashing his cheerful, gap-toothed smile.

His optimism and kindness briefly lift my spirits. As I clean and he washes dishes, Val tells me about his childhood in Ukraine, where he lived happily with his parents and seven siblings until his father, who was an engineer, died when Val was fifteen years old. His mother was left with eight hungry kids to feed, clothe, and send to school. This presented a huge challenge, because Val's mother didn't have a job or the academic qualifications to pursue one, as she had dropped out of school when she became pregnant with Val. After the death of her husband, and with no formal skills, she took every possible job she could find to take care of her family, working as a nanny, a cleaning lady in office buildings, and a hotel chambermaid, often working two or three jobs at once. I feel immediate empathy for Val's mother as I squash a cockroach with my foot and spray down the corner with roach killer. Even with all her hard work, his mother was unable to make enough money to make ends meet, so Val dropped out of school to help her, taking any odd job he could find. I can imagine that he stepped up to help with the same positive attitude with which he seems to approach everything.

He stacks the final dish in the drying rack, I put down my broom, and we sit down together at the newly clean kitchen table. One day Val's mother handed him an envelope full of cash and told him that she had been setting money aside every month to send him to London. She wanted him to find a proper job and build a better life for himself and their family. A year ago, Val arrived in the UK, and he is now studying engineering while working part-time at a recruitment agency; he is able to pay for his college fees and also send money back home. His story inspires me.

"Yes, my friend, my mama do this for me. Can you believe?" Val says, his voice cracking with emotion. "Ah, my mama!" He shakes his head and looks away. I look at the tears glistening in Val's eyes and feel similar emotions bubble up inside me. Although our home countries are thousands of miles apart, with vastly different cultures and languages, Val's story reminds me so much of my own. Like Val, I am the eldest in my family, and like him, my mother struggled to take care of me and my siblings. Like Val, my mother constantly searched for money for our family, doing all kinds of odd jobs. Val left everything behind to come to London to pursue his dream, which was also his mother's dream for him, and so did I. All of this was made possible by the sacrifices our mothers made, and by their determination to give us opportunities that would lead to meaningful lives full of purpose and joy.

I can tell that Val and I will become good friends, so I open up to him about my mother. It feels good to tell this story to a person I can trust. I tell him about the first morning after I arrived in Epworth from Goromonzi, when Amai gave me my first big opportunity—to attend school for the first time, when I was ten years old.

✛

I am startled out of sleep by Amai's anxious voice saying, "It's time to go. Wake up your brother."

I rub my eyes and look around at the siblings I have only just met, sleeping on the floor beside me, all huddled together under the same thin, brown blanket with frayed edges, dotted with tiny holes. I take in the small, stuffy room that is much smaller than Gogo's tiny hut, and empty except for a big pile of clothes heaped in one corner. A long wire suspended between the unplastered brick walls is hanging with children's clothes of various sizes. I look over at Osi and immediately decide that I am going to call him "The Boy," inside my head, so I will not start to like him. I gently nudge The Boy awake.

I stumble out of the dark house and find Amai kneeling next to a small fire in the yard, stirring porridge quick-quick in a metal pot. Other fires are burning in the neighbors' yards, and dark smoke tunnels upward into the gray sky. I notice that Amai's house, made of brick, is much nicer than the other homes, which are made of sticks and clay or scraps of metal covered by roofs of colorful plastic. The homes around me are built close together, and all of their yards combined are smaller than Gogo's yard. The air is fresh and crisp, the sky still dark and gray, and my longing for the bright yellow sky in Goromonzi feels like a stab in my heart. *Today*, I think, *I will run away, back to Gogo.*

Amai hands me a bucket. "There," she says, nodding toward a shack made of sticks and plastic at the edge of the yard. Inside, it smells like rotting cabbage. Small brown rocks are laid out over the damp ground and a single bar of cracked green soap sits in the corner. This is the washing shack for Amai and four other neighbors and their families. I splash my body with water, scrub my legs and cracked feet, and dry off with a small, scratchy green towel. When I get out, Amai hands me a blue dress and a matching sweater, just like the clothes I noticed hanging inside moments before.

"Are we going back to Goromonzi?" I ask hopefully, although I wonder why I wouldn't simply wear the other new dress she gave me yesterday.

"Hurry up," Amai says, ignoring my question. "The porridge is almost ready. Where is your brother?"

When The Boy comes out, he is wearing a pair of blue shorts and a sweater that matches my own, only smaller. We both eat porridge, as Amai shares the food with her neighbors.

"Where are we going?" I ask again. I really want to know. *Why won't anyone tell me what's going on?*

"Us, we are going to school, Lizzy," The Boy shouts gleefully.

I am confused and alarmed. I want to go back to Gogo, not to school with The Boy.

"Let's go," Amai says impatiently, balancing a large metal basin on her head. I decide that wherever this school is, I will wait for Amai to leave and then ask the teacher how to get back to Goromonzi, to my true home with Gogo.

"How far away is the school?" I ask.

"Aaaa, maybe one hour," Amai responds.

I don't know what "one hour" is. I don't know how to tell time. I have never had a watch. I decide I will know how long "one hour" is once we get there, and I follow Amai as we weave through the township, marching toward the school. I ask how long it will take to walk to Harare, and Amai says, "maybe five hours." I still don't know what five hours means–means, but I imagine it will be like walking from Amai's home to school five times. *I can manage that*, I think, remembering the long journeys to get water at the river in the Good Forest. I know how to walk fast-fast. When I ask, "How far from Harare to Goromonzi?" Amai's voice is irritated and weary, "Me, I don't know." Once again, I am asking too many questions for a child, so I keep walking and say no more.

"We are here!" The Boy cries when we reach Epworth Primary School, and I follow Amai through the gate into the schoolyard, which is packed with students in blue uniforms running around and making too much noise. On the edge of the schoolyard sits a white church with a wooden cross. Beside the church are classrooms arranged in a square facing each other. I stay close to Amai. I can hear my heart beating in my ears.

Amai walks with me into the classroom, "This is Lizzy. She is coming from our village, Goromonzi." After she introduces me to the teacher, all the students laugh. I am too terrified to respond. In my panic, the room begins to spin. The teacher rushes to my side and leads me to an empty chair at the back of the classroom while the kids keep laughing.

I slump into the desk chair, feeling miserable. Amai doesn't know that when I was supposed to go to school in Goromonzi, when I was seven, Gogo bought me a uniform, a book, and a pencil, but I only attended for a few weeks because there was too much work to do in the fields. Gogo needed my help. I can count to fifty and add simple numbers, but I cannot write a full sentence and it hurts my hand to hold a pencil. *What will I do now?*

The teacher writes numbers on the board and asks us to copy them down in our notebooks. It is the first day of the new school year and I am not prepared. I don't have a notebook or a pencil, because Amai didn't give me either one, so I pretend to write on the desk with my finger. I can't follow anything the teacher is talking about and I finally stop trying.

When the bell rings, I find The Boy, my brother, excitedly waiting for me outside my classroom. He grabs my hand, beaming with joy, and drags me toward the school gate. He asks me all kinds of questions without waiting for answers: "Do you like mathematics? Can you teach me grade four things, Lizzy? Me, I am smart-smart. Aaaa, do you play soccer, Lizzy? Me, I am fast-fast."

Outside the school gate, we step into the chaos of plenty-plenty *ambuyas* and *sisis* pacing up and down with huge metal basins full of mangoes, guavas, bananas, *mafatty* buns, crispy *madora* worms, sweets, and potato chips to sell as lunches for the children.

63

"She is there!" The Boy says, running to Amai. He throws his arms around her legs.

"How was class, Lizzy?" Amai asks, shaking the *mafatty* buns inside the basin she carried on her head to the schoolyard. She hands one bun to me and another to The Boy. I have no appetite, so I give my bun to The Boy and help Amai wrap up buns in old newspaper for her customers, the students.

After lunch break, when I ask the teacher how long it will take to get to Goromonzi if I walk fast-fast, she says, "It is not possible. You will never make it," and shoos me away to my desk at the back of the room.

I was clinging to hope that I might find a way out of here, but now that two adults—Amai and the teacher—have said that it is impossible to walk back to Goromonzi, I realize I am stuck here: in this unfamiliar place, surrounded by people who might as well be strangers. I miss Gogo terribly. All I want is to be with her back home. My heart is a weight in my chest. Tears form but I blink them away; I don't want anyone to see that I'm upset. I've been laughed at enough for one day. I make a pillow on my desk with my arms and set my head on it, hiding my face. I am lost and overwhelmed, and I have just realized that I am here for good.

The Boy is so happy to see me after school, and never stops talking and asking me questions, so I decide that if I am to stay here forever, I will call him by his real name, Osi. Osi talks and tells stories until we reach Amai's house. The moment we arrive, Amai says, "Lizzy, you must take care of the house and the children. Me, I am searching for money." I know how to take care of Gogo's hut, but I have never taken care of a house full of children. Amai offers no further instruction or information, overwhelming me again. *What does she mean by searching for money? How long will she be gone?* I am full of questions, but this time I do not ask them. I simply nod in agreement. I will do what I'm told.

The next morning, as the person in charge, I rise at the crack of dawn, just like I did in Goromonzi. I clean the house, sweep the yard, and make fire to cook porridge. I wake the children and feed them, rushing to get myself and Osi to school on time. After school I fetch water from the borehole, wash the dirty dishes, the dirty children, and their dirty clothes. I prepare dinner that night and then every night after, put the children to sleep, and then collapse, exhausted, on the blankets next to them, where I immediately fall asleep.

I miss Gogo every second of every day, but at school I make a new friend called Jeri, who is smart-smart and always at the top of the class. When I tell her about my struggle in school, she says, "Aaaa, don't worry, Lizzy. Me, I can help you with your schoolwork." She stretches her arm across my shoulders and gives me an affectionate squeeze, which makes me feel a bit better. Jeri tells me she wants to be a nurse when she grows up so she can take care of others.

"Me," I say, "I want to be the girl in the blue uniform."

"Who is that?"

"She is God's angel, Jeri. She feeds hungry children, and she once took care of me. Promise me, Jeri," I say, hooking my small finger with hers. "Promise that we will help other people when we grow up."

We raise our hands up, pinkies pressed together. "I promise, Lizzy, I promise," she says, and gently pulls our fingers apart.

Time goes by, as days turn into weeks, and weeks turn into months, and finally the school year has ended, and it has been nearly one year since I moved to Epworth. When I receive my report card, I see I have failed every subject. I am hugely disappointed. When Amai sees the results, she is equally distressed. "Eeee, Lizzy," she says, and I feel ashamed, knowing I have let her down.

One morning she calls me in from the yard, where I've been playing with Memo and Osi. I find her sitting on the sofa folding clothes into a small bag. It is a week before Christmas, a few weeks since the school year ended, and Amai has just come back from the Harare city center, where she goes each year to buy scraps from an Indian fabric store to sew the children's holiday clothes. Amai says there is never enough money to buy the children new clothes and shoes. Baba works for an Indian man, bagging groceries in his small shop, but it's not enough money to take care of the house and the children, and there is never enough to buy food, never enough to replace the two worn blankets or even to pay school fees. Amai is forever searching for money: selling *mafatty* buns outside the school; knitting school sweaters to sell to other parents; raising and selling chickens and rabbits; selling vegetables from a stand in the yard—eventually scraping together just enough, after paying for school fees and food, to plead with the store owner to sell her fabric scraps because she doesn't have enough for the real-real fabric which is too expensive.

I notice she is folding one of my dresses instead of stitching together fabric scrap clothes. This is odd.

"Where are we going?"

She says nothing, just zips the bag closed.

"Are we going to Goromonzi?" I feel a surge of excitement and wait anxiously for her answer. Amai promised me I could visit Gogo during the first school holiday, but when the time came, she said, "Eeee, Lizzy. Us, we need help searching for money." I learned how to braid hair, and I stayed in Epworth braiding as many as eight heads of hair per day. When the second school holiday arrived, it was the same: no money. I eventually gave up and stopped asking Amai about visiting Gogo. *Could it be that God has answered my prayers, that I am going back to Goromonzi after all this time? I will finally see Gogo!*

"Lizzy, you should get ready," Amai says, and I throw my arms around her and leave quickly for the washing shack before she can change her mind.

When I return from the washing shack, Amai says, "Here! It's yours," handing me a new green dress with a white ribbon around the waist. I haven't had a new dress from Amai since the day I left Goromonzi, and now I feel sad, because Amai has used money that she doesn't have to buy me a new dress. She sits down on the sofa and stares into empty space, looking completely lost. *How will she search for money when I am away?*

Who will take care of the house and the children? I feel guilty, but I put on the dress so as not to hurt her feelings. I am sad that Amai needs me, when all I want is my Gogo.

I thank Amai, and she wraps her arms tightly around me until a car horn sounds.

"Your uncle Sam is here," she says, letting me go.

Uncle Sam is married to Amai's older sister, Aunt Jane, and he has visited us when he occasionally drives Baba home from work. He speaks English and German from his time abroad, and when he speaks our Shona language, he sounds funny-funny. Still, he is friendly, and I am grateful that he is taking me to Gogo.

I turn to look at Amai's sad face and wonder if I should stay. But I know I must see Gogo; it has been too long.

Outside in the yard, Osi, Memo, and Chio are sad to see me go. "Don't worry, I will be back soon-soon." I promise to take them next time. "I will teach you how to pick juicy black berries in the Good Forest," I say then hug them goodbye. I get into Uncle Sam's car, set my head against the window and quickly fall asleep. I dream that I have fallen into the river in the Hyena Forest. As Gogo reaches for me, the water pulls me away and I scream and scream until Uncle Sam gently shakes me awake.

"We're here," he says softly.

I am so excited to see Gogo, but when I wake up, I see bright, flickering lights everywhere. I hear the voices of many people and cars honking. This is a city. This is not Goromonzi. *Am I still dreaming?* I blink, but when I open my eyes, the lights are still there. They seem even brighter, the city noises that much louder.

Still in shock, I follow Uncle Sam when he says "hurry up!" and we walk through a black gate, down a narrow corridor, then up four flights of stairs. He opens the door into a room and flips a switch, flooding the space with light. I have never been in a house before with this much light, and I blink several times as my eyes adjust. When they do, I realize I have never been in a house full of such beautiful furniture. A wide window is trimmed with lacy white curtains, pulled back to reveal a busy road and fast cars. A green, shiny sofa that looks long enough to seat three people faces a large television sitting on top of a wooden cabinet. Two small, matching chairs sit at both ends of the sofa, one directly below the window. In the middle of the room is a small glass table. I look down and see that the floor is made of small pieces of wood glued together. When I look to my left, I see a spotless kitchen through an open door.

"Where are we?" I ask. I feel as if I've walked into a dream.

"Home."

"Where is Gogo?"

Uncle Sam pauses and then asks, "Gogo?"

I ask him several times where we are, and he repeats that we are home. I follow Uncle Sam past a room with a white toilet like those I have seen in schoolbooks, but never for real. In what he calls "my room" is a real bed, but I have never slept in a bed before. He shows me a wardrobe—a big cabinet with wire hangers—where I can hang my new school uniform for my new school.

"What new school?" I am utterly confused and also wildly disappointed; I was meant to be in Goromonzi tonight.

"Didn't your *amai* explain? You're going to Admiral Tait Primary School."

This makes no sense. I was going to see Gogo and then return to school with Jeri.

Seeing the bewildered look on my face, he says, "It is one of the best private British schools. You'll like it, you'll see. You will learn English, and then you can speak English with me." Uncle Sam smiles at me before leaving the room.

I'm so disoriented I can hardly see straight. Didn't Amai say I was going to Goromonzi to see Gogo? No, she didn't. I asked her, but she never answered. None of it makes sense, unless . . . she has gotten rid of me for a second time. *Amai has abandoned me again.*

I feel a burning sensation in my body that spreads from the inside out. I hear a terrible ringing in my ears and I fall to the floor, curling myself into a ball. I stare up at a black spot on the wall and wonder what I did wrong. *Why doesn't Amai want me?* I tried so hard to take care of the house and the children. I tried hard to search for money, to make her happy, to make her love me. *How can this be happening?*

Eventually I fall asleep on the floor, and the river nightmare I had in the car continues, only this time Gogo is standing on the other side. She lowers her face and walks away, leaving me stranded with the rushing river between us and no way to cross. I wake up with my heart pounding and spring onto my feet, legs still shaking. *I must get to Gogo right now.* I don't know where I am or how far away Goromonzi is; I don't know which road I would take to get there, or even if it's possible to walk there on my own. All I know is that I cannot stay here. I need to get back to my home in Goromonzi. Just like God once parted the water and led the children of Israel to the Promised Land, I know that God will lead me back to Goromonzi. *Yes! He will lead me,* I say in my head.

I tiptoe down the corridor, careful not to disturb Uncle Sam, who is snoring loudly in his bedroom next door. I leave my bag of clothes behind so I can walk quickly to Goromonzi. Outside the sky is dark and the air is cold, so I tiptoe back through the house to pull a sweater from my black bag. There, sitting on top of my neatly folded clothes is a piece of paper. I unfold it carefully and read:

Dear Lizzy,

Uyu mukana wako. Wekuti uve munhu wandakatadza kuyita ini.
     (This is your opportunity. I want you to become what I was unable to be.)

Ndinokuda, Amai
(I love you, Amai)

When you educate a girl,
you educate a nation.

❨❩

—Malawian proverb

6

It is my second year in London, and I stand in the doorway, scanning the small room for an empty chair. The rows of neatly organized desks are nearly filled: Three young women draped in vibrant saris chat away in Hindi in the front. Five guys kitted out in urban streetwear—bright red-and-white Adidas tracksuits, slouchy gray sweatshirts, and baseball caps—huddle in the back. I flash a warm smile at an African girl wearing a colorful head scarf, who smiles back, then perch myself by the window, still reveling in the fact that I am here. I organize my pens and my notebook. *I am ready.*

"Welcome to your first lesson in International Relations," announces a neatly dressed man. I remember the moment I got my acceptance letter, the exact wording: "Congratulations, your application for admission to The London College, University College Kensington, as an undergraduate student, has been successful." Sitting at my desk, I feel the weight of the moment, anchoring me to this room and to this, my first day at university.

I did it, Gogo. I finally made it! I think to myself, thinking of the struggle it's taken to get here, to London College, one year after my arrival in London. The journey has been both harrowing and remarkable, sometimes in the same hour: I remember how I cried myself to sleep so many nights when I failed to find a job; how I skipped meals, drinking water to curb my hunger so I could save every pound I could for university fees; how I hid my pain from Gogo and my family in my letters so they wouldn't worry; how the hostel manager cruelly demanded I start paying rent with money I still didn't have, and tried to throw me out on the street a *second* time after I solved his pest problem. I look out over the room and wonder about everyone's unique stories and how hard they've worked to make the dream of attending university a reality.

The memories make my eyes sting with tears. I hide my face and stare through the open window, allowing crisp, cold air to filter in. Outside the weather is as glorious as I feel: limitless clear, blue skies. A sky for a new beginning. The classroom overlooks a high-rise building of low-income housing, where the apartments look like shoeboxes stacked one on top of the other. Television satellite dishes, colorful flowerpots, and wet clothes draped over balconies brighten up the building's lackluster façade, which is in stark contrast to its posh surroundings—Notting Hill Gate in West London, with its vintage clothing stores, quaint bookstores, and coffee shops. The building reminds me of the pictures Val has shown me of his home in Ukraine. So many stories in that building as well, I'm certain. This city is full of stories.

Val, my first friend at the hostel, has become a great friend, not only keeping me company and telling me about his life, but also helping me get a job in my moment of greatest need. When the bellowing hostel manager threatened to kick me out that second time, I pleaded with Val to introduce me to his boss at the recruitment agency. He had just quit for a better engineering job, but I would happily take his old one, and I did.

"Thirty calls a day, nothing less," the twitchy, cold-eyed boss shouted, directing me to an empty cubicle and slamming a large telephone book on the desk in front of me. With that, I finally got my first regular paying job in London, becoming a sales rep in charge of cold-calling information technology companies to secure hiring contracts for the company, which is where I still work part-time. I only earn a small base salary plus commission, but I have worked hard, quickly learning how to close small deals and then large ones, increasing my weekly earnings and then savings, month by month, until I had enough money to move out of the youth hostel, and eventually enough money to enroll in university.

I am finally an undergraduate student, working on my degree in International Relations, a prerequisite for a job with the United Nations, and back on track to achieving my dream. I searched for months for the right university. I wanted to go to one of the best universities, like Oxford, or Cambridge, or the London School of Economics, but when I looked at the fees, they were too exorbitant. I shifted my focus to the highly ranked but smaller universities that, while affordable, still offered accredited degree programs.

When I was wiping down kitchen counters and setting rat traps less than a year ago, this goal—which I have held for nearly a decade— seemed utterly impossible. I am the first of my immediate family to go to university, the first to have access to higher education. I am overcome with gratitude for this tremendous *mukana* (opportunity). It is one of so many in my life for which I am deeply grateful.

✛

The first morning after Amai sends me to live with Aunt Jane and Uncle Sam in Harare I storm into the kitchen, still clutching the note from Amai.

"What does this mean?" I ask Uncle Sam. I feel so broken and upset that I am no longer intimidated by him, and I can tell he is a kind man. I will demand an answer. Uncle Sam is sitting at the kitchen table eating white toast with marmalade jam and drinking a cup of coffee. He is smartly dressed in a crisp white shirt and pressed gray trousers. The light streaming in from the kitchen window bounces off his round wire-rim glasses, neatly tucked behind his small ears, that make his brown eyes look as big as an owl's, only more caring and kindhearted. That he is so nice to me only spurs me to press for answers to my questions.

He looks at me, reaches for the note, and says, "Your *amai* has asked that we take care of you. I thought she had explained everything to you."

I am breathless with confusion and hurt. No, Amai has not explained anything to me, because she never does, and now she has abandoned me for the second time. I don't need or want to be taken care of like a helpless child. Gogo taught me how to take care of myself, and I looked after the entire house and the children on my own at Amai's. I do not need to be watched or coddled or protected. I am eleven years old.

I look away from him, still brimming with pain. "I can take care of myself."

"Ohhh, I have no doubt, young lady. Your Amai just wants to give you the best education, that's all."

"I already go to school in Epworth."

"I know," he says. "But your grades aren't great. This is your chance for a new start at one of the best private schools." I don't know what a private school is, and neither do I care to attend one.

"Here, let's eat and then I will show you around your new school today," he says, sliding a piece of buttered toast toward me. I do not sit down. I don't want to eat, and I don't want to see any new school with him. All I want now is to go back to Goromonzi, and then maybe back to Epworth to see my best friend, Jeri. Even then I am not sure I ever want to see Amai again. I need to be as far away from her as possible, so she can never abandon me again.

"We will leave in just a few minutes," Uncle Sam says kindly, and takes a sip of coffee.

And so, like so many things that have to do with Amai, and what she does or does not tell me, it seems I have no choice in this school situation, as it has already been decided for me. I am going to a new private school, whether I like it or not. After breakfast, Uncle Sam walks with me to Admiral Tait, pointing out details and landmarks along the way.

"We live in an area called Eastlea, and these types of houses are called flats. Our flat is on the fourth floor," he explains as we walk down the stairs. I watch his feet land on each stair slowly and carefully, keeping the creased ironed lines of his trousers sharp and straight. I decide that Uncle Sam walks slowly, and not with purpose like Gogo. Once outside the building, I look back at the flats; now that it is daylight, I can see how tall the buildings are. The idea of living in a flat so high up terrifies me. What if there is terrible rain and the building crumbles around us, like some of the houses in Epworth do after a storm?

I keep my thoughts to myself and walk silently next to Uncle Sam up the busy road with plenty of cars that make so much noise—honking and speeding up and passing one another—that I can barely hear Uncle Sam as he continues to explain things to me: how the big road right in front of the flats is called Samora Machel Avenue; how if I turn right and walk alongside the avenue I will be able to reach the city center in less than an hour, and if I turn left I can be at my new school in forty minutes; how I should always make sure that I wait for the traffic light to turn green before crossing the street or a car might run me over. There are no traffic lights in Goromonzi or Epworth, so I stare curiously at them as they change from red to green, then watch Uncle Sam's gentle face, noticing the care and excitement in his eyes.

I know that Uncle Sam wants me to be excited too; maybe he wants me to be the child he never had. Amai has told me that when Uncle Sam and Aunt Jane got married, they tried to have children, but God did not hear their prayers, which made them both very sad. Now that I am here, I can tell Uncle Sam is thrilled to have me around, to teach me things, to have a child to care for. I want to be happy with him, but I still feel empty inside.

Along the avenue, we walk past women weaving baskets at a small market and people dressed in smart clothes moving up and down the path, clearly in a rush to get somewhere. We pass large, attractive houses, some surrounded by concrete walls and others with neatly cut hedges.

Beautiful, bright jacaranda trees line the avenue, carpeting the pavement with their bell-shaped purple flowers. I take in everything, remaining silent, until we finally reach the school.

"This is one of the best private schools in the country, called Admiral Tait Primary School. There should be plenty of British children in your class, which will be great for improving your English," Uncle Sam explains with a smile. He sounds so positive and hopeful, but I remain wary.

The classrooms are painted white and form a U shape around a large yard anchored by a huge rectangular flower bed brimming with yellow, white, pink, and red flowers. We poke our heads into the empty classrooms, taking in the brand-new desks and chairs, then walk to the back of the school, where there is a sparkling blue swimming pool surrounded by a fence. I have never seen a swimming pool before, so I stare at the clean blue water for a while, then follow Uncle Sam behind the pool to a playground with an evenly cut lawn.

Unlike Epworth Primary School, the school and its grounds are so nice—like something out of a magazine or a book—with freshly painted buildings, shiny corridors, lush playgrounds, and fragrant, blooming flowers that fill the air with their sweetness. Everything looks perfect, and for a moment I get excited about what I might learn here, and what this will mean for me. I breathe in the smell of freshly cut grass, look around the yard, and feel sudden joy cut through my sadness. But I also feel unsure, and I quickly begin to worry about all the things I do not know: I have never met anyone who is British. I don't know how to speak, read, or write English. *How does Uncle Sam expect me to go to school here and learn anything at all? How will I even fit in?*

"So, what do you think about the school?" Uncle Sam asks, barely able to contain the excitement in his voice.

"What if the other children don't like me?" This is a real concern, a real fear of mine. After all, this is a British school, and Gogo has told me that the British people have not always been kind to us Africans. *Will these children be nice?*

When I tell Uncle Sam this, he says, "Things have changed, and we are now one nation." I don't know what it means to be one nation, but I like hearing that things have changed; it eases my worries a bit. Uncle Sam places his hand on my shoulder and says, "I know this is not easy for you, Elizabeth. Your *amai* and all of us love you very much and we all want the best for you. We all want you to have the choice to do more with your life, and getting a good education gives you the *mukana* to dream bigger, to accomplish more."

I am moved and comforted by his words. I want to do more with my life so I can make Gogo proud. I begin to feel that I can trust Uncle Sam; that I can talk to him and he will listen to me. I feel immense gratitude for his caring and concern.

"Thank you for everything, Uncle Sam," I say, and I mean it.

When I start school at Admiral Tait, I find it extremely challenging. Unlike at Epworth, all the subjects are taught in English, which is incredibly difficult. Still, I like being in a classroom with fewer students, because the teacher is able to spend more time with each of us. I like having a nice library with plenty of English textbooks to read, and I like receiving milk from the school at lunchtime. I appreciate having all these things that I never had before.

I am yet to make friends at the new school, and I miss Jeri terribly, but I am always excited to spend time with Uncle Sam when I get home from school and he gets home from work. Uncle Sam explains that he is an economist. I don't know exactly what he does, but I know that he is very proud of his job, which he says will help our country, Zimbabwe, heal after *Chimurenga* and improve the lives of our people. Aunt Jane works at the hospital in the evenings, so I help Uncle Sam prepare supper as we listen to English language tapes on the stereo. We sit together at the kitchen table for dinner, and Uncle Sam asks me to tell him about my day in English, helping me find bigger and more precise words to describe things and feelings. "You may also use the word 'lovely' instead of 'nice,'" Uncle Sam says. "For example, you could say, 'I had a lovely day,' instead of 'a nice day,' or you could say, 'I had a brilliant day,' if your day was exceptionally great."

After dinner we clear the table and do homework, with Uncle Sam guiding me. He is attentive and supportive as he patiently teaches me how to read, write, and speak English with more ease and skill, asking me to repeat all the sentences after him. I pay attention to how Uncle Sam's mouth moves over and around certain words, then repeat after him, over and over again, until my pronunciation improves. I take it all in, my mind like a sponge that expands more and more each day. I want Uncle Sam to be proud of me, so I work extra hard, spending all my lunch breaks reading in the library, which becomes my sanctuary, as I am still without any friends at school.

One day at lunchtime, the weather is sunny and warm, so I decide to take my book out of the library and sit underneath a big jacaranda tree at the bottom of the playground and let my shins soak up the sun, just as I used to do outside Gogo's hut in Goromonzi. When I see the mean, pretty girl with her silky blond hair, and her two equally mean and pretty friends, approaching me, I feel panic set in. They always make fun of my kinky hair and thick African accent, giggling behind their hands whenever I speak, and whispering behind my back when I pass. Last week, after the teacher taught us about a famous British woman called Queen Elizabeth, the pretty girl demanded that I immediately change my name. "You can't use our queen's name ever again. Don't you have some kind of stupid Shona name?" she yelled in my face as her fingers pinched my stomach until it stung. I don't have a Shona name, and when I shook my head, she pinched me harder until my eyes watered with pain.

"Anesu," I blurted out. "You can call me Anesu."

I remember Gogo saying that *anesu* means "God is always with us."

It is what she says when we are going through a difficult time and think that God has forgotten about us. "*Anesu*, my dear child," Gogo says as a reminder that no matter how challenging the situation is, "God is always with us." I needed God to be with me and protect me from the mean, pretty girl, so I quickly decided that my new name was Anesu, which is what the mean girl and her friends began to call me.

Now this morning the teacher asked us to tell a story about kindness. I thought very carefully about my answer, because I didn't want to give the mean, pretty girl and her mean friends any reason to make fun of me, but I also wanted to tell this particular story that matters so much to me. I stood up and spoke about the kind girl in the blue uniform and how she saved my life.

"Hello," the pretty girl says now, with a big smile on her face. I can't believe she is being kind to me. I can't believe she finally wants to become my friend, when she's been bullying me, pulling at my uniform and pinching my stomach until it stings and makes my eyes water. She has made me so nervous and self-conscious that I have developed a stutter when I speak English at school.

I am glad that our lesson on kindness has encouraged her to be kind. *What a relief!* This will make my life at school so much more pleasant. I say a silent thank-you prayer to God, jump to my feet, smile, and nervously stutter, "H-h-hello."

"I brought you something," the girl says, and hands me a parcel wrapped in a white plastic bag. I really want the pretty girl to like me. I want to have friends. I calm myself so I don't stutter too much, and say, "T-t-t-thank you," in my best English accent.

"You are welcome," she responds, still smiling. "Let's go," one of her friends says, pulling at her hand. They all burst out laughing, then take off running away from me.

"B-b-bye," I shout at them, still grinning from ear to ear.

I sit down, excited about my gift. The package feels warm and soft against my hand, making my mouth water. I quickly open it, dig my fingers inside, and then just as quickly toss it away from me. I stare at my fingers, now covered in warm human feces, and feel my stomach churn. The smell is unbearable, and I quickly wipe my hands on the lawn. When I try to stand up, my body is trembling so violently that I drop to my knees and vomit up everything in my stomach. Finally, I pick up my books and take off running out of the schoolyard all the way back to the flat, leaving before school ends. I cannot bear to return to the classroom today. Weeping, I wash my hands over and over again, but a slight smell of feces still remains.

When Uncle Sam comes home from work, I am too embarrassed to tell him about the feces, or about the bullying and how anxious I've become as a result. Instead, I ask Uncle Sam why the other students laughed at my story about the girl in the blue uniform. Uncle Sam explains that the girl in the blue uniform works for UNICEF, part of the largest humanitarian organization, called the United Nations, which helps people in need, including starving children. By sharing my story, I had unintentionally revealed too much about my humble background and the fact that I too was once starving. And in return—I quickly realize after the explanation—the pretty girl, a true bully, had decided to feed me with her feces.

I am upset with myself for giving the mean girls a reason to be cruel to me, so I hang my head down and hide my pain from Uncle Sam. "Elizabeth, you should never let anyone make you feel ashamed of who you are or feel embarrassed of where you are from," he says, placing his hand on my shoulder. I know that he is right because that's what Gogo always says; she says "to be African is to be blessed, something to be proud of"—and in my bones, I know this to be absolutely true. But right now, I am too sad and upset to feel proud or blessed.

I struggle at school initially, but by the end of the term, with Uncle Sam's patient tutoring and my hours of hard work at the library, my grades improve and I get an A in my English class. As a reward, Uncle Sam finally takes me to Goromonzi to see Gogo.

It is the first time I have been back home since Amai took me away two years ago. We find Gogo sitting in the yard, underneath the big tree next to the hut, shelling maize. She is on her feet as soon as she sees the car, walking quickly and with purpose, her footsteps assured and her arms wide open. *It's my Gogo!* I can barely wait for the car to stop before I open the door and run to her.

"Gogo, Gogo!" I scream, throwing myself into her arms. She stumbles backward, I shuffle my feet forward, tighten my arms around her, and catch Gogo's fall. We stand there for some time in silence, realizing that no words will ever be enough. I can feel her heart beating against my ear, and I inhale her familiar earthy scent and wrap my arms as tightly as I can around her beloved body. We remain silent, then stare into each other's eyes, allowing our souls to speak to each other.

Finally, Gogo takes my face in both her hands and, still looking into my eyes, cracks a huge smile. "Aaaa, you are home, my dear child, you are home." I feel relief and excitement and gratitude and tremendous happiness. *Yes, I am finally home!*

That night, inside the hut, in my true home, to which my heart still belongs, I tell Gogo all about the new school and my time in Epworth: about learning English and about Osi and the children and my friend Jeri. Gogo listens with excitement in her eyes. She tells me everything about Goromonzi, including how they barely survived the last drought, and the sadness returns to her face. Although the rain has finally returned, bringing with it new life, there is still not enough food for everyone in the village, so together we get on our knees, hold hands, and ask God to protect our village.

I am thrilled to finally be back home, and I spend the following days visiting everyone. I am greeted by blessings and cheerful laughter. Throughout the village I notice promising signs of healing: chirping birds sit on new leaves in the Good Forest; water is flowing in the river;

and small mangos dangle from tree branches, waiting to be picked. But in the fields, I see skinny maize stalks that may not provide a plentiful harvest, and this worries me. Still, it is better than no crops at all, so I silently thank God and spend afternoons helping the *ambuyas* and the *sisis* pluck weeds in the fields, sharing stories and laughter. In the patchy grass pastures, I see only a few cows grazing slowly, and I help *sekurus* and *hanzwadzis* tend to them. Gogo has three new goats, which I help tie up in the bush every morning, just as I did when I was young.

I am home, and although it feels exactly the same, I see everything differently. As I spend more time talking and sharing with the *ambuyas* and the *sisis*, I begin to sense the burden of unspoken fear buried beneath their joy. I feel sadness return to me and then my own fear, as I viscerally remember what it's like to live through and barely survive a drought. Gogo says it is like living with a very sick child, when any moment their soul could be called back to the heavenly father, leaving you with an unbearable pain that never entirely disappears. You live in constant dread, fearful from not knowing when or if the moment of loss will come, and how you will survive if it does.

In Goromonzi, our land is all we have. The land is our provider. Just as Gogo taught me, we are children of the African soil. We survive and thrive with our land; we raise our animals off our land; we work hard and maintain our dignity and pride through our land. Without the rain, our land dies, and when it dies there is no life, and when there is no life we are left with nothing. We perish. And that is the fear I begin to see in the eyes of my people, in the eyes of each person in Goromonzi, young and old. Buried in each face, behind the strength and determination, underneath the smiles and laughter, there lies the deep fear that at any moment everything can change, everything can be taken away, leaving us with nothing: no crops, no cows, no food. Without the land's bounty, we will starve. I know how it feels to be hungry, how painful it is to want for food and water and have none. This frightens me. *What will happen to everyone here if the drought strikes again or a food shortage continues? How will Gogo survive?*

I take a break from plucking weeds to stand underneath the useless tree in Gogo's field of maize. I see myself at eight years old, lying helplessly underneath this very tree, unable to move from hunger. I see the girl in the blue uniform give me a bowl of warm porridge and a bottle of water, and I hear her clear, melodious voice say, "As Africans we must uplift each other."

Suddenly, I know exactly what it means: to uplift others. The meaning of the words clicks in my head the way so many new words have done while studying at my new school. I imagine extending my hand and pulling up every person in my village to stand beside me, together and beloved; I imagine them safe and fed, and able to work to fulfill their own unique potential. I turn my head toward our small village at the top of the hill, realizing that even though I am still just a child, I now have much more than the rest of the *sisis* and *hanzwadzis* in my village. Unlike them, I now have the *mukana* for a good education, so I can dream bigger and accomplish more with my life; unlike them, I no longer have to worry about ever being hungry, or even the possibility of dying of hunger should another drought return. *This is all too unfair.*

In this moment, I understand what I must do. I know that I must uplift others just as my life was once uplifted. Thanks to Uncle Sam, I now know that to be the girl in the blue uniform means working for the United Nations. I make a vow to God, promising that I too will become just like the girl who came to me on that fateful day, just in time. I will work to uplift my village and my community. This is my dream—to work for the United Nations. This is what I will do. No matter what.

Your dream is a dream for your community.

☾☽

—Zimbabwean proverb

7

"Miracles happen all the time, we just have to recognize them for what they are," Gogo always told me. It is 2003, three years since I first arrived in London, and a miracle has happened to me. I am still at the London College, completely energized by all that I'm learning, and still working part-time at the recruitment agency to pay my fees. To strengthen my knowledge of the United Nations, I also now intern once a week at the United Nations Association (UNA-UK), a charity organization dedicated to supporting the global work of the UN. My days are long, and although I am often weary and hungry when I step into the bus to head home, I always climb the stairs to the top deck on the big red buses. I marvel at the fact that when I arrived in London, I was an outsider trying to steal a glance through the windows. Now I am a passenger, and from this vantage point I can soak in all the different neighborhoods of the city as the bus shuttles past schools and shops and people from all over the world walking along the streets. More and more I feel as though I am a part of this place and I feel a satisfying sense of fulfillment, because each moment is saturated with meaning and purpose and challenge. Every day I feel myself growing, expanding, getting one step closer to putting my dream in motion.

So when I am sitting behind my desk in the windowless basement of the UNA-UK and read a job posting in the *Guardian* newspaper, my heart rate skyrockets. *Could it be?* I read the announcement carefully again and again, just to be sure I am not imagining it, my heart leaping in my throat. *Gogo was right.* I have witnessed a miracle. There is simply no other explanation.

The United Nations has just established a project team in London to work on a one-year assignment focused on HIV/AIDS in Africa. *This is it.* This is the *mukana* I have been waiting for. I look around the stark basement room and practically expect the walls to melt, it all feels so surreal. My hands start to shake and sweat beads on my forehead. It is as if God has brought the United Nations to me *from* Geneva. I thought for years I had come to the wrong place, but it seems I am in just the right place after all; it has simply taken three long years of hard work and keeping my faith to find it—or, more accurately, for it to find me.

I take a deep breath. Yes, it is absolutely the perfect miracle; sadly, I could not be less qualified. The job vacancy calls for a PhD researcher with twelve years research experience. Okay, I do not have that. But the post also indicates that this is an African project to be led by Africans for Africans—and I am African, *and* I speak several African languages, as well as French, which is spoken by most countries in the western region of Africa. Most importantly, I have field expertise that will be a real asset to any project team dedicated to this issue.

I set the newspaper down and close my eyes. *I will apply for this job*, I think, *and I will get it.* In my body I feel a visceral epiphany, that all those years working at the HIV/AIDS clinics in Zimbabwe must have been part of preparing me for this moment. I have the stories of patients and families seared into my heart and mind. I can practically see their faces and hear their stories as if they are happening now instead of years earlier.

✛

A year after Amai sends me to live in Harare with Aunt Jane and Uncle Sam, she shows up at my school unannounced. I see her standing outside the school gate one afternoon after the final bell. She has a big smile on her face and is wearing her best red dress, the one with the big white buttons, now slightly faded from the sun. Her brown canvas shoes are so worn in places that a hole exposes her right little toe. I don't want the British children to make fun of me because of Amai's clothes, so I walk away from her. After all, she left me *twice*, and I am not yet ready to fully forgive her.

"Hello, Lizzy." She chases after me, still smiling. I have not seen Amai since the day she abandoned me for the second time.

"What's wrong?" I ask, bracing myself for the worst. It seems that every time Amai comes back into my life, everything gets turned upside down without explanation.

She dances around the question, asking me about school, about my favorite subject, offering me a boiled egg from her bag which she should really be selling for extra money. She tries hard to be nice to me, but then finally says, "Eeee, Lizzy, things are tough. Us, we need you back home. Us, we need help searching for money," her words landing like a punch to my stomach.

Not this again! "What about my school?" I am caught off guard, and I speak sharply.

"Don't worry, Lizzy. It will not be all the time. You, you can stay here and go to school. Us, we just need you in Epworth on the weekends so you can help me with the house and the children while I search for money." She rests her hand on my shoulder and I quickly shrug it off. *How can she upend my life again?* I have to study on the weekends! I have promised Uncle Sam that I will earn good grades so that I can get into Roosevelt Girls High School, one of the most highly competitive private secondary schools in Harare.

When I explain all this to Amai, she says, "Eeee, Lizzy, your *baba* and I don't yet have enough money to pay for your secondary school fees.

Please, Lizzy." I feel a pit in my stomach. If I don't get into a good secondary school, then it will be difficult for me to get into university, and I now know that I must do this so that one day I can work for the United Nations. I have worked so hard at school! And now Amai is asking me to suddenly change course?

"I can ask Aunt Jane and Uncle Sam to continue paying for my fees." I offer what I think is a reasonable solution.

Amai is quick to respond. "Us, we pay for your fees now, Lizzy. Your aunt and uncle contribute, but your *baba* and I, we pay half." I didn't know this; it is just one more thing Amai never explained. I feel trapped, and also immediately guilty. Amai and Baba should not be paying fees for me to attend a fancy private school when there is barely enough money to feed Osi and the children. What is Amai thinking? Why didn't she just leave me at Epworth Primary School, which is a lot cheaper? Or, better still, why didn't she just leave me with Gogo? Then we wouldn't be having this problem. Gogo could have taken care of me; she had been doing so since I was a baby.

I feel my body go hot with anger, and then I blurt out all of my thoughts and frustrations to Amai. She is quiet and looks sad, and after a moment she calmly says, "Lizzy, you, you are our responsibility. Your aunt and uncle help, but it is our responsibility to give you the best education. Us, we want more for your life. We want you to have the *mukana* that your *baba* and I never had." I am moved by Amai's words and truly grateful for the *mukana*. I do not want to be a burden. I will do my share.

The following Friday I catch a bus to Epworth after school. Once again, I am in charge of taking care of the house and the children while Amai travels to nearby communities selling rabbits and chickens. In between my chores, I help Amai search for money, braiding women's hair and selling tomatoes, onions, and mangoes from the vegetable stand at the bottom of the yard. I am happy to be back, to see Osi and the children, but just like the first time I returned to Goromonzi, everything feels exactly the same but I see it differently now. It fills me with sadness that Osi and the children still live in this small, dark house with no electricity, no toilet, no bathroom, and no proper kitchen, while I live in a nice house in Harare; they still sleep on the cold concrete floor under the same worn-out blankets, while I sleep on a soft bed with clean sheets; they wear canvas shoes while I wear shiny leather shoes. The guilt consumes me at night as I struggle to sleep. I think again about my dream that crystallized during my recent trip to Goromonzi, when I made a promise to God to become the girl in the blue uniform. I still want more than anything to be just like her, so that one day I too can make life better for my family.

In the morning, my old school friend Jeri from Epworth Primary School comes to visit, and I find my joy again. "Uuuu, Lizzy, many girls stop coming to school. They are pregnant-pregnant. Me, I don't want to be pregnant-pregnant. Me, I still want to be a nurse," Jeri says.

I think of Aunt Jane. "You can also be a doctor, Jeri. If you want."

Jeri's eyes are wide and disbelieving. "Huhhh, a doctor?! No! Me, I am a girl, Lizzy. Me, I can just be a nurse."

"Yes, Jeri! Yes! You can be a doctor! My aunt Jane, the one I live with in Harare, is a doctor." I am beaming with excitement, remembering my own surprise when I first found out about Aunt Jane's occupation. I had never seen a female doctor in any of my textbooks at school, and it was an even bigger surprise when Uncle Sam told me that Aunt Jane wasn't just an ordinary or average medical doctor; she is *in charge* of the largest HIV/AIDS clinic at the leading medical center in Harare, Parirenyatwa Hospital.

I want Jeri to believe me, to believe that she can do more with her life should she choose to. "Yes, Jeri, you can be a doctor! My uncle Sam says you can do any job you want if you work hard at school," I say again.

Jeri holds her chin in one hand, looks at me out of the corners of her eyes, and says in a disbelieving voice, "Aaaa, you Lizzy. You, Harare has made you crazy for real-real now." She bursts out laughing, tossing her head back. I laugh with Jeri until tears roll down our cheeks and our stomachs hurt. It is as if I know deep down that this is the last time that Jeri will come to visit, the last time I will ever see her.

One evening when I'm back in Harare, having adjusted to my new school and settled into a familiar daily routine, Aunt Jane says, "Elizabeth, there is an HIV and AIDS crisis going on in our country right now." We are sitting with Uncle Sam at the kitchen table, having just finished eating supper together, which is very rare, because Aunt Jane is always at the hospital working and almost never at home. "Zimbabwe now has one of the world's highest prevalence rates," Aunt Jane continues. It is 1988, and she explains that already half a million people have been infected by HIV and that it will only get worse. I am curious to learn more from her.

Aunt Jane is Gogo's eldest daughter. She has a serious round face with two small eyes, one of them slightly lazy, which Aunt Jane calls her "useless eye," but she pays no mind to it. Her hair is short and curly, so she doesn't have to worry about braiding it. "I don't have time for that kind of nonsense," Aunt Jane says matter-of-factly, wanting to be efficient with her hair just as she is in the rest of her life. Because Aunt Jane is proud of her hair, I too wear my hair natural, unlike some of the African girls at school who use a special cream to straighten their hair so it looks silky and flowy like the British kids' hair.

When Aunt Jane was a teenager, she won an academic scholarship to study medicine in Poland, then after graduation moved to Germany, where she worked as a medical doctor. It was during this time that she met Uncle Sam, who had also moved from Zimbabwe on a scholarship and stayed in Germany, to work as an economist. After *Chimurenga* and Zimbabwe's independence, they returned home together in order to give back to our people, because that's what Gogo says we should always do.

"You must come to the clinic after school so you can learn for yourself what is going on in our country. Bring your books with you so you don't fall behind on your schoolwork," Aunt Jane adds, to my surprise and delight.

"Thank you, Aunt Jane," I say, excited to finally learn more about her work, and about an illness which has caused so much suffering to *sekurus* and *ambuyas* in Goromonzi. What I remember is that the *sekurus* would leave Goromonzi for the big city of Harare to look for jobs and money for their children, and they would be gone for a long time. When they finally returned to the village, some of them brought more than money with them; they brought back a shameful disease called HIV/AIDS, which Gogo and the *ambuyas* called "Satan's illness." Gogo told me never to speak of or ask questions about this illness, and so I didn't. But when I went with her to pray for the sick *sekurus* in their homes, I saw what the illness did to them: it made their heads small like a child's head and their eyes bulge. Their bodies were so thin that their clothes were practically falling off. At some point they were no longer able to walk, or stand, and finally they couldn't even sit. They slept all day and all night, defeated by Satan's illness, as helpless as small babies, unable to lift their heads from the blanket, or turn their necks from side to side, or eat food because of the painful pink sores that covered their mouths and noses. Gogo prayed and prayed for the *sekurus* to get better, but Satan's illness would always win, taking their souls and often leaving their wives and young children, who were now also infected by the illness and facing the same grim fate.

Finally, I will be able to ask Aunt Jane all the questions I have about HIV/AIDS. The following week I join her at the clinic, volunteering two afternoons a week. Inside Aunt Jane's small but functional treatment room, I sit to one side of her desk, waiting for the next patient to enter. A green curtain partially hides a green examination bed. A cream metal cabinet stores patient records and medicine. Between the metal cabinet and the examination room is a small metal chair, and that's where I sit.

I am surprised to see that most of the patients do not look as terribly sick as the *ambuyas* and *sekurus* in Goromonzi. Here, the patients are young women and men dressed in nice city clothes. Even the older, more impacted patients, with sunken faces and skinny limbs, look healthier than those in Goromonzi. When I ask Aunt Jane about the differences between the patients here and those at home, she explains that Parirenyatwa is a very expensive hospital, and that only those with money can afford the service and treatment. I feel sickened by the thought that the *sekurus* and *ambuyas* in Goromonzi don't have the same *mukana* to receive treatment and relief simply because of where they live and how much money they have.

I listen closely as Aunt Jane explains results to a new patient, watch as the patient sobs at the news, and observe as Aunt Jane offers consolation and explains the treatment plan. I learn a great deal about how to deliver the most difficult news in a factual way, but also with compassion and kindness. Gently but firmly, Aunt Jane will say, "You have taken an important step today in finding out about your status so you can best protect your loved ones. HIV no longer has to be a death sentence. There is treatment that can help." She encourages the patients to share their status with their spouses, recommending that they also get tested. She provides them with leaflets offering daily tips on how to manage the disease, as well as information on support groups. Aunt Jane works hard to make sure that every patient feels supported and that nobody feels shamed by their status. Her compassion is a force of good in an otherwise dark and lonely moment for her patients.

I pay close attention to every detail, writing down notes about how to help patients with the disease: how to speak to them; how to prescribe treatment and how to comfort and console; how to assuage as many fears as I can. Gradually, my knowledge and expertise grow, and when I have questions I ask Aunt Jane for answers. When I turn fourteen and start secondary school at Roosevelt Girls High School, I keep volunteering at Parirenyatwa Hospital until one day Aunt Jane says, "I must do more," and takes an additional job at the HIV/AIDS clinic at

Gomo Hospital. This hospital is on the outskirts of the city and within walking distance of the main Mbare bus station, which services all the surrounding villages in Zimbabwe, including Goromonzi. She keeps her job at Parirenyatwa, but also begins providing services to patients from underprivileged communities, including those who travel from rural areas seeking treatment.

I follow Aunt Jane to Gomo Hospital, where she works two afternoons every week; there, the patients look much more like the sick *ambuyas* and *sekurus* in Goromonzi. They are skeletally thin, their bones simply hangers for their clothes; their eyes are large and sad. Inside Aunt Jane's treatment room, I listen and watch as women hold up their hands with embarrassment, trying to cover the weeping wounds around their mouths and noses. I watch men with wilted hair slump over with despair. I watch sick young girls hold tightly to their dying babies, and see a terrible pain overcome their faces as their bodies refuse to recover, worsening day by day. When Aunt Jane throws her arms around her patients to comfort them, I look away and shield my eyes from the pain. Sometimes it is simply unbearable to witness.

At some point, Aunt Jane comes to understand that because more and more patients are flocking to both clinics, there is no longer enough medicine to treat everyone, and the little that is left is very expensive— much too expensive for most. "I must do more," Aunt Jane says, and takes a *third* job at the Blair Research Institute, where she works two mornings a week with other doctors to successfully manufacture HIV medicine that is affordable for Zimbabweans.

Eventually Aunt Jane realizes that HIV infections continue to rise because people don't want to talk about the disease. "I must do more," she says again, and takes a *fourth* job, as a radio doctor at the Zimbabwe Broadcasting Corporation, where she goes on the air for an hour once a week to give medical advice to all Zimbabweans around the country about how to prevent the spread of HIV. I help Aunt Jane by being her eyes and ears with young people my age so that she can better understand what we think and feel about the disease. Some mistakenly believe that young people can't get infected, and some are adamant that the disease is a hoax invented by Westerners. On the radio, in a calm and straightforward voice, Aunt Jane separates fact from fiction, calling on young people and communities to openly talk about HIV/AIDS in order to end the stigma and change their behavior accordingly.

When Aunt Jane realizes that she is still not reaching the most underserved communities, she says, "I must do more," and opens her own private HIV/AIDS clinic in Epworth, which I now understand is one of the most impoverished areas in Harare. I join her in Epworth, spending my weekends at the clinics, registering patients, helping the nurses clean the patients' sores, and administering medication.

I see more intense suffering at the clinic in Epworth than in any other clinic. I see the suffering of grandmothers raising as many as twenty grandchildren after AIDS takes the children's parents; the suffering of HIV-positive orphaned girls and boys living alone in the slums of Epworth, begging for food at the clinics; and the suffering of patients dying every day simply because they can't afford treatment. I bear witness to all of it. I also see Aunt Jane's own suffering, devastated by the pain of her patients, wanting to do more for them, as she starts handing out free medication and food, gradually turning her clinics into free clinics, using up all her savings to save her patients, doing everything she can to help. Despite all her efforts, we are not able to save everyone.

One day Nyari, a young patient, bursts into the clinic, hysterical and shouting something about her baby, who is strapped on her back. Nyari is roughly twenty years old, with a sweet, round face, long, braided hair, and wide brown eyes. "*Mwana wangu*—my baby, *mwana wangu*—my baby," she screams, untying the sarong around her waist.

I am in the clinic in Epworth with Amai, waiting for Aunt Jane to arrive from Harare. When Aunt Jane told Amai about how important it was for patients to be greeted by a person they could trust, Amai said, "I can help." This is Amai's community and she is known and respected here. She welcomes each patient warmly, making sure they feel no shame about seeking help and treatment.

I run behind Nyari and gently but quickly take the baby from her back. "What happened?" Amai asks, trying to calm Nyari, who will not be calmed. I rush into the empty treatment room with the baby and place her on the treatment bed.

"Hurry, Lizzy, please take Nyari outside," Amai yells, pushing me and Nyari out of the way as she shields us both from the baby, who lies lifeless on the bed.

"*Mwana wangu*—my baby," Nyari screams, then collapses on the floor. When Nyari regains consciousness, she explains to Amai that her child was born with HIV. I throw my arms around Nyari just as I have seen Aunt Jane do. I fail to console her, because I know as she does that consolation is impossible. I break down with her, and the two of us weep over her child, who does not survive. It is the first time I witness a baby die in front of my eyes, but not the last.

After the death of Nyari's innocent baby, I work even harder and more diligently, together with Aunt Jane and Amai, to spread real knowledge and facts throughout communities in Epworth. We encourage community and religious leaders to take the lead in addressing HIV/AIDS in their community. We tell the truth: that the situation will not get better—in fact, it will get far worse—if the disease is not talked about directly, and the stakes could not be any higher.

✛

"This way, madam," a cheerful young woman says, leading me down a carpeted hallway of the United Nations project office in London. She opens the door and I step inside. The narrow interview room overlooks the south bank of the River Thames. I sit across the table from Dr. Julia Cleeves, a United Nations senior policy advisor. I am thrilled to be finally meeting her. She has a firm handshake, a posh British accent, and a beautiful, perfectly tailored suit. This is the most important interview of my life, and I planned to look as confident and beautiful and capable as the girl in the blue uniform appeared to me all those years ago. However, the blue tweed men's blazer, cinched at the waist with twisted blue yarn, and the streaky blue-and-gray flared skirt that resisted my attempts to dye it completely blue—both from a charity shop—fall short of the impressive image I planned to project.

"You simply don't have the relevant experience," she says. "I need someone with solid research experience, as the job posting indicates." Dr. Cleeves pauses. "But I very much admire your tenacity." This last bit refers to my weekly calls, every Friday afternoon, to her office over the past seventeen weeks, which eventually resulted in this meeting. I know this is a pity interview, and that Dr. Cleeves has no intention to hire me, calling me here simply to find relief from my relentless phone calls. Gogo says we should never allow people to pity us, that we should never be seen as helpless, but this time, I am willing to accept the pity of Dr. Cleeves because it comes with a chance to achieve my dream, and right on the heels of the miracle of the United Nations coming to me. After all, a pity interview is still an interview. I feel like I'm standing on the threshold of an open door: all I need to do now is walk through.

"Given that this is an African project," I begin, "my practical experience is truly unique and invaluable, Dr. Cleeves." She looks irritated, but she is still paying attention, so I continue. "I grew up in communities devastated by HIV and AIDS, I worked with countless patients in several clinics, and I know firsthand how it feels to lose loved ones to AIDS. I lost so many of my relatives to the disease in Zimbabwe." Even as I speak, I feel the loss of those who suffered and died.

I tell Dr. Cleeves that I bring a perspective to the project that is representative of the Africa I know, which is about Africans uplifting each other—people like Aunt Jane who are always endeavoring to do more for their people. I am familiar with and have lived an African narrative that is not a simple story of poverty and despair, but one of hope and perseverance in the face of any challenge, coupled with a dogged determination to make life better for everyone.

Dr. Cleeves listens impatiently; she is clearly a very busy woman. Finally, she says, "Impressive, but it simply isn't enough." Her eyes subtly direct me toward the door, as if to say, *This interview is over.*

In a clear and confident voice I say, "Dr. Cleeves, I know all about patient care. I know how to test for HIV/AIDS. I know how to administer treatment and speak to patients with compassion. I have washed the seeping sores of AIDS patients with my own hands. I have watched babies die and held their wailing mothers in my arms." As I speak, these heartbreaking scenes float through my mind: the broken families; the many funerals; the grieving relatives and friends; the orphans; Nyari's innocent baby; the hollow eyes of sick *ambuyas* and *sekurus* waiting in the clinics for treatment or a diagnosis.

Anxiety ripples through me. I haven't struggled in London for these three long years, refusing to give up on my dream, doing any kind of work I could get, saving every pence and pound for university, to walk away now when I'm so close, with one foot already in the door. I stop short of shouting, *I can do this! Just give me a chance!* Instead I say to myself, *Shinga.*

But even as the stories spill from me, I feel doubt spreading. *Who do I think I am?* I am just a girl from Africa. Maybe my dream is too ambitious, as so many people have told me so many times. Once again, I feel less than, unequal—just as I had at my British primary school. There, I experienced three levels of inequality all at once: racial inequality, because of the color of my skin; social inequality, because of my humble upbringing; and gender inequality, because I was born a girl, and like so many other girls in my village, my education was never prioritized and I lagged behind in my learning and knowledge. Now here in London, I can see that Dr. Cleeves doesn't believe that I have what it takes.

She looks at her watch. My time is running out. And yet I have made it this far, and now stand face-to-face with the woman who can help me achieve my dream. I tell Dr. Cleeves the story of Zimbabwe's terrible drought and the girl in the blue uniform who saved my life. I tell her how this encounter has helped define my dream, which acts as the engine for everything I do.

Dr. Cleeves's serious face softens suddenly, and she looks thoughtful, as if she understands everything. I hold my breath. She thanks me again for my time, and begins to shuffle files and papers on her desk. I turn and begin walking toward the door, but I feel as though I'm moving through water, about to sink. I know that if I walk through the door, I will never walk back through it again, and my dream will never come true. I put my hand on the doorknob and feel as though I'm drowning. This is my last chance; there will not be another one. *Shinga!* I say to myself, and then I turn and ask, "Would your senior researcher perhaps need a research assistant?"

Surprisingly, a bemused smile crosses her face. She sets down her files. "I've never thought about that before, but yes, perhaps. I don't have money to pay you, so it would be an unpaid volunteer position."

I am deeply disappointed that I will not be paid, as I need to make money in order to keep up with my university fees and living expenses, but of course I do not refuse. "Yes! I will do it! Thank you, Dr. Cleeves."

"Welcome to the team, Elizabeth," Dr. Cleeves says, this time with an inviting smile on her face. And with that, I step through the door to stand in the room that I always believed was waiting for me.

I grip her hand in mine, and feel a surge of gratitude wash over me with such force that it takes my breath away. *This is it. I have done it.* After all these years, my dream, that I have held for myself and for all the people who have supported and believed in me, has finally come true.

I breathe out. The voices of self-doubt and insecurity fall silent. In this moment, I accept myself for who I am. I feel the pride of my identity fill me from head to toe. Yes, I am a girl from Africa. Yes, I am good enough. Yes, I am!

If you pick up one end of the stick,
you also pick up the other.

✪

—Ethiopian proverb

8

The sharp smell of antiseptic cleaning solution lingers in the air like a strange perfume. The antiseptic and the sickly sweet scent of illness worsen my nausea, which Dr. Cleeves, whom I now know as Julia, warned me I might experience in Ethiopia, ten thousand feet above sea level. "Women and their children are dying here every day. Our hospitals are operating at maximum capacity and we simply can't cope: we don't have enough beds. We don't have enough staff to care for our patients." Standing in the dimly lit corridor outside the HIV/AIDS ward at Zewditu Memorial Hospital in Addis Ababa, Ethiopia, the doctor looks exhausted, her face drawn, as she describes the situation to Julia and me. Although the ward in Harare where I worked with Aunt Jane was often crowded, this one is *overflowing* with female patients. Some lie on thin, shiny metal beds lined up on either side of the hall; some curl up next to their wailing babies on the concrete floor; others lean their frail bodies against the wall wherever they can find space.

The doctor goes on to explain that women and girls are disproportionately impacted by the disease: housewives alone constitute over a quarter of all the admitted cases. And with that, I sweep the nausea away; altitude sickness is nothing compared to the suffering of the women here. My heart aches to see the pain etched on their faces. I am reminded of the huge responsibility that comes with my new job, making me more determined than ever to play my part in bringing much needed healing to the women here and in other communities across Africa.

During my first few weeks as an unpaid researcher, the learning curve was massive, and I struggled to keep up. My first research assignment, to map the prevalence of HIV/AIDS across all fifty-five African countries, challenged my perspective and many of the things I thought I knew about my home, revealing a continent with rich ethnic, religious, and linguistic diversity. Even the HIV/AIDS infection rates differed from country to country, as did the unique approaches taken by governments and communities to address the epidemic. I felt anxious that I might fail at the task and so I bravely asked Dr. Cleeves if I might join her during lunch to learn as much as possible from her directly. Over steaming plates of fish and chips and mushy peas in the bustling cafeteria, I learned more about the project, her methods, and even her character.

For the first time ever, our innovative project seeks to address the HIV/AIDS epidemic in Africa using "scenarios," an extremely efficacious decision-making tool used in the private sector to inform needed action in the future. "When everyone is involved, everyone will be invested," Dr. Cleeves said one afternoon, explaining that this new approach to combating the illness will bring together more than 120 stakeholders across Africa—including governments, communities, civil society, international donors, and the private sector—to collectively design policies to address the HIV/AIDS epidemic on the continent. "Real and lasting change is only possible when Africans lead and inform change in their own communities," she continued. I enthusiastically agreed. After a few of these amiable, chatty lunches, Dr. Cleeves turned to me and said, "You know you can call me Julia, right?"

Soon after, Julia invited me to accompany her on this latest mission, and now I am thrilled to be in Ethiopia, back on the African continent for the first time since I moved to London. This is the first time I have ever been to this part of the continent, commonly known as the "horn of Africa." This is one of the world's oldest countries, home to "Lucy"—arguably the most famous of human skeletal remains, more than 3.2 million years old. When Julia and I arrived in Ethiopia last night, the hospitality from those we encountered was nothing short of the warm and inviting African hospitality to which I am accustomed. Yet everything else felt different: the weather, the language, the food, the culture. Here the weather is tropical, and the official language is called Amharic, a Semitic language with its own fascinating alphabet that I have never seen before. Here the women do not have coarse hair like mine, but rather naturally soft and flowy curls that perfectly frame their long and slender faces. Here we are not served *sadza* for dinner, a staple meal for most Sub-Saharan Africa countries, but rather one of Ethiopia's national foods, injera, a sour, fermented flatbread paired with different meat and vegetable stews and plated in a colorfully woven basket large enough for everyone to eat from. The differences I observe fascinate me as much as the beautifully embroidered white dresses worn by some of the patients in the ward.

"We have an Ethiopian saying, 'If you pick up one end of the stick, you also pick up the other,' so we are explaining to communities that it takes all of us working together to end the suffering," the doctor at the Zewditu hospital says, echoing the community values that Gogo always talks about. I smile at the thought. "We are so overwhelmed that we have started to advocate for community involvement and engagement," the doctor continues, "by asking people to help take care of HIV/AIDS patients in their own homes."

I take detailed notes about how we can advocate for funding and resources with our partners to support the hospital's vital work as this battle-worn doctor describes the need for more equipment and resources and staff. Then I share with the doctor some of my front-line experience caring for patients at the clinics in Zimbabwe, and the methods and practices that were most effective in that particular context. As I'm talking, I think about all three of Gogo's sons in Goromonzi, who contracted HIV/AIDS and then passed it on to their wives and some of their youngest children. In our village alone, we buried at least ten of Gogo's relatives and cousins while I was growing up, including Sekuru Chop-Chop, Gogo's middle son and my favorite *sekuru*.

✛

When I am fifteen years old and arrive in Goromonzi during a school holiday, Gogo says, "Eeee, you must go see your Sekuru Henzi; Satan's illness has visited him," referring to my favorite *sekuru*; there was no one quite like him, and as a child he was my hero. He called himself "*Muramba Tsvina*" ("one who refuses filth"), which was not his real name. His real name was Sekuru Henzi, which is what Gogo called him. But I called him Sekuru Chop-Chop inside my head because of his behavior. Gogo said that when he was young, Sekuru Chop-Chop always got into too-much-too-much trouble, and he continued to do so as an adult. In my memory, he was always sharply dressed and happy-happy until he was no longer happy-happy. That's when he would say "Chop-chop!" and grab his clothes from his wife, Ambuya Chop-Chop, pack a bag, sling it over his shoulder, and disappear to Harare without saying another word to my *ambuya*, and without hugging his crying children or saying good-bye to Gogo.

Gogo would comfort Ambuya Chop-Chop and apologize for her son's bad behavior, telling people that she had lost her son to Harare, except Sekuru Chop-Chop was not lost for real-real, he just went back and forth to Harare looking for money, and bringing back nice things for

Ambuya Chop-Chop, enough of them for her to forgive him, until the next time he said "Chop-chop!" and packed his bag, to disappear again without an explanation. One day he was no longer able to travel, because he fell ill.

As soon as Gogo tells me the news, I drop my bag inside the hut and run to Sekuru Chop-Chop's house. When I arrive, I find a small boy sitting on a grass mat in the yard, propped up against a tree next to the sleeping house. I don't recognize the small boy, so I announce myself. "I come in God's name, *hanzwadzi*," I say. "We welcome you," the small boy answers faintly, and his voice sounds familiar.

I keep walking toward the small boy, until I suddenly realize that it is Sekuru Chop-Chop, except he looks nothing like my *sekuru*. His body has shriveled to almost half its size, leaving him drowning inside his favorite brown trousers, now faded and full of holes. He was always so fastidious about his appearance, but his once crisp white shirt is worn and dingy. His face is an image of a startled ghost, with shiny, dark skin, stretched tightly over sunken cheeks, and bulging owl eyes. His lips look bright red and raw, his hair is soft and curly, and his feet are bare and cracked. I have never seen Sekuru Chop-Chop without his shiny shoes, and now he is barefoot. I am startled by how lost and shrunken he looks, as if he is disappearing before my eyes.

I notice that he hasn't recognized me yet, so I say, "It's me, Sekuru," and approach the mat. I want so badly to throw my arms around him, to show him how much I love him, but I am afraid of hurting his frail body. He looks practically breakable. Instead, I sit next to him on the mat and place my hand inside his bony hand.

"Aaaa, is it really you, my niece?" Sekuru asks, looking down at our locked hands.

"I am so happy to see you, Sekuru," I respond, looking away from his face, overwhelmed by the situation and his appearance. I have never seen Sekuru Chop-Chop this weak and sick before. I have never seen him look so helpless, as helpless as a young child. He was never afraid of anything. Now he is clearly too weak to move.

"How are you feeling, Sekuru?" I ask.

Sekuru starts coughing uncontrollably. Finally, he stops, clears his throat, spits out a string of slimy saliva, and says in a pained voice, "Eeee, me, I am sick, my niece," admitting to things he has never admitted to before, emotions he would have labeled weakness when I was young.

"Are you taking medicine, Sekuru?" My question startles him because here in Goromonzi we are never to talk about HIV/AIDS. I don't want to make things uncomfortable, so I quickly explain that I now help Aunt Jane at the clinics in Harare and that I have seen her patients recover after receiving treatment.

Sekuru Chop-Chop remains silent and still refuses to meet my gaze. I remember how Aunt Jane cares for her patients, so I place my hand on Sekuru Chop-Chop's back and repeat my question in a low, comforting voice, "Are you taking medicine, Sekuru?"

I watch Sekuru hang his head with shame: the shame of being offered help by a child, and the shame of suffering from AIDS, or "Satan's illness," as it is called here in Goromonzi. Even in the city, in Harare, people call HIV/AIDS *chirwere*, which simply means "disease." This is particularly odd because in our Shona language we call every other disease by its true name.

"Eeee, medicine is too expensive, my niece. But also you, you are a junior-junior, I should be the one taking care of you," Sekuru says sadly. I want to help so badly, but I know that I don't have a job or any money to buy Sekuru Chop-Chop medicine.

"We need a deal, Sekuru; you can't go to heaven yet," I respond, tears stinging at the back of my eyes. "Deal?"

I watch fear fall over Sekuru's face like a blanket, his eyes saying everything that he does not or cannot say: *I am fearful of not living up to the deal. I am afraid I will let you down.* I see this, but I need Sekuru to agree to our deal and do this for us. I keep staring at him, pleading silently with my eyes, until he clears his throat, smiles faintly, and says, "Okay, deal."

Only a few years later, Sekuru Chop-Chop breaks our promise and his soul is called back to the heavenly father.

✛

I refocus my attention on Julia and the doctor and explain my experience building trust within communities. I share how I once traveled with Gogo and the *ambuyas* to the village next to Goromonzi to pray for a sick *ambuya*, but when we arrived the sick *ambuya* wasn't there. A young girl led us down a hill, deep into the forest. There we found the sick *ambuya* shackled to a tree in order to prevent her from spreading "Satan's illness" to the rest of the village. Gogo explained to the village elders that there was no risk of getting the disease through regular social contact, and that isolating a sick person was punishing and harmful. The village elders set the sick *ambuya* free, and she returned to her home, where she received care from her community. "It is important that community elders—in particular traditional and religious leaders—are effectively engaged as a way to successfully address the taboos and stigma that are associated with HIV/AIDS, and to stop misinformation that leads to unnecessary suffering and increased infection rates," I say.

Julia nods. "You are absolutely right, Elizabeth, we need a holistic approach if we are to be successful. Most of the HIV prevention programs are primarily focused on preventing transmission through behavior change. This alone is not enough. Behavior influences health, but culture influences behavior. One must take into account underlying social and cultural norms, especially here in Africa, where culture and tradition are so important. These things really matter."

I feel proud to have Julia validate my experience and contributions, so I smile and nod. I am impressed by how deeply she, a Western scientist, understands and acknowledges the critical role played by social and cultural norms in determining how a community will respond and behave. I think of Aunt Jane, telling her patients in the clinics and the listeners on the radio to "call a spade a spade," and calling HIV/AIDS by its real name, not "Satan's illness" or *chirwere*. The more Julia and I work together, the more my respect for her grows.

Back in London, I am promoted to the paid position of events organizer, in charge of organizing all the consultative workshops and meetings with the project stakeholders across Africa, seeking their input and expertise to inform the scenarios project and help stem the tide of the epidemic ravaging my continent. I think to myself that I have never done more difficult but important work—which I am also finding to be well suited to my abilities and on-the-ground experience.

I continue my work in London, but after I've been in Africa, however briefly, I am homesick for its familiar sights and sounds. I am twenty-eight and it has been a little over three years since I've seen my family, but it feels much longer. As soon as I can afford a plane ticket, I fly home for a visit.

I arrive to a Zimbabwe that has changed a great deal since I left. My country is experiencing a critical food shortage due to political turmoil and erratic rains. As we drive through Harare's city center, I notice flocks of young boys and girls milling on the streets, begging for money and food. Aunt Jane explains that according to official statistics, at least ten thousand Zimbabweans died the previous year from hunger, and that six million people, roughly half of our country's population, will need food assistance in the upcoming year. The food insecurity is astonishing, and its devastating impact is only beginning.

It is heartbreaking and disheartening to hear and see these troubling realities, so I feel thankful to spend time with my siblings as we catch up on life at Amai's home. Osi now works in the city fixing computers, and Memo is a hairdresser; both are married and living with their families in

Harare. Chio, my baby sister, is now twenty-two years old, still living with Amai and still looking for a job.

When I tell my brother and sisters about my life in London and the constantly rainy weather, Memo teases me: "Lizzy, me you can't pay me a thousand cows to live in a place that is lacking sunshine."

"Memo is right," Osi agrees. He cannot imagine living as I do, in a small apartment that is nowhere near a park. "You live like a small-small chicken in a small-small coop, Lizzy. But eeee, me I think a chicken has it better than you; at least it can go outside and eat fresh grass! Me, I will stay here in Africa," he adds, leaning into me, chuckling—making us erupt with laughter.

Our conversation reminds me of how precious life is here in Africa, where I am always surrounded by my family's love, open space, and the beautiful African sun. Chio chimes in with her own tease: "Me, I hear you guys over there in London eat fish and chips every day. That is not food, Lizzy. *Sadza*—now that is food," she says, and we all burst out laughing again, and just for a moment we are able to forget our country's food shortage, and Amai's own struggles.

The price of rabbit and chicken feed has more than doubled due to the food crisis, and Amai is having trouble searching for money because she cannot afford the food to raise the animals and sell them. Still, we get down on our knees on the concrete floor after dinner and pray to God in gratitude for our blessings, thanking him for Baba's new job at a local tavern in Epworth, which pays slightly more than his old supermarket job. We thank God especially for my new paid job with the United Nations, which will make it possible for me to send money back home to Amai so she can buy food. I am so grateful for the *mukana* that my family has given me, and proud that my job will make life better for my family in return.

Back in Goromonzi, Gogo slaughters one of her goats to feed the *ambuyas* and *sekurus* and their children who all gather in her yard, bearing small baskets of whatever food they have to celebrate my return home, however brief. When I remind Gogo of the food crisis and suggest that they save their food, she says I should never speak like that again.

"You, my dear child, you are a child of this soil. You have brought us all immense pride." Gogo stares into my eyes, gently folding my hand into a fist between her palms, and says, "I always wondered why a child is born with their hands clenched into a fist." She pauses and continues, her eyes never leaving my eyes. "Now I know, my dear child. Now I know. You, you were born clenching your blessings," she says. Her words fill me with happiness.

The *sekurus* chop wood next to Gogo's goat shed as the *ambuyas* slice cabbages under the big tree next to the hut. The children shell dried beans into a large woven basket. I help Gogo build a large cooking fire in the yard. She is still the same Gogo, but she looks frail to me, and it pains me to see it. Still, I am happy to be side by side with her again, cooking food and sharing laughter.

At dusk, the sky is bright orange, and by the time we sit down to eat, it is nightfall, and our beautiful, seemingly endless African sky is teeming with so many shining stars it would be impossible to count them all. We sit around the big fire, sharing *sadza* soaking in fresh goat stew. On one side of the fire, the *sekurus* sit on empty water containers and wooden stools. On the other side, the *ambuyas* and Gogo sit on colorful sarongs spread out over the ground. I sit on the dusty ground with the children, and I am happy there, remembering my childhood years in the village. The flames of the fire rise into the sky, illuminating the faces of the people I have known all my life. We sing songs of praise as we dance around the fire, thanking God for bringing me safely home to Goromonzi.

On my last night in my village, I am teary as I say goodbye to my beloved Gogo. She is getting older, and every moment with her becomes that much more precious. I know she will not be around forever, but I can't bear to think about losing her—not yet. I commit to coming home every year to see Gogo and my family. I am grateful for my new life and job in London, but I know without a single doubt that no matter where I am in the world, Africa will always be my home. It is here on the African soil where I truly belong, here with Gogo, where my heart and soul feel nourished and rejuvenated. Gogo takes my hand in her palm and places it on my heart, just like she did when I was young. I feel the warmth of her hand, both its gentleness and strength, when she says, "Whenever you need me, I will always be right here with you, inside your heart, my dear child. Never forget that, never forget." I hug her as tightly as possible; I wish I never had to let go.

When I return to London, I place my hand on my heart and speak to Gogo whenever I miss her, which is every day, even as I continue to love the work I do, traveling with Julia to more African communities impacted by HIV/AIDS and deepening my knowledge of the crisis and of the African continent. In Egypt, an Arabic-speaking country in North Africa, I am encouraged to learn that the country has a less than 1 percent HIV/AIDS prevalence rate, and I ask policymakers to share any lessons they've learned that could prove effective if deployed in other parts of the continent. In Nigeria, a vibrant West African nation that is Africa's most populous country—a place where hundreds of languages are spoken—community leaders teach us how to speak to people accurately and effectively about the epidemic within their diverse communities. In East Africa, a region populated by more than 160 different ethnic groups, patients in Kenya share their agonizing experiences in accessing treatment due to stigma and discrimination. The crisis is different in each unique place, and therefore requires unique approaches to prevention and care.

I witness the way Julia manages high-level meetings with African government officials across the continent, advocating for the rights of communities to access healthcare services. Like Aunt Jane, Julia is a force, a formidable mentor, and a woman who is always ready to "do more." She works patiently and tirelessly to help people change and better their

111

lives, and the more I watch her, the more I learn. I watch in awe as she refuses to take no for an answer: *Your Excellency, we firmly believe that your country can be a role model for many on and off the continent.* She chooses her words carefully and delivers them calmly until she gets a yes. As we grow closer, I spend weekends with her family—her husband Andrew and sons Jacob and Oliver. She gives me a second home in London, for which I am deeply grateful. It is amazing to think that in these few years this city that for me was once so unfamiliar and cold has become a place of community and connection and professional fulfillment.

One afternoon Julia calls me into her office and tells me she's been asked to send someone to the UNAIDS head office in Geneva to support the second phase of the HIV/AIDS scenarios project. After twelve months of intense work, the African stakeholders have now developed a report with clear, actionable policy recommendations that will empower African governments to combat HIV/AIDS in their respective countries. Solutions by Africans for Africans—this is a huge accomplishment, and once again I feel truly humbled to be part of the project.

"I would like to send you to Geneva," Julia says.

I know just how significant this next phase will be; it will require someone with astute communication and diplomacy skills to support African governments as they begin to implement the policy recommendations. Such a position was, not so long ago, beyond my wildest dreams. I start to panic. I have never done this work alone. Julia reassures me that I have grown in confidence in my ability to engage with African governments and communities. She has faith in me, but although I am grateful, I cannot imagine my work without her as an integral part of it. She has been my mentor, my guide. "Will you be moving too?" I ask, praying silently for her to say yes.

"I need to stay in the UK now," she says.

My head starts to spin, thinking of all I will need to learn and do. And without Julia? Impossible. I can't do this work by myself. I can't be the *only* person at the head office in Geneva with intimate knowledge of this project. It's too much responsibility, and I am terrified that I will fail at the job and disappoint this woman I respect so deeply and who has taught me so much. I put my hands on her desk and clear my throat.

Julia, sensing my hesitation, reaches across and puts her hand over mine. "Elizabeth. I have complete trust that you will do a brilliant job."

I feel as though my heart might burst. "Thank you," I say. "Thank you, Julia, for the opportunity and your trust," I finally manage to say, my eyes full of tears, and my voice thick with emotion, as I think of the weight of this next opportunity: to be part of supporting the efforts of my continent—what an honor!

I quickly find a furnished apartment in Geneva, at the top of a small hill in the center of *Vieille Ville* (Old Town), a maze of charming cobbled streets and picturesque squares with quaint water fountains, cafés, restaurants, souvenir stores, galleries, newspaper stands, and the famous St. Pierre Cathedral, which overlooks my apartment. The church bell keeps the time, chiming every hour on the hour. The apartment is clean but basic, and it is also eerily quiet. The minute I set down my bags, I miss the familiarity of my life in London and my home in Africa, but I also think about this girl from Africa who, just a few short years ago, believed that making it to the "nearest" UN office in Switzerland was utterly impossible. Now here I am, living in the shadow of the Swiss Alps, working for the United Nations. I push open the small window to let in the crisp mountain air. I hear birds chirping in the trees outside my window, reminding me of the colorful birds in the Good Forest in Goromonzi. I hum along with the birds' songs in an effort to cast away my loneliness as I slowly unpack my suitcase and settle into my new home.

Over the coming weeks, I mobilize all the skills I've learned from Julia, explaining our scenarios project as an innovative case study, arguing that the lessons we learn from a successful implementation of this strategy to address HIV/AIDS will provide tactics to approach other developmental challenges—like entrenched poverty, food insecurity and hunger, and gender inequality.

I travel across Africa, engaging with African governments and their communities, encouraging them to implement the policy recommendations, determined to create lasting change from the inside out. "While there are enormous odds to overcome, there is much that African countries can do with their collective strength to overcome the disease and grow economies," I tell the ministers of health. I emphasize the need for unity and integration between individuals and their communities, and between African countries. My goal is to ensure that our scenarios project alleviates infection rates in order to support the ambitious goal of UNAIDS that by 2020, at least 90 percent of all people living with HIV/AIDS will know their status and have access to treatment.

In communities, I work with religious and traditional leaders as I did with Aunt Jane in Zimbabwe, to evolve beliefs and values so that HIV/AIDS is no longer seen as a sin, or a punishment, or a risk or a curse—and mobilizing entire communities to seek testing or treatment. I am thrilled with our accomplishments, which reenergizes me to do more. And when I learn that one in five new HIV infections happen among adolescent girls, who constitute just 10 percent of the population in Sub-Saharan Africa, due to cultural, social, and economic inequalities, I work tirelessly with healthcare providers, advocating for the creation of youth-friendly sexual and reproductive health services.

I am ecstatic and truly grateful when I join the head of the organization, Dr. Peter Piot, executive director of UNAIDS, on a trip to the United Nations headquarters in New York City to present our HIV/AIDS scenarios project to the UN secretary-general, Mr. Kofi Annan.

When we pull up to the UN headquarters, an imposing, modern glass building surrounded by the flags of every nation in the world, I feel a jolt of excitement and also disbelief. *Here I am! Finally!* I think back to my first full day in London, when I went to what I thought was the United Nations and was told it was in the United States in New York City, the very place I am now standing. If only I could go back in time and tell that girl, who thought her dream was crumbling, that a few years later she'd have made it to *both* offices, doing the work she was inspired to do all those years ago by the girl in the blue uniform. A smile spreads over my face, one of joy and pride and deep gratitude. I think of all the times I told myself *"shinga,"* reminding myself not to give up and to find a way, no matter the sacrifice or amount of work, and no matter how many times it felt like this dream was, as so many told me, far too audacious for a girl from Africa. And yet, here I am. I am working for the UN in Switzerland and am now moments away from presenting this important work to the secretary-general of the United Nations in New York City.

It is difficult to digest the fulfillment of this lifelong dream, so along with excitement I also feel a tightness in my chest and a nervousness that makes me tremble. As we cross the shiny lobby full of people from all over the world, and then travel up to the executive suite on the top floor, I manage to calm down. I am about to meet the very first United Nations secretary-general *from Africa*. I need to gather myself together in order to be truly present for this remarkable moment. When I finally shake hands with Mr. Kofi Annan, I think of how astonishingly powerful a dream can be; to think that my dream has come full circle, that the words that once inspired my dream—"As Africans we must uplift each other"—constitute what I am doing and what I have done.

After I have known Julia for a few years, she is diagnosed with ovarian cancer. I visit her in a London hospital, where she lies in a narrow bed with a thick tube in her nose and a skinny one in her arm attached to a drip. We have walked through so many hospital wards together and witnessed so much suffering, always trying to find ways to better help sick patients. I long to do more for her now.

"You are going to be fine, Julia," I say, squeezing her hand and trying not to panic. I know that ovarian cancer is not always fatal if detected early. *Julia can't die*, I think.

I pray silently to God to take care of her, and for a time it seems my prayers are heard and answered, and Julia returns to work—but not for long. Nine months later, I visit her in her London home. Lying in bed, she looks small and frail, a breathing tube in her nose. As soon as I enter the room, she reaches for me.

"Elizabeth, I don't want to die," she says. I sit on the edge of her bed, hold her hand, and see in her eyes a terror I have never seen before. I long to lift her pain, to take it all away, but of course I cannot. This amazing, strong, and compassionate woman who fought the good fight for so many—how could it be that her light would no longer shine in the world? My heart is breaking.

"How long?" I start to cry.

In a trembling voice, without letting go of my hand, she says, "A month. Two months maximum."

A week later, back in Geneva, I receive a call from Julia's husband, Andrew. "Elizabeth, Julia has just passed."

I sit in my apartment, stunned and devastated. I can hear people chatting and laughing in the street, and the buttery smell of croissants drifts in through the window from the bakery next door. How can it be that Julia is no longer here? What am I going to do without her? The woman who taught me how to do this work in the world; the woman who believed in me wholeheartedly and treated me like family; the woman who gave me the once in a lifetime opportunity to fulfill my greatest dream. She was my ally, my colleague, my mentor, my friend, my family. Now she is gone, and the world seems smaller, narrowed to a point, and less friendly, as if a light has truly gone out. I put my head in my hands and sob, overcome with a sense of loss that is overwhelming and far too familiar.

I am because we are,
and because we are, you are.

◐

—African proverb

9

Stumbling through a dense forest in rural Uganda, practically breathless, I finally slump over. I have been walking for six hours. Breathing the humid air feels like trying to breathe water. I fall to the ground, then quickly leap to my feet; I've been warned about the rattlesnakes. The rhythmic pulse of insects surrounds me. Dripping with sweat, my skin is sticky and hot to the touch, and I am light-headed from dehydration. I have a throbbing headache, and my heavy backpack seems to grow heavier with each step. I start walking again, putting one foot in front of the other. I must find a way to manage the hike through the jungle, the punishing humidity, and my physical fatigue. I also carry some trepidation about what I am marching into.

The Budongo Forest is a four-hour drive from Kampala, the capital city. Ernest, my gregarious driver and translator, is a local Ugandan who will accompany me to a village affected by river blindness, a devastating disease that, once it spreads in a community, seems intractable.

Ernest notices that I'm struggling. "Now we rest a little, my sister," he says in his choppy English, lifting the backpack from my shoulders and setting it on the ground. Ernest speaks many of the more than forty indigenous Bantu languages spoken in Uganda; English is not his first language. He is sweating too, but doesn't seem terribly bothered by it, as I am.

"I am so sorry, Ernest. Yes, ten minutes rest, please." I am frustrated with myself, as I normally handle intense heat and humidity well; I simply hadn't expected this kind of physical effort, at least not today. Unlike my last visit, two years ago, Ernest wasn't able to drive us to the end of the dirt road, where the village would be just a ten-minute walk away. This time, when we entered the forest, the road had been washed away by a recent torrential rain and we faced an impassable, muddy brown river. My heart sank. "Eeee, road not safe," Ernest said. "Us, we leave car. Us, we walk. Me, I lead, my sister," he said with an energy I did not share. I followed him; there was no other choice.

"You, you wait for me, my sister." Ernest disappears for a moment into the thick forest. I take a few deep breaths and try to gather myself.

It is 2007, four years since I started work at the United Nations. I am still living in Geneva and am now a technical officer with the World Health Organization (WHO), which is fully committed to the fight against river blindness. As part of my role, which entails providing programmatic advice to governments and communities on how to best address river blindness, I am returning to Budongo to check on the community's progress in terms of treatment and prevention of the disease. Although every part of my body hurts, and I'm feeling muscles I didn't know I had, this pain is a far cry from the suffering I witnessed during my last visit. I try to prepare myself for the people I will meet again and the stories I will hear. To be of service, I remind myself, is worth any difficult and seemingly endless trek through a jungle.

Ernest finally reemerges with a huge grin on his face, clutching a handful of green leaves. "This is a good one, my sister. Eat." He hands me some leaves and shoves the rest into his mouth. As I chew, the bitter juice perks me up. "Thank you, my brother," I say, truly grateful for his kindness.

"Now we go, my sister, yes?" Ernest asks as he helps me strap the backpack over my shoulders. It seems lighter somehow, and I am able to carry on. I'm reminded of the *sisis* in Goromonzi; when they saw me struggling to carry my water container, they always offered to relieve my burden for a moment so I could make it all the way home.

Ernest and I march on; I'm still breathing hard, but I'm reenergized enough to notice how the forest hums with life: leaves scratch together and birds call from trees. The day's light is fading; when we emerge from the forest, night has fallen completely and the world is dark apart from millions of twinkling stars scattered across the sky. The bright light from my flashlight reveals a cluster of round grass-thatched huts, similar to those in Goromonzi, and I feel nostalgic for my village. I glance at my watch. We have been walking for over ten hours. No wonder I feel as though I could fall asleep standing up.

"We are here, my sister," Ernest says. He knocks on the door of a hut—not the same hut where I was welcomed on the last visit—and shouts something in the local Bantu language. He turns to me, saying, "So, my sister, you, you sleep here tonight."

When I step inside the hut, I am overjoyed to see an old woman sitting by the fire—she looks to be roughly Gogo's age. We exchange basic greetings in the local language and she smiles at me warmly, as if she's known me a long time. I feel instantly connected to her as if she is my own Gogo. As I settle myself next to the warm fire, every limb and muscle in my body aching in pain, I have a sudden longing for Gogo. I see her in my mind, sitting next to the fire cooking *sadza* in our smoke-filled hut, teaching me valuable lessons about what it means to be African, stories that would shape the vision of my life and work.

✤

It is nightfall in Goromonzi, and Gogo is busy-busy making *sadza* over the roaring fire. Plenty-plenty smoke swirls inside the warm and cozy hut. Gogo stirs the porridge and then asks me to sit down. "My dear child, I must tell you a very important story. Listen carefully. Open up your ears wide-wide."

I love learning about our land and our people through Gogo's stories. There is so much about the world I long to know! I sit at Gogo's feet and train my attention on her. I hear *ambuyas* and *sekurus* in neighboring huts laughing and talking, and every once in a while, a baby's cry. The wind rustles the trees; animals shuffle and howl in the forest. The familiar night sounds of home.

"A long, long time ago," Gogo begins, "there was a lion and an elephant who lived happily in the forest with the other animals." Gogo always uses animals to teach me. I learned to count by pinching all ten fingers, one finger for each goat. *This is how many goats we have. Never forget.*

"In the middle of the forest stood the big-big Tree of Harmony. The elephant ate its leaves, and the lion and her baby cub escaped the hot sun in the shade of the branches. They shared the Tree of Harmony happily, until one day a hungry hyena from a different forest tried to eat the lion's baby as it slept." I shiver. I do not like hyenas.

"The lion told the elephant, 'I must sleep on the tree's branches so I can see the hyena coming.' 'No, lion,' said the elephant, 'those leaves are my food and I want to eat without being disturbed.'" Both arguments make sense to me.

"The lion suggested the elephant find a different tree. The elephant suggested the lion also finds a new tree," Gogo continues. "Now both animals were angry. They argued and argued and finally decided to fight for the Tree of Harmony. The next morning, the buffalo, the zebra, the giraffe, and the leopard gathered to watch the battle. The lion roared and the elephant stomped, shaking the earth, both charging to destroy one another."

Gogo's eyes gleam in the firelight. I have forgotten about dinner, lost in the story. "In the middle of the battle, the zebra stood between them and said, 'Stop. You can't fight. There is a better way to solve this. Together.'

They continued fighting and charging until the buffalo stepped in. 'Stop! The lion and her baby can cool off with me in the river!' The giraffe stepped in offering the elephant leaves from her tree. The leopard promised to protect the baby lion from hyenas."

Gogo pauses. I can feel my heart thumping. "The lion and the elephant stopped charging, realizing their great mistake; they were best friends, and the tree belonged to both of them. There was no need to fight; and to keep fighting would destroy them both, as well as the lives of the other animals. From that day on, the lion and the elephant shared the Tree of Harmony again. On hot days, the lion and the cub played in the water with the buffalo; the giraffe shared her leaves with the elephant; the leopard watched over the lion cub, chasing away the hungry hyenas. The animals lived happily together in the forest, sharing whatever they had and protecting one another."

A smile crosses Gogo's face. "Now, my dear child. What do you think this story teaches us?"

"That we should be nice-nice to each other," I respond. "And not fight."

"Very good," she says, and then looks at me intently. "Just like the animals, we must always take care of each other. We have a word for this: *UBUNTU*." She says the word slowly, articulating each syllable. *"U-bun-tu* [*Ooo-Boon-too*] is what connects us as human beings—here in Goromonzi, but also everywhere in the world." Gogo blows on the fire, sending sparks into the air like shooting stars. "*Ubuntu* is the essence of who we are as Africans, a lesson we learned from our ancestors, who understood that we are all part of one human family. We need each other, and we are responsible for each other."

This is exactly my experience of village life, people helping others for the good of all, but the word is new to me. "What does *ubuntu* mean-mean, Gogo?"

"*Ubuntu* means: I am because we are, and because we are, you are."

I understand that I have seen *ubuntu* in action all the time. We share the weight of work and sorrow, and the lightness of joy and abundance. We pray for sick *ambuyas* and *sekurus*; we bless one another each time we meet; we pray for rain and celebrate together when it arrives. "And," Gogo says, "we must always treat each other with humanity and never cause others to suffer, because when we do, we in turn cause suffering to ourselves." I think of the times when I have been unkind and resolve to do better, in honor of our ancestors and the gift of *ubuntu*.

Gogo takes my hand and folds it into hers, gripping tightly until our hands make a ball. "You are special because of *ubuntu*. We all are. Never forget, my dear child. Never forget."

I am because we are, and because we are, you are. I squeeze Gogo's hand and feel connected to my ancestors, to my family, to my village, to my community, and even to myself, since this special word is my birthright. Gogo and I hold hands in silence as the fire fades. The village is quiet now; even the animals in the forest are asleep. In this moment, everything is as it should be—peaceful.

Over the coming days, Gogo further explains how *ubuntu* shapes every aspect of our lives, how we live in the world, how we treat one another, and even how we dream for the future. Gogo teaches me what it means to have and pursue a dream as part of an *ubuntu* community. "Aaaa, you have to dream big, my dear child, because your dream doesn't just belong to you, it is a dream for all of us," Gogo explains. I don't fully understand, so I wait for her to continue. "You are part of *ubuntu*, which means that your dream must be big enough for all of us, big enough for all Africans. Never forget that my dear child. Never forget."

The values of *ubuntu* guide my upbringing and, in particular, my understanding that a dream is a shared, inclusive vision for all; rather than just an individual ambition or desire, a dream represents the hope of a future for the people you love, for your family, for your entire community.

The *ubuntu* worldview is this: there is no "I" without a "we." So when

I am in secondary school at Roosevelt High in Harare, an all-girls school named for Eleanor Roosevelt, a former first lady of the United States and a pioneering women's rights activist—I know just what to do when the teacher gives us a special assignment to write an essay describing each of our personal dreams. I write about the dream I have held firmly in my heart and mind since I was young: the dream to become the girl in the blue uniform so that I can uplift the lives of others. I work as hard on the essay as I have ever worked on anything, so I am baffled when my English teacher gives the paper an F and summons me to her office.

"Elizabeth, what happened?" Her slender face is serious as her eyes scan each page of the essay. "This is not a dream, Elizabeth. A dream must speak to your personal ambitions, and not all this nonsense that you have included about your village and family. This is neither ambitious, nor focused. That's why you failed."

I am legitimately shocked, as I had expected to get an A+ mark for the essay. I knew it was passionate and well written, and more than that—it was the truth. I did exactly as Gogo taught me, clearly articulating how my dream held within it the hope that I might improve the lives of my family, my community, other Zimbabweans, and even fellow Africans who might be positively impacted by my humanitarian work one day. I imagined all of these people, known and unknown, with access to education, adequate food and safe shelter, quality healthcare. A world free of violence and strife, where each person lived with meaning and purpose and joy.

I try to explain all this to the teacher, but she doesn't understand. I am dismissed, failed essay in hand.

At night, after supper, I share my essay as well as my deep frustration with Uncle Sam. Since the moment I arrived at his home in Harare, Uncle Sam has been my champion, my tutor, my family, my sounding board, and my source of total and unwavering support. To call him a father figure would be an understatement, because I can bring to him my anger, my triumphs, my confusion, as well as my anguish, knowing that each and every time he will not judge me, but instead patiently support me to find a solution, always encouraging me to try harder, challenging me to embrace new ideas and pushing me to reach my goals—just as he does tonight.

"You must understand something very important. The word 'dream' means something entirely different in the West than it means to us Africans. In the West, people mostly have a dream for themselves, a dream to better their individual lives and fortunes, and the assignment you were set was to explain how you interpret this definition. Your essay uses our African understanding of the word dream, which is important. However, you should also take this opportunity to see things from a new perspective, to understand the importance of having a dream for yourself."

I am confused. "Does it mean that I can no longer have a dream for others?"

Uncle Sam shakes his head. "A dream can be both things. Take your aunt Jane, for example. The dream she had for herself became a dream for her community. When we first met, she was chasing after her dream to become a medical doctor. It was something that she wanted to accomplish for herself, to prove to herself that she could do it. She also told me then, as you've said here, that she was driven by the dream to help others, the dream to give back to our people. Your aunt Jane's dream was both things."

Uncle Sam pauses, places his hand on my shoulder, and says, "Always remember, if your dream benefits others, it will ultimately benefit you. *Ubuntu* teaches us to think of ourselves as part of a whole, so if one person is uplifted, then others also rise." I listen intently to Uncle Sam's words. I begin to understand that improving the lives of others will improve and enrich mine as well. A shared dream is a true give-and-take. A dream can be for one, *and* it can also be for many. In that moment I know, without a doubt, that as long as my dream continues to be a dream for others, it will also be my own.

✦

In the morning, I wake to the unique and stunning yellow African sky, which always makes me feel at home, hopeful, and ready to work. I thank the *gogo* for her hospitality and step out to see the village of Budongo in the bright light of day. Before I take my first step, a young girl I do not recognize practically tackles me in a hug.

"You are back, you are back! Me, I can be your teacher now. Me, I go to school."

I immediately recognize her voice. "Betty! It's so good to see you." I pull her toward me for another hug. It is almost impossible to believe that this is the same girl I met two years ago when she was ten years old. During that visit, she was one of the first people I encountered in the village. I found her sitting underneath a tree in her parents' yard, wearing a short brown dress with shoulder straps. Her entire body, including her pretty round face, was covered in a bumpy red rash and she scratched her skin incessantly.

This constant itching was caused by the millions of baby worms that squirmed beneath Betty's skin: a telltale symptom of having contracted river blindness. An adult parasitic worm—transmitted to humans through the bites of infected blackflies that breed in fast-flowing streams and rivers—will, once inside the host, produce baby worms that cause severe itching and a constant need to scratch. Eventually the worms travel to the eyes and can cause permanent blindness. This corrosive disease impacts approximately 25 million people of all ages, primarily in Africa, and fell particularly hard on Betty's community.

When I introduced myself to Betty two years ago, she stopped scratching her skin for a moment to laugh.

"Aaaa, you, you can't speak well-well," she said.

"Aaaa, maybe you can be my teacher, Betty," I said, playfully.

Her smile dissolved and the light disappeared from her eyes. "Me, I can't be a teacher, because me, I can't go to school because my skin is itching all the time." Betty's suffering was palpable, and I wanted so badly to ease her pain.

Now, only two short years later, I pull away from this revitalized, energetic girl so I can take a proper look at her. Betty's skin has cleared up apart from some minor scarring, and she is no longer scratching. As I look into her lovely brown eyes and feel her youthful energy, I choke up with emotion. Two years ago, I held the image of Betty digging into her skin at the forefront of my mind as I encouraged the communities to equally prioritize treatment for children impacted by river blindness, which was not yet happening. If Betty's story is any indication, the issue of inequities in the distribution of available medicine, supported by me and my colleagues at WHO, is clearly being resolved.

Unlike most diseases, there is no vaccine to prevent river blindness, but there is a medication called ivermectin that controls the impact of the disease by killing the baby worms, reducing painful itching, and preventing permanent blindness. Ivermectin is donated by WHO to affected communities free of charge. The medicine is not a cure, and in order for it to be effective it must be taken orally each year, without interruption, for a minimum of twenty years in order to kill the baby worms annually for the duration of the predicted natural life cycle of the parasitic worm. In the early 1980s, distributing ivermectin became a formidable challenge. Neither WHO nor any African government was able to develop the resources or infrastructure to sustainably deliver medication annually to each impacted community for the required period of time.

But then something amazing happened: the communities themselves recognized the great suffering caused by this illness and took action, stepping in to lead the necessary change. Guided by *ubuntu*—which teaches that one suffering person is everyone's responsibility, and that our ability to flourish as individuals is inextricably linked to the ability of our community to thrive—the communities self-organized, appointing individuals in each village as local community distributors of the medicine, donated by WHO. Each year these community distributors took turns delivering treatment, volunteering their time and effort completely free of charge. Communities had complete ownership of these programs; the solutions arose from within, rather than from an external "benevolent" source. As a result, high treatment rates were recorded, the spread of this devastating and pervasive disease was significantly stalled, and those who had contracted the disease got their lives back.

Humbled and grateful, I give Betty a tight hug and delight in her strong and youthful embrace.

"Ready?" Ernest asks, signaling that it's time to get going. I watch Betty bound away, healthy and happy, and I am filled with hope that I will encounter many other children like her, in this village and others; children who were living in terrible pain but who are now attending school, laughing and running, their suffering a distant memory.

"Ready!" I follow Ernest to our first meeting with the community leaders, still brimming with joy at the sight of Betty, and ready to hear about all the impressive progress the community has made in addressing river blindness. I know challenges remain, but I am positive we can work together to address them.

I recognize most of the leaders who are gathered in a small yard, the men sitting on wooden benches and the women on the ground. The warmth in their voices when they greet me feels like being hugged by the African sun. I sit with the women, prepared to listen and learn and strategize. They thank me for the increased medication and are happy to report that everyone in the community has equal access to treatment.

I ask how they have been able to reach everyone. Although overall we have seen high treatment rates across all river blindness–impacted communities, there are still pockets with low treatment coverage despite the availability of medication. One woman eagerly jumps in. "Aaaa, us, now we are also in charge. Now that we have enough medications, us women are also involved as community distributors." Another woman, looking up at the men with a cheeky expression on her face, says, "Yes, and us we do a better job. We are more patient and refuse to give up until everyone takes their medicines, even if sometimes we have to go back to the same house every single day." She erupts in laughter, and the women and some of the men join her. I take mental notes, filing away these stories, even more convinced that substantive, lasting change happens only when communities work together to lead from the inside out.

As Ernest and I venture into the community over the following five days, the changes are obvious. There are still blind village elders being led with a stick by young girls and boys as a result of river blindness, but we speak to more children who are now in school, all thanks to the additional treatment and the community's efforts to deliver it equitably. Inside smoky huts we speak to mothers with blotchy skin, the dark pigment having been literally scratched away by their own hands, but at least now they are no longer isolated and are able to concentrate on our conversations.

When we go to the maize fields, my heart swells with joy to see crops sprouting on what was once barren land. We find one woman, Apio, and her children busily plowing their maize field. The sun is shining, the sky wide open, endless and bright.

"Aaaa, my sister, us, we are winning!" Apio exclaims, smiling. Her voice is cheerful. Her baby is strapped to her back with a bright orange-and-red sarong that matches her dress and head scarf. Her other children—three daughters and a son—are plowing a few meters away. In the early 1970s, most communities, including Apio's, abandoned their homes and the fertile land near the rivers for fear of contracting river blindness. The results were devastating: hunger, poverty, and a high drop-out rate in schools. Now these same families are returning to their homes and farms and thriving once more.

"Look at all this, my sister," Apio says, pointing to her maize field. "Look at God's blessings."

"Praise God, my dear sister," I say, remembering the same joy on Gogo's face every time the rain—which Gogo called God's tears—blessed our fields.

"Aaaa, us, we did it ourselves, my sister. Me and other women are now community distributors, working together with the men," Apio says proudly. "My sister, us, we realized something important, you know. We realized that we have to take care of each other, because what is done for us, without us, is not for us," she adds. There is conviction and passion in her eyes. She reminds me again of Gogo, always fighting for what's right, refusing to give up.

"Why do you think you have been so successful, Apio?" I ask.

"Aaaa, this one is simple, my sister." Apio laughs and throws her head back. "Us, we always take care of each other, my sister. All this work, distributing treatment, we all do it for free. Yes, we do it for each other. Because, us, we are a community, we are one family."

Standing proudly over her maize field, full of hope and purpose, her family at work beside her, Apio has articulated what lies at the heart of who we are as Africans. I reflect on Gogo's many teachings and think of how fiercely proud she would be to see the manifestation of *ubuntu* in Apio's community. Change was happening in Budongo because the community understood that being part of a collective means treating each other with compassion and respect—the central belief of *ubuntu*. When we support others in their suffering, even when it's hard—especially when it's hard—everyone benefits. Apio and her community understood that prosperity was only possible if they all worked together to be each other's keeper, and that's what they did, to terrific success. Their story proves this singular truth: that no matter the hardships and suffering Africans experience, we always find a way to uplift one another as a community, because of our *ubuntu*. Our individual and collective resilience is astonishing. I feel great pride, once again, that I am a girl from

Africa, here and now, doing this work, meeting these incredible people and hearing their stories.

As I leave Uganda and visit more communities across Africa, thoughts of my second trip to Budongo lift my spirits and reinforce the importance of the work I do, as well as the power of *ubuntu* in accomplishing this work. Gogo's valuable lessons show me again and again that we are all connected, and that "*I am* because *we are.*" With my boss, Dr. Uche Amazigo, a fearless Nigerian parasitologist, we also realize that we must encourage gender balance in the distribution of river-blindness treatment. We need more women like Apio creating greater impact in their communities; we need more stories like Betty's.

I continue my journey across Africa, encouraging more women distributors to be involved in the fight against river blindness. But as I meet and talk with more people, I come to understand that it's not about encouraging only women to be a part of the solution; I also need to convince the men, because in keeping with cultural and social norms in many of these traditional, rural communities, men still make the majority of the important decisions. The question is: how to sway them to the importance of this approach?

"No, no, no! Me, I will not allow my wife to go outside the home!" a man shouts, jumping to his feet and pumping his fists in the air.

I make every effort to remain calm as I look out over the faces of the men I have invited to this meeting, with the support of the community chief, in the Mahenge Mountains district of Tanzania, a five-hour drive from the lively hustle and bustle of the capital city, Dar es Salaam. Here, in Tanzania, home to Mount Kilimanjaro, the highest mountain in Africa, the East African mountains are green and lush, not at all like the icy Swiss Alps I see through my office window in Geneva. Here, the mountains surround you. In Switzerland, it is as if the mountains were cut out from some sharp material and pinned to the sky. Here the air is heavy with humidity, while in Geneva it is often wintry and thin.

"No women distributors!" The men are adamant, some of them angry.

I politely address the man who is still standing. "Let me ask you a question, my brother. If your wife is taking treatment and she experiences some of the side effects, would you be more comfortable with her discussing how she feels with a male or a female community distributor?" Without saying it out loud, I am referring to a commonly known side effect of the treatment: itching around the genitals.

I can tell this lands powerfully, and there is a brief moment of silence. "Okay, okay," he finally says. "Definitely a woman community distributor."

By engaging with both women and men, instead of excluding the men's voices or opinions, we actually welcome more women distributors, and more people receive the life-changing medication. When everyone's effort is equally accepted, then everyone is equally invested in solutions and success. *This* is how hope and healing emerge in communities affected by river blindness.

After my trip, Dr. Amazigo wants us to do more. Her mind is always working, thinking and strategizing about new solutions that will better the lives of more people. Sometimes I wonder if Dr. Amazigo ever sleeps or grows tired. "We must maximize the benefits of this community-driven development approach," she says. Guided by this methodology of solutions by Africans for Africans, we eventually launch a curriculum of "Community-Directed Interventions (CDI)," at fourteen African universities.

Of course, there is always more to do. River blindness is not the only disease that takes or destroys lives in Africa. Every year, millions of children die due to a vitamin A deficiency, and every year millions of adults and children die of malaria in countries across the African continent. Dr.

Amazigo decides that we need to empower our community networks to more effectively and efficiently address other diseases, like malaria, and also child mortality.

Three months later, my colleagues and I launch these pioneering pilot projects in Cameroon, Nigeria, Uganda, and Tanzania. Together with the river-blindness medicine, entire communities—women and men—coordinate the distribution of vitamin A supplements and insecticide-treated nets, as well as repellant and medication for malaria prevention and care.

When I travel to the French-speaking country of Burkina Faso in West Africa, also known as "the land of honest people," I share the stories of people like Apio and others who are harnessing the wisdom of *ubuntu* to practically and effectively address their challenges as a community, acknowledging the agency they have over their own lives instead of applying the traditional "savior" approach that assumes "those with less should have no say at all in how they are helped by those with more." This is not a formula for success; instead, real sustainable change comes from the inside, driven by the people for whom the change matters most and sustained by the community that best understands their own needs and culture. This always creates the most concrete and lasting impact.

While in Burkina Faso I contract malaria; not for the first time, but this strain is particularly severe, so much so it takes the life of a fellow UN colleague. My fever is so high it triggers hallucinations, and I am utterly flattened, devoid of energy. When I am eventually rushed to the hospital, there is a great deal of panic about my dire condition. My fever won't break and I am growing weaker by the day. The doctors sedate me heavily, and for two weeks I lose consciousness as my body fights its way back to health.

When I come to, I am still weak, but well enough to be discharged from the hospital and return to Geneva. There I find several voice messages waiting for me; Amai has been calling me for a week, and each message is more desperate than the last.

I play the first message over and over again, willing it to change, for the news to be a terrible nightmare, and each time I push play, I pray to hear different words, for a miracle.

"Gogo has passed. We need you back home." Amai's voice is raw with emotion and also a fair bit of panic and concern; she's likely wondering where I am and why I have not answered the phone or responded to her messages.

At first, I'm simply numb, on my knees in front of the machine, listening again and again to the words: *Gogo has passed*. I think to myself, *It's not possible*. I just saw her when I was home for Christmas only months before; she never said anything about being sick. She looked frail, which made sense given her age, but death? Gogo was ninety-three, but two of her older sisters lived past one hundred. She has always been so formidable, so strong and capable—it's hard for me to believe that death would stand a chance. I pace around my apartment, gasping for breath, still feeling the effects of my protracted illness. We were supposed to have Gogo around for at least another seven years.

I sob myself to sleep that night, and when I wake up, I think, *Perhaps it was all a terrible dream*, but I know I must face the brutal truth. And with that, my world falls apart. It's like I've fallen into a great crack in the ground, falling down and down, even though I am still in my clean, white apartment.

By the time I make it home to Goromonzi, Gogo has been buried in the family cemetery next to her field of maize. I stand next to her grave, place my hand on my heart, and hear her voice as if she is sitting right next to me, or speaking into my ear. *Whenever you need me, I will always be right here with you inside your heart, my dear child. Never forget that, never forget.* The pain is unbearable. It seems impossible that I will never hold her or speak to her or laugh or cook with her again. Without the anchor of her presence and guidance, I feel unmoored and untethered from the world as I have always known it, and lonelier than I've ever felt in my life. I collapse onto her dusty grave, curl myself into a ball, and wail like a wounded animal, crying over her, blessing the soil and her soul with my tears.

Gogo: my rock, the woman who knew best my whole heart and loved me with hers. The first to teach me what it means to be a proud girl from Africa, *Mwana Wevhu*, child of the African soil. The first to teach me how to see and relate to the world and others in it, to live according to *ubuntu*, finding my humanity by finding it in others. The first to teach me that to be human is to belong—here in Africa and everywhere in the world.

I stay for a long time at Gogo's graveside, until the shadows lengthen and the light fades. As the magic of dusk falls across the familiar landscape, I place my hand on my heart and promise to carry and share her teachings, all the days of my life.

Where there is love,
there is no darkness.

○○

—Burundian proverb

10

I wrap my hands around a steaming bowl of dumpling soup, trying to get warm. It's nightfall, and I'm sitting on a wobbly wooden chair in a dimly lit, cramped, and absolutely freezing room. The walls are painted bright green, bringing a touch of cheer to the otherwise depressing space, which is barely big enough to fit a couch, a coffee table, two wooden toddler-size chairs, and a tiny television on a black metal stand. Hanging on the walls are photographs of a happy-looking woman and man and their two children, a girl and a boy, inside cherrywood picture frames embellished in gold. The room has no heat, and the bitter cold is made much more intense by the drafts moving through the cracks in the broken window. The house reminds me of Amai's shanty neighborhood in Epworth, the way everything felt close to falling apart, and the shabby rooms that were always either too hot or too cold.

I am in the rundown Ortachala neighborhood of Tbilisi, Georgia's capital city, where some of the most impoverished residents live in densely populated and dilapidated apartment buildings and small houses with colorful metal tin roofs. This is in complete contrast to the sleek and beautiful city center just a twenty-minute drive away, with its art nouveau buildings, quaint cafés, and chic clothing boutiques that remind me of the allure and urban beauty of Geneva's old city. Through the broken window I see a grimy apartment building; colorful clothing flaps from clotheslines strung across balconies, which are lit by bright fluorescent lights. People are constantly moving in and out through the different apartment doors, their voices and laughter filling the otherwise cold, gray evening with lively energy.

Keeping my hands around the hot bowl of soup, I try not to shiver, and say, "Tell me about your experience," looking first at Ana, a petite, auburn-haired woman in her late twenties, with a round face and tiny brown, bright eyes, the size and color of a hazelnut. Her friend Elene is roughly the same age, with a slim face framed by loose curls of long black hair that match her dark eyes. The two women sit together on a sagging maroon couch directly opposite my chair, inside Ana's home.

"It is very upsetting, you know. My sister didn't deserve to die," Ana says, and I can see the pain swallow the youthful sparkle of her eyes. "When she went into labor, she didn't have enough money to go to hospital. She was forced to labor at home and bled to death, killing herself and the baby. She was only twenty years old, you know."

"The government doesn't care about us. Everything is too expensive: the hospital, the medicine, the treatment, everything," Elene chimes in, her voice heated.

I think about the death of Gogo and how losing her has changed everything. I felt so lost in the world without her. Her death and Julia's before her prompted me to reevaluate my life and purpose. One early morning, unable to sleep, I stood in the kitchen holding a cup of peppermint tea and thought, *Gogo and Julia are gone. But I'm still here.* I wanted to do more, to make more of a difference for others in their honor. I enrolled at the London School of Economics and Political Science (LSE), which would have been impossible a few years before. My degree at the London College was the stepping stone for a master's degree in Political Science at this prestigious school, and this education eventually led to a position at the World Bank, where I work now, in 2009. Based in Washington, DC, I am part of a small pharmaceutical policy team charged with ensuring that underserved communities around the world—like Ana's and Elena's—have access to affordable healthcare services and lifesaving medicine. I report directly to the head of the unit, Dr. Andreas Seiter, a tall, efficient German man with a serious, angular face and wispy blond hair, and in my role I support governments around the world in developing pharmaceutical policies to improve the availability, affordability, acceptability, and utilization of essential medicines.

Yesterday, on the car ride toward the Tbilisi city center, Ana, acting as my local Georgian translator, said, "We have the best hospitality in the world, because the word *Tbilisi* comes from the old Georgian word *Tpili*, which means 'warm.'" She invited me to have dinner at her home, which I happily accepted: spending time with the people the humanitarian programs are designed to serve is the best part of my job. When I am with the people—hearing their stories, listening to their fears and dreams and ambitions and struggles—I experience the same feeling of community and deeply shared humanity that I knew growing up in Zimbabwe. Visiting people in their homes and having frank conversations, witnessing how they live and seeing the intimacies of their day-to-day lives—all create opportunities to learn about the real issues impacting ordinary citizens. It is on the ground, in the field, in homes and kitchens and community centers, where I can see firsthand what's at stake, and what's working and what needs to be changed. All of this is completely different from the other aspects of my job, which include highly sensitive diplomatic negotiations in official meetings; talking to government bureaucrats and other power brokers; and developing policy recommendations to create systematic and structural change. Here, with the people, is where my heart lives and belongs, and what motivates me to do the other part of my work.

Elene stops eating, places her bowl of soup on the floor, and continues, "I lost my son three months after he was born. He had a rare heart disease, and my husband and I couldn't afford the surgery which could have saved his life. There is not a day that goes by when I don't blame myself for failing to save my own son." She looks suddenly pained, her face hollowed out by grief, as if the loss happened just the day before.

As Elene blinks back tears and Ana puts a comforting hand on her friend's back, my head begins to spin with emotions and ideas. Elene and Ana are only two of so many others who suffer globally from lack of access to healthcare and lifesaving medicine.

I heard so many stories in so many countries during my time working for and traveling on behalf of WHO, the largest institution of its kind in the world. What I learned is that access to healthcare is not just a problem in what are often referred to as "developing countries" in Africa, Eastern Europe, Latin and South America, as well as parts of the Middle East and Asia. Health inequality exists everywhere, on every continent—even in countries with great wealth, like the United States.

In Chicago, Tina, a young college student, explained that "there are the 'haves' and the 'have-nots.' I mean, us African-Americans are often seen as the have-nots because we can't afford healthcare. It is almost as if our lives are valued less; as if we are expected to feel less pain." When Tina rushed her mother to an emergency room at the nearest hospital, she never expected that it would be the last time she saw her. "My mother was having complications with her breathing due to high blood pressure. I mean, we sat in the ER for four hours, and every time I went up to the counter to ask for assistance, the nurse told me to sit down and wait to be called. I mean, hours went by and they never called us, and during that time I saw them attend to other patients who were clearly the 'haves.' They knew that my mother didn't have private health insurance, and so we were not a priority. At one point the nurse even snapped at my mother and told her to 'control' herself as she groaned in agony on the floor. I mean, can you even believe that?" Tina pauses, and then says, "Eventually my mother drew her last breath and died right there on the cold ER floor, clutching my hand. I had just turned eighteen and still blame myself for not having been more forceful with the nurse. I mean, can you imagine that we were just right there inside a hospital, a place that was supposed to save my mother's life, but instead took her life?" Tina's voice was hollow with pain. No, I couldn't imagine losing a parent under such circumstances. Tina's mother had died not because there were no healthcare facilities close by, or because medicine didn't exist that could treat her condition; it wasn't an issue of not having qualified healthcare specialists, as is sometimes the case in rural hospitals and clinics in the developing world. No, Tina's mother died a terrible death because she was a disadvantaged woman of color. She died because she didn't have access to the resources that should be available to all people.

Her story was painful to hear, and I knew as I opened my mouth to say the same thing I had said over and over again to numerous grieving families—"I am so sorry for your loss"—that as heartfelt as my words might be, they were both too late and fell drastically short of what Tina and her mother deserved.

All across the African continent, I witnessed people's unbearable suffering from treatable diseases like malaria, cholera, and measles, de-spite the availability of safe and effective medicine. In the Republic of the Congo, a francophone county in central Africa with a population of five million, I spoke with a bereaved father, Tony, two of whose children had died from measles. He explained, "Huhhh, this one is very-very dif-ficult, my sister. We have enough money for food or for medicine, but not for both. When the children got sick, we had to choose. I said okay, is it better to buy food, but then they die from disease? Or it is better to buy medicine, but then my five children die from hunger? God knows, my sister, that is not a choice, that is a punishment," Tony said, sadness consuming his eyes. I exhaled and searched for the right words to say. "I am so sorry for your loss, Tony," I said, remembering how a South African economist had once described it to me: "The situation is dire. Most developing countries, including here in Africa, don't have price regulation policies in place for pharmaceutical products, and as a result the cost of medicine is now the second largest expenditure after food for most African families." Tony's was one of those many families im-pacted, and choosing between food and medicine, as he pointed out, is not a choice, it is a punishment—one that no parent or person should have to endure.

I stop eating my soup now and look up at the sad, drawn faces of Ana and Elene. "I am so sorry for both of your losses," I say, getting choked up, knowing full well that just like Tina, Tony, and many others, Ana and Elene weren't looking for my sympathy; what they wanted, what they all deserved, was equal access to healthcare services for themselves and their families.

I feel determined to set right the health inequality that led to Ana and Elene's great suffering and grief. I know I must do more, just as my aunt Jane always endeavored to do more at the HIV/AIDS clinics in Zimbabwe, where she worked tirelessly to alleviate the suffering of her patients, especially those in impoverished areas like Epworth. I explain to Ana and Elene that my work here in Georgia on behalf of the World Bank is to support their government in providing accessible healthcare to all Georgians. Three years ago, the World Bank helped the government of Georgia launch a medical insurance program for impoverished and underserved communities. My job over the next five days is to evaluate the impact of this program, to measure its successes and failures. "Hopefully our work will be able to create meaningful change and save people's lives, here in Georgia," I explain to Ana and Elene. They nod, but of course any of these changes are too late to save Ana's sister or Elene's child. Those losses, as I know far too well, are forever.

When I finally meet with the Georgian government officials the following day, they tell me they are making significant progress. However, my visits to communities over the course of the week paint a slightly different story, one not in keeping with the official report. For example, I learn that medicine is still too expensive for most Georgians. "We self-medicate with cheap, unsafe medicine that we find on the black market, which is dangerous, but we feel we have no choice," I'm told.

At Tbilisi Central Hospital patients express a similar concern—that even when they are admitted to the hospital, they still can't afford the medicine. The physicians I talk with are equally frustrated, citing long hours and old hospital equipment as unsustainable conditions of care. Clearly, more must be done.

As I depart Georgia, the heartbreaking stories from all the people I met stay with me. It is clear that there is much more that the government needs to do to accelerate progress. The idea of risking one's life with counterfeit medicine in order to try and save one's life is unjust and unnecessary. It is heartrending to realize that most of the medical tragedies that impact ordinary Georgians every single day reflect the continuing disparities in healthcare globally.

As soon as I am back in Washington, DC, I make recommendations to Dr. Seiter. I advocate for the allocation of more resources to the government of Georgia in support of the rapid scaling of the medical insurance program.

Dr. Seiter is not afraid to challenge the status quo and demand that systems do more, or at least make an ardent attempt. Just after he hired me, during our first weekly meeting, he said, "Every citizen deserves the right to affordable and quality healthcare services, *ja*. Equally, those in the developing world must have access to the same quality medication and healthcare services as those in the developed world. *Ja*, this is fair. Even if it means naming and shaming governments to deliver those services."

After my experiences in Georgia, I lean into Dr. Seiter's passion to create change and make a plea on behalf of Ana, Elene, and the many women and girls in similar positions. "The new system needs to work for women, which is currently not the case. We must invest more funds and work closely with the government to ensure universal provision of free reproductive health services to all women in Georgia as part of the country's new insurance program," I suggest as part of my recommendation. Over the next three years, the government of Georgia, with the support of the World Bank, makes huge investments to improve the quality of neonatal care; more than 750,000 Georgians are able to access healthcare as part of the medical insurance program; and policies are put in place to ensure access to quality and safe medicine, with the country eventually expanding its insurance program to all Georgians, even covering drug purchases.

Shortly after my return from Georgia, I learn that one of our World Bank partners in the private sector has announced the establishment of a philanthropic initiative that will invest half a billion dollars toward combating maternal mortality globally. And it is desperately needed, as the statistics are alarming: one woman dies every two minutes from complications related to pregnancy and childbirth globally. Knowing that more than half of these deaths occur in Sub-Saharan Africa alone is devastating to me, and I know I must find a way to advocate for my home continent in the crucial distribution of these resources. I join the team as director of external affairs and policy for Africa, traveling to several African nations, meeting with communities and government leaders to identify countries with the greatest needs. I am energized, but also troubled; as we visit each country the story remains the same: there simply aren't enough affordable and accessible healthcare services to meet the demands of citizens or prevent maternal mortality.

In Zambia, a southern African country bordering Zimbabwe, I travel to a small town, Mumbwa, in the Central Province, three hours from Lusaka, the vibrant capital city. During community meetings with women's groups, I hear about the challenges faced by women within the country's limited healthcare infrastructure. "Us, we are suffering, my sister. Sometimes we have to walk for ten hours to find a clinic while in labor with our child. And then when we get there, we can't even find a midwife," they tell me.

At one of the local clinics, Grace, a nurse, says, "Eeee, my sister, one of the biggest challenges in our village is maternal and child mortality. There is a lot of teenage pregnancy, which as you know is causing many young mothers and their children to die. I have witnessed girls die from complications during delivery because their bodies aren't strong enough; some bleed to death, some have obstructed labor, some end up with life-threatening infections post-delivery." Grace pauses; she looks sorrowful and tired. "Eeee, my sister it is hard; even the girls who make it, sometimes their babies die of illness, or because the young mothers don't know how to take care of them, or they are so poor that they have no food to feed them." As I listen to Grace recount story after story of young children dying, I am reminded of the fact that even though the world has made remarkable progress in child survival in the past few decades, over five million children under the age of five still die annually, with half of those deaths occurring in Sub-Saharan Africa. I almost became one of those statistics myself.

✛

The first time Gogo saved my life, I was only a year old. Amai had abandoned me with Gogo when she ran away from the village with Baba. Gogo says I was so malnourished that death came looking for me. Death, she said, made my head swell until it was the size of a large pumpkin; my arms and legs looked tiny-tiny, like baby tree twigs in the bush. Death made my liver big-big until my belly looked like it was about to explode and a burning rash covered my entire body.

Panicked, Gogo threw me on her back and trekked to the nearest clinic. By the time she arrived, I was extremely weak. I could no longer open my eyes or respond to Gogo's words. When the clinic nurse saw me, she burst out crying. "Huhhh, you are too late, Gogo. The child is no longer with us." Gogo did not cry and she did not flinch. Instead, she stared at the nurse and said, "Nurse, please give me medicine."

The nurse shook her head. "Uuuu, it is too late. The medicine will not work. The child has severe kwashiorkor [acute malnourishment]." Gogo said nothing, but her eyes filled with tears. The nurse placed a comforting hand on Gogo's back and said, "Gogo, please take the child back home. Please pray for the safe return of her young soul back to the heavenly father."

Gogo stared at my nearly lifeless body, lying so still in her arms. Her tears cleansed my face, blessing me with her pain. "Nurse, please give me food for my dear child, please," Gogo begged. The nurse looked down and said, "The food is too expensive, Gogo."

Gogo did not have any money. She felt so ashamed for not having the money that she needed to buy the food that would save me, her dear child. Gogo had only ever begged God, but never a person, never like this. This time, she was desperate. This time, her spirit was broken. This time, she knew what she had to do to save my life. And so she begged. She hung her head down and looked at the ground. "I am begging you, Nurse. Please help me."

The nurse saw Gogo's shame and felt ashamed herself for having any part in creating it. She went inside the clinic and returned quickly with a bottle of powdered milk mixed with water; she handed the feeding bottle to Gogo.

"Thank you, Nurse. May God bless you," Gogo said, her head still hanging low.

Gogo never made it back to the village that night. Instead, she slept underneath a tree when night fell, afraid of disturbing the lions in the forest with her movement. That night, Gogo prayed, but she did not pray for my young soul's departure to the heavenly father as the nurse had suggested. Instead, she prayed for a miracle, and God answered her prayer. God opened up the heavens and it rained all night, blessing us with his tears. As soon as she got back to the village, Gogo went to every *ambuya*'s home, asking for extra food to feed her dear child. People gave generously, and the kwashiorkor, which would have stunted my growth and learning abilities, was stopped in its tracks. With love and determination, Gogo nursed me back to health. With the help of everyone in our community who gave when they were asked to give, in the spirit of *ubuntu*, she chased away death, and I survived. I lived because my community committed to uplifting one another, even in the most difficult and life-threatening situations.

✛

In 2012, I return to Zambia after many months of hard work crafting legacy projects for the maternal mortality initiative. It is winter in Lusaka, and the air is crisp, but nowhere near as brutal as the winters in Switzerland, where the wind from the Alps makes the cold settle deeply in your bones. Together with my colleagues, the delegates of our donor partners from the United States and Norwegian governments, as well as the Zambian government delegates, we are launching our inaugural pilot project, *Saving Mothers, Giving Life*, a five-year public-private partnership aimed at dramatically reducing maternal and newborn mortality in Sub-Saharan African countries.

On this early evening I am deep in conversation with Chilu, one of the few women invited from a local community to join this gathering of high-level dignitaries for the launch event. As our voices bounce back and forth over the soulful African music playing softly in the background, she says, "Aaaa, my sister, God did not forget us. Me, I almost died with all of my pregnancies, like so many women in my village. So, eeee, us, we thought God had forgotten us. But, today, my sister, today I know that God did not forget us." Tears glisten in her eyes.

I can feel myself tearing up as well. "God never forgets us, Chilu. He never forgets us." I place my hand on her shoulder.

Up above our heads the sky is slowly turning bright orange as the sun races toward the horizon, creating an enchanting, colorful dusk that reminds me of Goromonzi. I let go of Chilu's shoulder, look up, and lose myself in the beauty of the sky. I think of the power of *ubuntu*, that when we uplift one person, we are all uplifted, that every person's life has value. I feel truly humbled to have been part of uplifting Chilu's community and bringing lifesaving access to healthcare across Zambia. Still, I know I must do more.

How else can I create more impact for other women and girls across Africa and globally? I want to search for more impactful solutions, and I resolve to do just that. To persevere in my work with passion and persistence. What I don't know in this moment is that ten years later, the maternal mortality initiative that I was part of championing in Africa will have eventually impacted 10.2 million women globally, creating the necessary conditions to experience healthy pregnancies and safe deliveries across forty-eight countries, the majority of which are in Africa, my beloved home.

Now that Gogo is gone, I place my hand on my heart and speak to her for answers. I feel the soft weight of her hand against my chest, I feel again her big-as-the-sky love for me that has sustained me for all these years.

Sticks in a bundle are unbreakable.

&

—Kenyan proverb

11

My heart is pounding wildly as I enter the room. "It is such an incredible honor to meet you, Your Excellency," I say, and I mean this wholeheartedly as I extend my trembling hand to a stately African woman in her late fifties. She wears a bright pink tailored jacket with large pink and yellow buttons and a blue, yellow, and pink African print head scarf that perfectly frames her round face and bright brown eyes. When she takes my hand, her handshake is firm, her demeanor friendly, and I immediately feel my anxiety subside.

We sit down and she gets right to the point: "We must liberate women from gender inequality. It is unjust that half of the world's population continues to face inequalities at all levels of society."

I nod enthusiastically. I'm struck by her choice to use the word "liberate," which Gogo also used when she talked about Zimbabwe's independence from colonialism.

"This is the greatest injustice of our time. One in three women and girls globally will experience some form of violence in their lifetime." The powerful conviction in her voice tells me she is determined to do something about it.

Injustice? Yet another revolutionary word. I am transfixed, mesmerized by her fierce determination, the kind I have only ever seen in Gogo's eyes in quite the same way.

I think of how I have looked up to this woman for so long, since she was a freedom fighter in the anti-apartheid movement in her home country of South Africa. I vividly remember the first time I heard her name—Phumzile Mlambo-Ngcuka—when I was still a young girl.

✢

I am in Epworth for the weekend, sitting on my favorite branch in the mango tree, watching over Osi and the children as they play soccer in the yard, waiting for customers to come to the vegetable stand. Suddenly, a tall white man charges into the yard, rounds up all the children in the community, and shouts "ACTION!" at the top of his lungs. He does not explain anything or seek permission. I hide up in the tree, behind the mango leaves, watching as the confused and frightened-looking children scatter wildly in all directions, while two other white men holding large cameras on their shoulders charge toward them. *What exactly is going on?*

Back in Harare, Uncle Sam explains that I have just witnessed the making of an upcoming film—*Cry Freedom*—about Steve Biko, a student activist who died fighting to end apartheid in our neighboring country of South Africa. I don't know what apartheid is, so Uncle Sam explains: "It is racial segregation imposed by white South Africans against black South Africans, forcing them to avoid contact with white South Africans, forcing them to live in separate areas and to use separate public facilities." I am deeply perplexed and upset by this explanation, which doesn't feel like an explanation at all.

"But the country belongs to black South Africans, no? So, how can they be discriminated against because of the color of their skin, they are Africans in Africa? Where are they supposed to go live, exactly?" I am bewildered.

The next day, Uncle Sam buys me the book *I Write What I Like* by Steve Biko, a chronicle of his efforts fighting apartheid. The story grips me totally, and I become instantly fascinated with all the stories of South Africa's anti-apartheid freedom fighters. I think of Gogo and the *ambuyas* and *sekurus* who fought for freedom in Zimbabwe, liberating our people and finally bringing an end to colonialism. I feel connected to this South African story in a deep and lasting way.

Several years later, in 1990, another freedom fighter, Nelson Mandela, is released from prison following twenty-seven years of incarceration by the white South African oppressors. Instead of retaliating against those who mistreated and oppressed him, Mandela forgives them in the spirit of *ubuntu*, becoming South Africa's first black president and bringing an end to apartheid: a landmark moment for the African continent. Among President Mandela's handpicked cabinet members is a female freedom fighter called Phumzile Mlambo-Ngcuka, who fought alongside him in the anti-apartheid movement.

This is the first time I learn of Phumzile and all she has done and fought for. Just like Gogo, she stood up for what was right, liberating her people and restoring their dignity. In that moment, Phumzile becomes my role model, and I carefully follow her trailblazing career full of "firsts" for women as covered by the media: first, she is an integral part of President Nelson Mandela's cabinet; and then she is elected as the deputy president to Mandela's successor in 2005, becoming the highest ranking woman in the history of South Africa.

✛

Now I am meeting Phumzile for the first time. Six months ago, she was appointed as the United Nations under-secretary-general and executive director of UN Women. She now leads the United Nations entity in charge of advancing gender equality and women's rights globally. She's still fighting for freedom, only now in a different way.

Phumzile pauses, looks at me, and says, "You must come work for us. You must join the fight." I could lift off my chair, I'm so alive with excitement. I am thrilled by the opportunity to work for my role model of so many years, and even more humbled to play my part in globally empowering and uplifting women and girls, many of whom live in the developing world and come from humble backgrounds similar to mine.

I accept the job offer with a full and grateful heart, and join UN Women in late 2013, as Phumzile's senior advisor in charge of building strategic partnerships with communities, governments, and public and private sector partners, to develop, fund, and implement initiatives to advance equality and women's rights around the world. I am now based in New York City, living in a one-bedroom apartment in downtown Manhattan. I hit the ground running, traveling from country to country, crossing the globe as part of my responsibilities. In rural villages, cities, community halls, and classrooms, I speak directly with women and girls who share with me their experiences and challenges.

"People keep saying that women should be more confident, more vocal, more assertive, but the reality is that there is only so much we can do when power systems and structures are set up against us. It's hard for women business owners to get seed funding from investors, because investors expect us to fail." This is Molly, an impassioned women's rights activist in Sydney, Australia.

"I don't know what to tell you. The whole thing is just fricking crazy. When I got pregnant, I had to beg my male colleagues to donate their sick leave to me so that I could go on maternity leave. You bust your ass to work for one of the most innovative companies, but then you decide to start a family, and you are suddenly seen as an inconvenience, a burden, because the company doesn't have a maternity leave policy." This is Laura, a senior engineer at the headquarters of a large technology company in California, in the United States, the only country in the developed world that does not provide national paid maternity or parental leave.

When I travel to other parts of Asia and Africa, I hear stories marked by similar frustrations: "Women here in Japan are still expected to conform to traditional societal roles. When I decided to go back to school to pursue a degree in medicine, my husband left me with two young children. He said I had brought shame to his family, because there is still this general belief that women should stay at home and raise children." This is Akiko, a medical student at a leading Japanese university.

"*Hawu wena*—hey you. Us, we grow up in charge of everything in our homes, cooking, cleaning, taking care of the children. But then one day when we say we want to lead our countries, we are told that we're not useful or capable, yet we have been leading all this time in our homes. Is that fair?" This is Nkosi, a young political activist from South Africa who shares her perspectives with me over a plate of piping hot French fries doused with malt vinegar in a trendy café in Johannesburg.

Nkosi is right: it's not fair, and neither is the painfully slow march of change.

The stories are vastly different, but share a common thread: regardless of nationality, race, physical ability, color, or culture, women and girls everywhere continue to face some of the greatest inequalities in the world, simply because of their gender. I am moved by the collective resilience and determination of the women and girls I meet, and their agonizing stories fuel my passion to create more impact, to improve the circumstances of more lives, and to do it more quickly. I search for solutions and answers, because I am, as I have always been, full of questions. *Why is it that despite all the progress made by the women's rights movement, no country or company or institution in the world can yet claim to have achieved gender equality?*

This question leads me to the realization that many issues of gender inequality are ultimately about power: who has it, how they use it, and for whose benefit. Currently, men still make the majority of decisions across all levels of society, often with less regard for the impact of those decisions on women and girls. In my small village of Goromonzi, the *sekurus* make all the important decisions, even though the *ambuyas* and *sisis* do the bulk of the work. The *sekurus* decide who goes to school, and it is often the boys. *Sekurus* decide who owns land, property, and livestock (usually the men), while *ambuyas* are left with no security or wealth of their own. I observed similar gender dimensions in my humanitarian work. In the field of HIV/AIDS prevention and care, it was often the husband who made decisions about whether his wife would get tested or receive treatment. In some communities impacted by river blindness, women community distributors needed the men's permission to serve their communities. It becomes clear to me that if we are to achieve gender equality, we need to have more women in positions of leadership, making decisions that will benefit women and girls now and far into the future.

In my office, and during meetings and conference calls with colleagues and external partners, I can't stop thinking and strategizing about how to enable more women to lead. So I head to the country that has modeled female leadership in an exemplary—and truly extraordinary—way. I travel to the African country of Rwanda.

Despite having experienced almost unimaginable violence and suffering in the 1990s caused by genocide, in 2003 the government of Rwanda accomplished what at the outset appeared an impossible task: they elected women to 48.8 percent of the seats in parliament, making it the biggest such accomplishment of any country *in the entire world.*

Now, eleven years later, Rwanda continues to have the world's highest number of women in parliament, with 61 percent representation. In my meetings with the minister of gender and the female members of parliament, I learn about their journey to success, how women rallied together in villages and cities to ensure that more citizens saw them as viable candidates.

"It was not easy; these positions were not just handed to us. We worked hard. We educated ourselves not only academically and intellectually, but also socially, spending months and years in communities, listening to the various issues women face so that we could properly advocate for them," one woman explains to me. "Yes, in the beginning it all seemed impossible. There was the bias that politics was a 'man's job.' In fact, even some women were not convinced. You will be in a community and you ask women if they agree with your policies, and they say yes. But then you ask them if they will vote for you, they surprise you by saying, 'Eeee, I am not sure. I think maybe the male candidate will do a better job.' We had to prove ourselves, and thankfully we did, with the support of our fellow female activists and, of course, our families." Another woman chimes in, saying, "But first we had to overcome the intimidation, the violence, the sexism, and the personal attacks. Some men wanted us to stop, but we said no and showed them that us women, when we stand together, we are unbreakable. In 2006 we showed them what we are capable of achieving, when our country passed a landmark bill to address gender-based violence. In this bill, us, female members of parliament, we were able to categorize rape as a punishable crime for the first time in our country. Prior to that, perpetrators went unpunished."

Their fortitude is palpable—a tangible force in the room. It is, I think, truly uplifting. This is *ubuntu* in action! And what an extraordinary feeling, to be surrounded by women leaders who listen, take charge, and are enabled, *by the power of law*, to make transformative changes in the lives of women and girls.

As I visit communities in Rwanda over the next few days, it is easy to see the results of these female leaders. Women-owned businesses are thriving. Schools are educating young boys about the importance of respecting girls, and how to show this respect through action and thought. More girls are in school, with a greater percentage studying Science and Technology, a field traditionally dominated by boys. There are more women landowners and property owners actively contributing to their country's economic growth. Women making decisions that empower other women and uplift their communities: this is indeed incredible progress, and a working paradigm for what is possible on a global scale.

I leave Rwanda elated and full of hope. It is truly exciting to see a country from my home continent lead in such a pioneering way, on such a vital issue. This African country is a role model for every country in the world. If Rwanda, a country that went through one of its darkest periods in the 1990s, was able to rebuild with so many women in leadership roles, then surely other countries can do the same. *We can do this globally*, I tell myself.

However, the reality in other countries is sobering. When I travel to Mongolia, a county with only 4 percent female representation in the national parliament, women share with me their hesitation to get into politics, or even consider it: "It is too expensive, too time-consuming, too risky," they say. Their hesitation echoes that of women from many other parts of the world. In India, women observe that "it is demoralizing to be held to different standards than our male opponents. To be judged by the way that we dress, or talk, or walk. To be called 'shrill' or 'too emotional' for expressing our views." They risk not being taken seriously, and sometimes, they risk their lives or the lives of their families.

"Eeee, when I announced my political campaign, the following evening two men came to my house past midnight," a female candidate from Zimbabwe shares with me in a pained voice. "My husband answered the door and they said to him, 'You better put your dog on a leash unless you want trouble,' referring to me. Huhhh, the next day, me, I dropped out of the race to protect my family."

In the United States, in Tennessee, a female candidate shares her terrifying experience with me. "Well, the male candidate I was runnin' against called me to his office one day. He'd been runnin' a smear campaign against me, sayin' all kinds of terrible things, and I'd asked to meet with him to resolve things. Well, when I arrived in his office, he closed the door, pushed me up against the wall, and threaten'd to rape me if I didn't stop my campaign. Of course, I refused to give up. But he still won; he threw money at it and bought the whole darn election."

The work is intense but exhilarating, and I can almost hear Uncle Sam say to me, *You must learn to find balance in life, Elizabeth. You can't live to work like your aunt Jane. You must also* live. Yet there is so much more work to be done! I continue to live on planes and in hotel rooms, moving from one country to the next to meet with communities and policy makers and advocate for laws that will accelerate progress toward gender equality.

On the rare occasions when I am back in New York City, I catch up with my friends from the African diaspora community over long lunches after Sunday church services. In bustling restaurants in Harlem, a neighborhood rich with black history, we share stories from back home and celebrate all that is great about our African continent: how it now has the largest mobile phone market in the world; how communities in Kenya pioneered the development of financial technology (fintech), which is now used for mobile banking globally, including in the US; how our remittances, the money that we members of the African diaspora send back home to support our families, continue to be greater every year than the total amount of aid money our continent receives from all Western donors combined, a fact that is rarely ever reported. We remind ourselves of our *ubuntu*, and that before we are Nigerian or Zimbabwean, or Senegalese or Moroccan or anything else, we are first and foremost Africans. We reminisce with gratitude over the *mukanas* given to us by our families to be here, remembering our African values—"to whom so much is given, so much is expected"—as we remind each other of our responsibility to uplift not just our individual countries, but our entire continent.

This connection with fellow Africans affirms my belief in everything Africa has to offer the world, fueling my passion to bring Rwanda's exemplary model of female leadership to every country and every woman who seeks to lead and create change. I get the chance to test my theory when my UN Women colleagues in Uruguay mention that this small South American country of 3.3 million people is gearing up for elections; I seize the opportunity and immediately jump on the next plane.

It is the middle of winter when I arrive in Uruguay's capital city of Montevideo, but the weather is mild and pleasant; leaving the airport we drive along the coastline and its sandy white beaches. The city is noticeably quieter than New York City; there are fewer skyscrapers and more art deco buildings, and the winding streets are lined with small museums and quaint colonial homes.

Arriving at the parliament building, an impressive neoclassical structure, I am greeted by a female member of parliament. "It is really unacceptable that women make up less than 13 percent of Uruguayan parliament," she says. "Today we are determined to make history." Her excitement and hope are contagious. The country's vice president is present, and the room is packed and buzzing with close to fifty women's rights activists, female politicians, and members of parliament.

For the past year, these groups of pioneering and passionate women, backed by the support of UN Women, have been working tirelessly to ensure that the country's upcoming elections will, for the first time in history, be governed by a national quota law guaranteeing that 30 percent of the seats on the ballot be filled by female candidates. Their efforts have paid off, and today they will present the signatures from their petition to the country's vice president, with the hope of the law being adopted.

I can feel the energy in the room, and along with it an undercurrent of anxiety. There is so much at stake here, and everyone present feels the weight of this moment. The passing of the law must succeed; otherwise it will be a very demoralizing setback that will significantly delay our progress in Uruguay. "All of us here are from different political parties, we are competitors. But we realized how important this moment is, that we are stronger when we work together, so we set our differences aside for our equality and our county's future," one of the impassioned activists tells me, and I think again of *ubuntu* and that "when we uplift others, we in turn uplift ourselves." I know this to be true, and I long to see it come to fruition here and now.

When my colleagues and I finally meet with the vice president for a bilateral meeting after the petition's submission, I make a bold suggestion: "Your Excellency, there is a huge opportunity for Uruguay to make great strides toward gender equality with the adoption of this law. It would be an incredible signal to the rest of the world if the law became permanent after this year's election."

A few months later, Uruguay goes to the polls, and the results are impressive. There is significantly higher voter turnout of female and young voters than in previous years. Most importantly, the 30 percent rule of representation is adopted as a permanent standard for all future elections in Uruguay. It is inspiring to see that by working together, the women in Uruguay have created real and lasting change for themselves and for their country. I feel proud and humbled by the work we have done to contribute to this historic milestone.

Still, I keep thinking about Rwanda. *Surely there has to be a way to accelerate progress for other African countries to follow Rwanda's phenomenal example,* I think. The equation is simple: when women lead, the lives of women and girls dramatically improve. When I share these thoughts with Phumzile, she says, with her usual determination: "We must send a signal to the world that African women can and will lead." Over the next months, my colleagues and I work with the African Union and the government of Germany to launch the African Women Leaders Network (AWLN), a network of over one hundred former, current, and aspiring female political leaders across Africa, empowering them with the resources, networks, and mentorship required to build political campaigns and run for office in their respective countries.

I search for more answers. How can we rapidly accelerate progress on gender equality around the world? How can we reverse the false notion that in order for women to win, men must lose? I know that gender equality is not a "zero-sum game," with one gender conceding power to the other. Equality means just that—being equal. As a child of the African soil, I also know through *ubuntu* that no one is truly equal until we are all equal; that real and lasting change happens only when we all work together, for the benefit of everyone. I start to wonder: *How can we use* ubuntu *to create solidarity among all genders in a way that benefits all of us?*

If you want to go fast, go alone.
If you want to go far, go together.

◖◗

—African proverb

12

I take a deep breath, scan the packed room, and feel my heartbeat gallop away. I can't believe that we are finally here, gathered in the UN assembly hall, which is absolutely packed. I am intimately familiar with this room—the yellow chairs, the name placards, the people mulling about dressed in their best attire and traditional outfits—but today the room seems different, and so do I. This is not just any meeting; this is the culmination of literally thousands of hours of work. Creating change is certainly not easy, but I have never in my life worked so hard, and with such significant resistance, to see a project come to life.

I'm exhausted and it all feels like a dream. *Is this really happening?* I worry that I will wake up to find that nothing has changed; that I am still working to convince our leadership team, our staff, and our partners of the wisdom and possibility of this vision. It has been an arduous journey, and though I've received intense pushback as well as fantastic support from my colleagues, doing so has taken more time and energy than I could have imagined. As I continue to marvel at the rows of people gathered here, I feel the full extent of my exhaustion settle in. I am a mix of bone-tired and ecstatic with relief. There have been many times when I have felt like giving up, but now here I am. Here *we* are.

"*Shinga*," I murmur, to remind myself that no, this is not a dream; in fact, it is the *fulfillment* of a dream. Around these semicircular tables sit a diverse crowd of United Nations dignitaries, including the UN president of the general assembly, Sam Kahamba Kutesa, and the UN secretary-general, Ban Ki-moon, both in beautifully tailored suits; our UN Women executive director, Phumzile; our newly appointed UN global goodwill ambassador, British actor Emma Watson; women's rights activists, ambassadors, students, and UN staff. The hum of conversations and laughter floats through the air as the voices of the ushers cut through the chatter: "Sorry, we are at full capacity, but there is an overflow room next door. You can watch the event from there," and hordes of people are guided out of the room. This is one of the largest crowds I have ever seen at a UN event. The thought makes my stomach churn with anxiety. It's a make-or-break moment like none I have yet experienced. Right here and right now, all our hard work is on the line. And, especially for me, the outcome is intensely personal. I have given this my all.

It is September 20, 2014, and we are gathered at the United Nations headquarters in New York City, to officially launch a new initiative to advance gender equality called *HeForShe*. The murmurs in the assembly hall fall silent as the UN president of the general assembly takes the stage, then UN secretary-general Ban Ki-moon. As the secretary-general begins to deliver his remarks, I tremble with nervous excitement, remembering the bumpy, winding journey that has led us here, to this very public and electrifying moment.

Six months after joining Phumzile as her senior advisor, she tasked me to design an innovative initiative that would help accelerate progress toward gender equality on a global scale. I immediately knew that we needed a transformative idea, and I thought perhaps the African philosophy of *ubuntu* could be a crucial component for an initiative's success. I began to explore ways in which we could make the fight for gender equality more inclusive by inviting all other genders, in particular men and boys, into the conversation.

For centuries, the women's rights movement has worked tirelessly to end the grave inequalities faced by women and girls in every country across the globe. The efforts of countless activists have paid off; thanks to their sacrifices and hard work, women's rights are seen more and more as *human* rights, with more girls in most countries going to school, more women entering the workplace, and many countries passing laws that protect women and girls from gender-based violence. Yet despite all this progress, no country in the world has achieved gender equality; and at current rates it will take at least another *one hundred years* for gender equality to be realized, according to the World Economic Forum Gender Index.

This is a deep source of frustration to many women who have dedicated their lives to the fight for equality, many of whom perceive men as an obstacle to their forward strides. I heard the same sentiments over and over during my consultative meetings: *men are the problem; they are holding back women; men constitute the majority of the perpetrators of gender-based violence, raping and sexually harassing women, marrying underage girls, trafficking vulnerable women and abusing them; men oppress women in the workplace and pay female workers less than they pay themselves; men rule countries and create wars that leave women destitute and in refugee camps; men value women's lives less, while expecting women to take care of the home and family, sometimes at the expense of their own dreams, and without financial compensation.* Their views and perspective are understandable. How could you not expect a level of resentment when progress is this slow?

There were others, of course, who held different views, and these voices encouraged me when I faltered or became discouraged. Like me, these supporters believed that achieving gender equality requires everyone working together to make the playing field level and fair. Despite some colleagues still insisting that I find a solution that would dismantle male privilege and flip the power dynamics in favor of women, that's not what I had done. Instead, I decided to make men an integral, fundamental, absolutely necessary part of the solution, because I believe that they *are* part of the solution. I knew that when everyone was involved and everyone was invested in creating change, greater progress could be made, and more quickly. I understood the pain and frustration experienced by my fellow women, many of whom had been dismissed and mistreated by men personally. But I also knew all too well that anytime one gender dismisses or devalues another, it is a missed opportunity, a loss for all of us. I had experienced this myself, even painfully so, with my own *baba*.

✛

One Friday afternoon, on my way to Epworth to stay with Amai and Baba for the weekend, I stop by the grocery store where Baba works to pick up groceries as Amai asked me to do. I am still a student at Roosevelt Girls High School. Baba wears a blue overcoat over a white shirt and his faded gray trousers fall only to his ankles, exposing dingy white socks and a pair of plastic brown shoes. He is his usual cheerful self, busy packing groceries for customers. His demeanor, as always, is calm and assured and he has a wide smile that lights up his face as he chats with each customer. He remembers all of their names and works hard to satisfy their needs, because, as he says, "the customer is always right."

I still don't know Baba that well. I rarely see him. Like Amai, he is always at work searching for money, apart from the one Sunday a month when his Indian manager gives him half a day off. Then he is at home, where he spends hours sitting quietly on a wooden stool, his head leaning gently against the chalky, unpainted wall of the house. His eyes stare into the distance. I know him in that moment as a man lost in his thoughts, smiling softly and at rest. There is a peacefulness about him on those afternoons. It is as if Baba is able to manifest his own happiness, to visualize a happier future, one that no one else can see, one far removed from our immediate humble surroundings, one that I too have often dreamt of for myself and for my family.

Amai says that for a very long time, Baba couldn't find a job because he had no education. He spent months walking from house to house in the city's nicest neighborhoods—Highlands, Avondale, Borrowdale—pleading for a job, any job. Finally, one day, a British family hired Baba as their gardener. They didn't pay him much money, so he taught himself basic English by forcing himself to speak English with the family each day. He used his improved language skills to find a better job as a milkman. When that job didn't pay Baba much money either, he once again searched for ways to improve himself and his situation, quickly learning how to politely engage with his customers and ensure their satisfaction. He used these customer service skills to secure a better job in a grocery store. He aspired to be a cashier, but the Indian man who owns the store, impressed with Baba's charm and customer service skills, agreed to hire him only to bag customers' groceries. Even though Baba was initially disappointed, he counted his blessings and accepted the job. At least now he would be able to make a bit more than at his previous job, and also enjoy the status and comfort of working inside a building, away from the blistering sun.

I steal another glance at him, as I occasionally do when he is in his contemplative state, and think to myself, *I hope that, just like Baba, I too will always find a way to create my own happiness, no matter my situation.*

After he's finished helping customers, I follow him to the loading dock, marveling at his unique and easily recognizable gait: perfect posture, straight shoulders, his feet bouncing lightly as if he's not just walking but dancing to some secret music in his head. We sit on the metal platform, and with his wide smile still illuminating his face, Baba hands me a cold bottle of Fanta.

"Thank you," I say, then take a sip. Baba is always warm and kind, but I don't talk to him that much, so I busy myself taking small sips of my Fanta, feeling slightly awkward.

I am surprised when Baba says, "Aaaa, I am so proud of you, Lizzy." He has never said anything like this before, and I feel a sudden rush of annoyance and anger.

"Why did you leave me in Goromonzi?" I blurt out. The question startles both of us. I feel heat in my face, as if I might begin to cry.

Baba's wide smile fades a bit, and for a moment he is quiet before saying, "To save you, Lizzy."

"You abandoned me!" I am unable to hide my emotions. "How is that saving me?"

"Huhhh, our situation was serious-serious, Lizzy. Your *amai* and I had no choice." Gogo says that people always have a choice to do the right thing, so I let Baba know what Gogo taught me. Frankly, I simply don't believe him.

Baba nods, looking thoughtful. "Eeee, the story is long-long, Lizzy. When your mother fell pregnant with you, we were both so young." He explains that he was one of twelve children, and his mother's favorite son. His mother, he tells me, saved the little money she made from her crops to send him to school, because he was the smart one in the family. He was expected to finish school, get a good job in the city, and then take care of the rest of his family. When Amai got pregnant with me, everything changed for Baba; he had to drop out of school and find a job to support Amai and the child he would soon have.

"My mother was very upset and disappointed with me. She never forgave me," Baba says, choking up. I don't know anything about Baba's family. Gogo said we were never to talk about Baba and his family, so we didn't. It is painfully clear to me now that Baba's mother, and then Gogo, wrote him off as a useless man. They didn't want anything to do with him anymore, and because I know what abandonment feels like, I feel for him in this moment, even though for so long I have blamed him and Amai for my own suffering. No wonder I didn't know how to imagine Baba's role in my life, or even how to talk to him when I was living with him and Amai in their home. He clears his throat, and I watch his face and eyes travel to a dark place. I put down my Fanta and listen carefully.

"Us, we tried living with my family, as is tradition, until you were born, but there was not enough food," he says. "Me, myself, I tried to find a job, but eeee, it was not possible. And my mother, she became more and more upset; she even stopped giving your *amai* and me food. You, Lizzy. You, you were just a baby and you were hungry and crying all the time, but Amai couldn't feed you because she was now thin-thin and so sick from hunger that she had no milk. Then you got very-very sick." He pauses and swallows hard. I feel heat in my chest, imagining this—angry that his mother would refuse to give him food, and that she would allow Amai to starve, a feeling I know far too well.

"My mother wanted nothing to do with me. She wanted us gone, so she chased us from the village. Huhhh, it was do or die, so we ran, leaving you behind with Gogo. Us, we had no choice, Lizzy."

Again, this business of not having a choice! Forgetting all my manners, I snap at Baba. "Do you know that I almost died? Do you know that, Baba? Gogo had to beg for food or I would have died!" I flush with anger as I yell, remembering the story of how Gogo chased away death when it came looking for me.

"Me, I am so sorry, Lizzy. Us, we wanted so much to take you with us, but we had nothing. We had no food and no money to feed you. I was afraid you would die. Right then—I promised myself and I promised God—that me, I will work hard and find enough money. I promised to one day bring you home. And now, here you are, Lizzy. You are home with us, and your *amai* and I feel truly blessed. I am so proud of you."

I feel a flood of emotions: guilt, sadness, anger. I want to feel happy. I know I should. I know that it was difficult for Baba to tell me these things, but now his words feel like a burden. For so many years, I have not known what to do with this Baba person, from the first time Gogo told me about him to the first time I met him and was unable to utter a word. I thought that he and Amai had left me behind because they didn't love me enough, but I know from the emotion in Baba's voice and the way he told this story that they did, and they do.

I understand that Baba made an incredible sacrifice, leaving every-thing and everyone he knew and loved behind—his parents, his family, his home, his community, even me—just so that I might survive. I am happy to know the truth, but sad that the world is such that Baba had to make such sacrifices and such choices. I put my hand on Baba's hand, and for the first time in my life, I can look at my father with love, admiration, and gratitude. I understand how much my father sacrificed for me, and how complicated and difficult his choices were, and that he made those choices not to benefit himself, but out of his great love for me.

✛

My *baba*'s story wasn't unique. In the course of my life, I've had male role models, like Uncle Sam, who gave me equal opportunities to pursue my dream, and who encouraged me every step of the way. My experience isn't uncommon, and I wondered what the world would look like if all men played a more active role in creating equality. *What if everyone took action?*

When I met Phumzile in her office to discuss my idea, I said, with conviction, "We should use *ubuntu* as our guiding principle to create an initiative that inclusively engages everyone, especially men and boys, as part of the gender equality movement." When I saw her face light up, I continued, "Just as we did in Zimbabwe and South Africa, we can harness the spirit of *ubuntu* to solve for this inequality, to create true solidarity among all genders to work together toward a more gender-equal world. We will call the initiative—*HeForShe*."

After my home country of Zimbabwe was liberated from British colonial rule, we faced a difficult choice: to forgive or to retaliate against those who had oppressed us. Now that the power was rightfully back in our hands, we had every right to chase away all the British people from our country for the years of suffering they had caused us. But we didn't do that; we chose another way. In the spirit of *ubuntu*, we forgave the oppressors and worked alongside them to build a new, unified Zimbabwe. No matter how painfully raw our physical and emotional scars felt, we recognized through *ubuntu* that, just like us, the oppressors were human, and because they were human, we were connected, which meant that any suffering we would cause them would also impact us. By acknowledging our shared humanity, *ubuntu* brought us closer together as a country and proved to be a useful, restorative tool, a worldview that created stability and peace in the months and years following Zimbabwe's independence. Yes, we were free, but as with any change, there was a period of adjustment that included the hard work of rebuilding; the residual effects of colonialism are not in any way easy to resolve. During colonialism, our people had been split up into different tribes, and often these tribes spoke different languages, and divisions were created and reinforced by the ruling powers. So, although this was a healing time, it was also a volatile time as people adjusted their mindsets and hearts to these seismic changes. Now that we were an independent country, everyone had to work hard to align with the spirit of *ubuntu* and commit to putting it into practical action.

Phumzile shared similar sentiments about the role of *ubuntu* in re-building her home country of South Africa. Only a decade after Zimbabwe's independence, *ubuntu* became the rallying call in the fight against apartheid in South Africa, under the leadership of President Nelson Mandela; Phumzile saw this firsthand as a minister in Mandela's administration. The *ubuntu* philosophy paved the way for reconstruction, providing much-needed healing for black South Africans as they sought to live and thrive in this new world where they were finally, by law, considered equal to white South Africans. Those essential lessons in *ubuntu* left Phumzile and me with a strong belief that solidarity was absolutely integral to successfully addressing any inequality. Now we hoped to use it to address gender inequality. I left her office that day feeling exhilarated.

Phumzile and I may have been united on this, but I struggled to galvanize and secure wholehearted support from UN leadership and some of our external partners. I was not doing what they'd asked me to do in the way they had hoped I would. I was asking them to embrace and accept men as part of the solution, not solely as the source of the problem, and even more so advocating to launch an all-inclusive initiative for gender equality (*HeForShe*).

The initiative would raise public awareness online and in communities around the world about the real and harsh challenges faced by women and girls in every country. It would invite and encourage everyone, especially men in those countries, to stand together as allies with women and take small, individual actions on these key issues as part of their personal commitment to *HeForShe*. The idea hinged on a behavioral science theory, that once men self-identified with gender equality and became aware of the atrocities faced by the women and girls in their own families and communities, they would be more likely to act and inspire others to do the same. However, trying to convince our internal and external partners of this vision proved challenging and sometimes provoked dissent. After all, I was working with UN *Women*, and there were concerns that including men would detract from the organization's imperative of empowering women and girls.

"I am fully aware that women's empowerment is my priority, and that is precisely the reason we need to engage everyone—men and boys in particular. We will never achieve true equality if the pursuit of it remains a struggle between women and men, where one gender's gain is another gender's loss. We need solidarity; we must find an inclusive way to work together." I provided the rationale behind my strategy and approach over and over again. "If men perpetrate most of gender-based violence, then shouldn't we engage them to bear the responsibility of not raping women, instead of placing the burden on women to not get raped? Shouldn't we engage men to say *I will not marry a child*, instead of expecting young girls to figure out how to escape a child marriage? Shouldn't men share the responsibility for creating more equitable workplaces, instead of asking women to constantly fight to remove barriers such as the 'glass ceiling'? If men had access to family-friendly policies, such as parental leave, they could better share the burden of taking care of the home and children or even become the primary caregivers, unburdening women to further pursue their professional dreams."

I pushed and pushed, building internal consensus, knowing full well that I could never do this alone, that I needed the support of my colleagues and the organization as a whole—until I finally secured internal approval to move ahead with the initiative's launch. However, since my approach was quite innovative, it was viewed as risky, and therefore was approved to run for twelve months as an awareness campaign only and thus was not allocated any resources or funding from the organization's limited budget.

I was deeply disappointed when Phumzile conveyed this message. I knew I would need a small team in order to fully execute the vision, yet I had not been provided with a budget or resources to *launch* the initiative, let alone hire a team. Quite simply, I would need to find another way, and I decided that no matter what, I would do just that. I felt grateful for the opportunity to prove the potential power of *ubuntu* in addressing gender inequality. I quickly thought of creative ways to move forward: I reached out to external stakeholders and secured support; I found creative agencies willing to provide pro-bono work and partners to fund the launch event. I was always on a call, or responding to an email, or making lists of what to do or whom to call or whom I might engage to solve for each arising challenge. Every night when I finally returned to my apartment, I couldn't stop thinking of ways to make this happen. I lived and breathed *HeForShe*, never losing my resolve and conviction that this was the right way forward, the approach aligned most with the *ubuntu* principles that the initiative was meant to embody.

And today the launch is finally happening. I watch the secretary-general, now finished with his remarks, trade places with Phumzile, who moves behind the podium to deliver her speech to officially launch *HeForShe*, dressed in an elegant, flowy white African-style floor-length gown with green, red, and orange embroidery zigzagging around the neck and across the chest.

As Phumzile begins to speak, my heart pounds wildly. The fact is, no matter what happens tonight, one thing is for certain: there's a great deal at stake, for all of us as an organization. What if the initiative is not well received, given the sensitivity around male engagement in gender equality? What if I am wrong, and this ends up damaging the United Nations' credibility? How will I be able to live with myself? I feel my confidence begin to fade a bit, but then I remember why I am doing it this way, why I've fought so hard for this to happen against all the odds. For our *HeForShe* initiative to be successful, it must build upon the incredible work of the women's rights movement, to which I am deeply indebted, but it must also flip the script, engaging all genders to find solutions to the complex issues of gender inequality. It must be innovative enough to disrupt the status quo in order to truly accelerate progress, but do so without upsetting or putting off our core stakeholders and donors who have stood behind this struggle for so long. I feel like I am balanced on a wire between skyscrapers, delicately placing one foot in front of the other, praying I will not fall. When the applause begins after Phumzile finishes her speech, which calls for solidarity and inclusivity in the movement, I sigh audibly with relief.

Finally, Emma Watson takes center stage to issue a global call to action. In her passionate and carefully delivered speech, she invites men and boys to become advocates for gender equality, reframing the issue from one that is exclusively about women to one that inclusively engages everyone. As she delivers her remarks, the audience is entirely rapt; a pin dropping would make a sound like a tree falling. Her impassioned words captivate the audience, and her speech gets a standing ovation.

What happens next is a global response that exceeds our wildest dreams. In the first five days following the launch of *HeForShe*, the initiative goes viral with tens of millions of views online, reaching men and boys from the streets of Mumbai, India, to classrooms in Buenos Aires, Argentina; from garment factories in China to prisons in the United States; from tea plantations in Kenya to rugby fields in New Zealand;

and from sleek offices in Japan to grubby police stations in the UK. The response is diverse and inclusive, cutting across all lines of nationality, culture, race, gender, religion, age, ability and occupation, culminating in a remarkable outcome: in just three days, more than one hundred thousand people—with at least one man in every single country *in the world*—join *HeForShe*, making a personal commitment to work alongside women for gender equality.

Supporters take to social media in millions, sharing their thoughts and hopes for a gender-equal world—a phenomenal response that generates more than 1.2 *billion* conversations across all social media outlets and platforms in the first week alone. When I hear that Twitter has declared *HeForShe* one of the most catalytic moments of 2014, I feel intensely gratified.

I immediately recall Gogo's teachings and my promise to carry her wisdom forward into the world. And now we are witnessing what is possible when we all work together in the spirit of *ubuntu*; when my colleagues and I embrace the richness of our diverse views and opinions in finding solutions; when all genders work together to accept each other as equals; when our humanity exercises compassion toward one another by acknowledging that what we share is more powerful than what divides us. We had issued a call for compassion to alleviate the suffering experienced by women and girls, and the whole world had responded.

Those who want the rain,
must also accept the mud.

✹

—Ghanaian proverb

13

"**What the heck is the** United Nations doing? What exactly are you engaging these men to do?" The woman on the other end of the line is clearly upset. This, the first backlash a week after the successful launch of *HeForShe*, hits me like a smack in the face, even though I've been bracing for such a reaction for months. The rapid transformation of *HeForShe* into a global movement has created a host of new dilemmas for me, not all of them expected.

"Surely you don't think that men talking about how they are *HeForShe* on social media is actually going to create change, do you?" The more she talks, the more heated and intense her voice becomes. I feel a bloom of panic in my chest as she continues, "This is insulting to us feminists. These men must be given direction and concrete actions to take in order to end gender inequality. Why are you giving them so much power when they already have it!" I try to answer, but she is not having it. I have no choice but to sit in my office, stay silent, and listen.

What I don't know in this moment is that this phone call is just the beginning of what will become the most challenging phase of my career, a nightmarish period that will leave me questioning absolutely everything about my work and what I've struggled so hard to achieve. In the coming weeks, the criticism cuts deep and comes in thick and fast, not only to me, but also to my boss, Phumzile, and the rest of the senior leadership team. I wake up every morning and wonder what irate emails and phone calls I might receive that day, and how I will respond diplomatically. The critique is wide-ranging: I am accused of being "naïve" for thinking that men actually care about making things equal for women and girls; my feminist values and credibility are both called into question; my ideas are considered "too disruptive." Despite the overall positive press, when a few harsh comments from journalists and media outlets hit the news, I feel myself beginning to tense up with doubt, even though deep down, I still hold to my conviction that true and sustained equality will only be possible if everyone is involved and works together to create change.

Proving this to everyone else will become the most important endeavor of my career so far. Our external stakeholders want results from men, and they want them now. I am equally impatient for progress, but I also recognize that transformative change cannot happen overnight—especially on an issue as complex and multifaceted as gender inequality, which has remained unresolved *for centuries*. Yet the pressure continues to rise, like water on the boil, together with demands that I create measurable change overnight.

When I am summoned to a *HeForShe* crisis meeting with UN senior members, I am nervous, but also fully prepared to address their concerns. I share with them the positive feedback from literally *thousands* of supporters who tell me how they are beginning to understand gender equality in ways they had never considered before. In the letters of solidarity and support, men write that the awakening feels as if the scales have fallen from their eyes, creating a "click" moment that allows them to finally see things from a different perspective, a new vantage point that demands real and lasting shifts in their behavior toward other genders. I know that the first step to creating change is for people to personally identify with the issues—to be invested in the problems at stake and the possible solutions. I share some of the messages I've received:

I thought gender equality was just a women's issue before, but now I understand that it is my issue too.

I believe in gender equality. I believe that my sisters should have the same opportunities as me. I just didn't know how to get involved, but now I do.

I have always been a feminist—in support of gender equality. But at some point, I got tired of all the male-bashing, of being made to feel guilty for the sins of other men, and so I just disengaged from the conversation. It's great to see this positive and inclusive approach, which makes me feel more welcome, like I can be part of the gender equality movement again.

I also read out loud an unexpected and deeply moving letter from a man serving a sentence at a maximum-security prison in New York City:

Two weeks ago, I was sitting in prison watching television, when I saw Emma Watson deliver the HeForShe speech at the United Nations mentioning that gender equality should liberate all of us and that "...If men don't have to be aggressive in order to be accepted, women won't feel compelled to be submissive. If men don't have to control, women won't have to be controlled. Both men and women should feel free to be sensitive. Both men and women should feel free to be strong." I found myself in these words and for the first time in my adult life I broke down and cried. Thank you for setting me free. While I remain consumed with loneliness in my small prison cell, I feel free.

At the bottom of his letter, he drew a bird flying out of a cage—a metaphor of how the movement had liberated him. When I received this letter, I got chills up and down my spine. His story reinforced my firm belief that transformation and positive change are possible, no matter our circumstances.

The leadership team is impressed and moved by the stories, but they insist that this must translate into *tangible* change in communities. This is a relief to me, as I have proof of change sparking all over the world. I tell them about men in Kenya standing up against gender violence; about students in India, France, the UK, and the US uniting to address the rape culture on college campuses; about a man in my home country of Zimbabwe who started a "husband school" to teach other men in his village how to become better husbands and fathers. These individuals are taking visible and concrete action for equality within their communities, as part of their personal *HeForShe* commitment, as part of their pledge.

It is still not enough. The leadership reminds me that because we are the United Nations, we must create large-scale systematic and structural change, especially now that the movement has become so highly visible. We have to prove that it works, not just that it's a good idea that has inspired many people. One senior member remarks, "Given the magnitude of success that *HeForShe* has achieved, we must have quantifiable impact." Another colleague adds, "Some of our biggest stakeholders now think that we are pumping hundreds of thousands of dollars into the work with men and boys at the expense of women and girls," expressing concerns that are completely valid. Other colleagues in the meeting back me up, acknowledging that like anything new and unknown, engaging all genders in an inclusive manner needs more time to be accepted and understood by everyone.

I listen carefully and maintain my composure, but inside I feel a sense of sinking defeat. After so much hard work and time and effort, when there is finally solid proof of success in this inclusive approach, there are more questions, more challenges, more demands.

I quickly suggest to the committee that we might be transparent that *HeForShe* isn't funded using UN Women's limited resources, but is instead funded exclusively by external partnerships that I personally established, as Phumzile requested. Even so, their concerns remain; some even argue for the discontinuation of *HeForShe* in the interest of safeguarding critical relations with the organization's core stakeholders. Although I understand and respect their perspectives, it is a difficult place to be in.

The situation does not get any easier when I meet one-on-one with Phumzile. "I need you to urgently find a way to concretize the work of *HeForShe*. I know that you are trying to empower communities to come up with their own solutions, an approach which I fully support. However, right now we don't have the luxury to experiment. We must assure our colleagues and partners that our initiative will indeed create tangible impact. And remember, Elizabeth: failure is not an option." The strain is visible on her face.

Phumzile is right; failure has never been an option, and under normal circumstances I would find her words energizing. I have never backed away from a challenge, however formidable. That is how I arrived here to do this work in the first place, and the experiences of that journey are what shaped my firm belief that achieving gender equality requires everyone.

However, these are not normal circumstances, and when I leave Phumzile's office, I feel hollow and deflated. I thought the almost overnight success of *HeForShe* would be proof enough that my conviction was correct. I was sure that I would soon be returning to the best aspect of my job: engaging directly with communities and meeting people, hearing their stories of struggle and triumph, listening to their hopes and dreams, and working to uplift their lives and create lasting change. I spent the months leading up to the launch working eighteen-hour days, pushing myself far beyond my limits, all in the interest of improving the lives of women and girls globally. But now I must do more, when I am already physically and emotionally exhausted. *How can I deliver more measurable impact? Is my plan too disruptive? If the organization loses critically needed funds to improve women's and girls' lives due to misperceptions about the* HeForShe *movement, how will I live with myself?*

When I return to my office, I finally unravel. On my desk I make a pillow with my arms and set my head on it, just as I did on my first day at school in Epworth when I was a child who felt sure I had landed in the wrong place. Or when I sat in the youth hostel kitchen in London, unable to find a job after trying so hard to do so, worried I might have to return to Africa, worried I would not make the best use of my *mukana*. And now, years later, *HeForShe*, meant to be a highlight of my work and a high point of my mission to uplift others, may not be everything I wanted it or meant for it to be. How could I have allowed a movement inspired by *ubuntu*—the very essence of what it means to be African—to have been all for naught? I want nothing more ardently or sincerely than to fight all forms of inequality, especially those impacting women and girls like me and like so many others I have met. But as I sit at my desk, near tears, I wonder if I should just give in, if I should finally give it all up. *I feel defeated.* After what I thought was a great achievement, and after all the impact that we have created, everything seems to be falling apart, in a way that feels all too familiar.

✛

A month away from the triumph of completing secondary school, I still live with Aunt Jane and Uncle Sam in the city during the week. Each weekend and school holiday, I split my time between Epworth, helping Amai search for money, and Goromonzi, plowing and harvesting Gogo's crops. Amai decides where I go, what work I will do, and when I can visit Gogo.

One blazing hot Sunday afternoon, Amai and I are marching to church. We walk quickly down the dusty road, our feet kicking up an orange haze that hovers in the air behind us. Amai leads, dressed in her cream church uniform, a white hat, and a pair of brown canvas shoes, while I walk barefoot behind her wearing my gray church skirt and a white shirt. I am excited—talking about my hope to go to university in anticipation of my high school graduation—when Amai says, "University? Eeee, Lizzy, what about work?"

"But I must go to university, Amai." A university degree is necessary for me to work for the United Nations, a critical part of my dream.

Amai stops walking abruptly and says, "Eeee, me, I thought you were going to find work, Lizzy. University is very-very expensive. Us, we don't have money. I wish . . ." She stops talking and a look of sadness falls over her face. I quickly look at the ground; her sadness makes me feel guilty, but it doesn't change my desire.

"Osi's secondary school fees are very high," she continues. "And, us, we need help with Memo's and Chio's school fees too." I know all this already. Osi, extremely intelligent, was always outperforming the students at Epworth Primary School, so the headmaster encouraged Amai and Baba to send him to a private school in order to challenge him and accelerate his progress. Amai did what she does best: she searched for more money and got Osi into one of the best private boys' high schools in Harare. I still can't look at Amai, but I'm searching for the right words to explain.

"Me," she says, "I am just asking you to make a small sacrifice so that the children can have the same *mukana* you had." And with that, I am trapped. I cannot be selfish and deprive Osi and the children of the same *mukana* given to me, especially knowing the sacrifices that Amai and Baba have made. I say nothing, but I feel a pit of sadness lodge itself in my stomach, weighing down my body, heavy with disappointment.

Amai places her free hand on my shoulder and says, "Eeee, Lizzy, you, you have already become more than me and your *baba*. Us, we are so proud. You, you have become someone we were not able to be."

When I finally look up at her, I see immense pride in her eyes. But there is sadness as well: yes, she gave me the *mukana* to complete secondary school, which she and Baba were not able to do, but it is clearly painful for her to realize that no matter how much she would like to send me to university, she will never find enough money, and like her, my own life will forever be full of sacrifices. She locks eyes with me, pleading silently for me to understand that even though things are changing for our family, nothing ever really changes; even though our lives are moving forward, we seem to stay exactly where we are: always searching for money, always making sacrifices, always taking care of the people we love.

When I finally graduate from secondary school, at seventeen, I look for an office job that pays a good salary. But despite all my efforts, I fail to find one. There is a job shortage in Zimbabwe, and my secondary education on its own simply isn't enough anymore. I must get specialized training in a specific industry, except there is no money for me to attend even the cheapest community college. I must help Amai search for money for the children, and I must also quickly save to pay for my own university fees. I tell myself: *I will find any job.*

At the industrial areas on the outskirts of the city center I join thousands of *ambuyas* and *sekurus* and young people my age flocking in from neighboring urban and rural areas, vying for the scarce manual labor jobs in the factories. Outside the tall fences surrounding the concrete factories and under the blistering sun, we stand together for hours that quickly turn into days and weeks, and then into months; we stand until our backs ache, our legs go numb, and our feet swell. Still we stand, wiping away from our faces thick orange dust stirred up by the passing trucks. Still we stand, as our eyes sting and our nostrils bleed from inhaling the thick smoke billowing from the factory chimneys. Still we stand, pleading for God's mercy, until the British factory foreman emerges each day through the gate and yells "Speak'n English?" and we stampede toward him like a crash of rhinoceroses, hoping to be picked.

Because I "speak'n English," one day I respond at the top of my lungs and shove my way to the front of the line, almost knocking the foreman off his feet. He asks if I have sales experience, which I do from selling Amai's fruit and vegetables. "I also have impeccable people skills from working at the HIV/AIDS clinics," I add.

"Very well then. That will do," he says. "You will start tomorrow morning at nine o'clock at the OK Supermarket next to Market Square. Your job is to cook soybeans inside the store, encourage customers to sample the food, and then convince them to purchase boxes of beans. The job is commission-based only, and you will receive ten cents for each box of beans that you sell. I expect you to sell a minimum of three hundred boxes each week or you will lose the job. That's all," the British foreman says, and shoos me away with a dismissive flap of his hand.

With that I get my first official job, after months of trying. I am glad that I will be able to help Amai search for money for school fees, but when I thank the foreman for the offer, a cloud of sadness consumes me. This is not the job I wanted, especially after my great education at the best private schools. I feel disappointed with myself. I can't believe that I have ended up right here, working in a supermarket, just like my uneducated *baba*. I feel like such a failure for wasting the *mukana* that my family gave me. I feel miserable and defeated, and right there at the factory gates, I begin to cry.

✛

Now, in the aftermath of *HeForShe*, I lie awake each night in my New York apartment, unable to sleep. My mind spins with questions: *How can HeForShe create more impact? How is this even possible with our resources? What if I waste this opportunity to create more impact for women and girls?* Eventually I fall asleep to the sounds of the city: garbage trucks rumbling along the busy streets; sirens in the distance; snippets of conversation floating up from the narrow street below my apartment. I wake up the following morning determined to find a solution.

As soon as I get to my office, I call one of the leading strategy consultant firms and, to my surprise, successfully convince them to provide two pro bono consultants to help create a flagship pilot initiative within the *HeForShe* movement. My brief to the consultants is highly ambitious; I emphasize that the pilot initiative must deliver tangible results for women and girls in only five years. It must engage the most powerful and influential male leaders, individuals who are willing and able to use their power to end specific issues of gender inequality in their communities, businesses, and schools. These leaders will be known as *HeForShe* Champions, because they will lead by example, championing targeted gender issues and committing to specific goals within their institutions. Each must agree to complete transparency, beginning with their gender parity data and then mandatory annual public reporting on their progress toward their gender equality commitments.

At first the consultants are skeptical. "This is way too big of an ask," they respond. "It is one thing to ask leaders to champion issues with concrete commitments, but it's another thing to bind them to mandatory transparency and reporting. Most institutions have embarrassingly low numbers when it comes to gender parity. They will never do it."

But Phumzile and I are adamant. "This has to answer the 'so what' question for the *HeForShe* movement," Phumzile insists. "We have to concretely demonstrate the kind of change that is possible if men are fully engaged as allies for gender equality." As ever, I am so happy to have her as a mentor and an ally.

Just a month later we come up with a concrete road map. Our goal is to create a five-year pilot project, *HeForShe IMPACT 10x10x10* initiative, convening 10 world leaders x 10 global CEOs x 10 university presidents to work together as Champions for gender equality. Our hope is that these Champions will implement transformative policies that will change the lives of women and girls, from ending gender-based violence (child marriage, sexual harassment, violence on campus, domestic violence) to ensuring gender parity within corporations and universities, that is, ensuring that women are equally represented in senior roles, receive equal pay for equal work, and have access to parental leave policies, and that girls have equal access to science, math, and technology classes. When I present the initiative to the UN senior leadership team and receive their sign-off, a palpable relief washes over me. I return to my office, sit at my desk, and feel alive with this unprecedented win, when not so long ago I thought I had failed.

In January 2015, just three months after the official launch of *HeForShe*, I arrive at the World Economic Forum in Davos, Switzerland, to launch the *HeForShe* pilot project. The crisp air and bright, cold sky, as well as the heaps of gleaming white snow on the Swiss Alps, remind me of my time in Geneva.

As the UN secretary-general, Mr. Ban Ki-moon; our executive director, Phumzile Mlambo-Ngcuka; UN Women's global goodwill ambassador Emma Watson; inaugural *HeForShe* Champions (including the president of Rwanda and the prime minister of Sweden); and global CEOs take center stage to officially break ground on our initiative, I feel a powerful sense of pride for what we have accomplished in such a short span of time. With Phumzile's sheer determination, in addition to the support of my colleagues and our UN Women partners, in only three months we have gone from launching *HeForShe*—a global movement that has reached all corners of the world—to engaging the world's most influential men to use their power to create more equitable societies. Most importantly, we have shown the world what is possible when we work together in the spirit of *ubuntu*, transforming the lives of *millions* of women and girls globally.

Years before, when I was working with Amai selling vegetables, then in the supermarket, then pounding the London pavement looking for a job, finally working as a janitor, and then transitioning to a fast-paced office, and then ultimately applying for a job with UNAIDS that I knew I had the experience for but not the academic qualifications—I kept going, no matter what. Through these struggles I built resilience and fortitude that have served me well in keeping the dream of *HeForShe* alive. *Gogo taught me well*, I think, and I close my eyes and thank her for teaching me to never, ever give up.

After the success of Davos, I fly home to Zimbabwe for my yearly visit to my family. I find Osi waiting for me at the airport in his "new" car, which is in fact an old, beat-up, secondhand Toyota Corolla. From the airport we drive straight to Highlands, one of the affluent suburbs in Harare. As we drive up the wide, paved boulevards lined with their famous blossoming purple jacaranda trees in this wealthy, predominantly white suburb and pull up at the end of an idyllic cul-de-sac in front of the freshly painted green metal of a motorized gated driveway, I feel as though my heart might leap out of my chest.

Behind the white gate is a white, bungalow-style house that sits on an acre of beautifully landscaped gardens sprawling with lush vegetation, yellow African daisies, and pink and white roses. The house has eight rooms, including three bedrooms, a bathroom with a stand-alone toilet, a dining room, a large kitchen with built-in blond wood cabinetry, an electric stove with an oven, and a large sink tucked underneath a window that overlooks an orchard of banana, peach, avocado, and mulberry trees at the back of the house. The living room at the front of the house has dark, hardwood floors, plenty of windows, a fireplace, and French doors that open up to an expansive veranda. The house has all the modern amenities of Aunt Jane and Uncle Sam's flat, but it is even more expansive: it is bigger than any house I have ever lived in. To its left sits an open-air garage for two cars and a stand-alone guesthouse with its own private bathroom. To its right is a shimmering swimming pool and a built-in grilling area with a grass-thatched gazebo. Colorful birds chirp and fly between the blooming jacaranda trees surrounding the yard, filling the otherwise peaceful air with cheerful music and sounds that remind me of the Good Forest back in my village, Goromonzi.

Several years ago, I was finally able to fulfill one of the promises that I made to myself when I was eleven years old, the day I realized that I needed to find a way to uplift the lives of my family; the day I noticed for the first time the economic disparities that existed between my life in the city with Aunt Jane and Uncle Sam, and the poverty my family faced in Epworth. So, when I was able, I bought this home as a gift for Amai and Baba, a thank-you for all the sacrifices they made while raising me and my siblings, and for giving me the *mukana* that made it possible for me to pursue and finally achieve my dream.

I remember that first day in the new house as if it was just yesterday. After I helped Amai and Baba move from Epworth into their new Highlands home, we all knelt down in the living room as we waited for Gogo to bless our home with a prayer. As I looked around the room at Amai, Baba, and my siblings and their children, I felt immense gratitude and pride bubble up inside me. Here we were, the Nyamayaro family, having achieved something that had seemed impossible for most families we knew, let alone for ours. Here we were, rising up together, uplifting ourselves as we uplifted each other. Here we were, living proof of God's love and the power of believing in a dream that includes more than just your own individual hopes, but also the hopes and dreams of many. For the very first time, Amai's eyes brimmed with unburdened pride knowing that things had finally changed. Even Baba's knowing smile was bigger than ever, silently saying, *See, I knew that everything was going to be fine*. Our sacrifices for each other had finally moved us forward, changing our lives for the better. As Baba's eyes glistened with joyful tears, so too did mine.

In a moment of crisis,
the wise build bridges.

—Nigerian proverb

14

I scan the small, cozy room painted a crisp white color and notice the plush, patterned burgundy rugs covering the wooden tiles. Newspapers, neatly stacked on a cherrywood rectangular table in the center of the room, are written in a language unfamiliar to me. Although sparsely furnished, the space feels intimate and regal at the same time. I fix my eyes on the closed brown door at the opposite end of the room and feel a surge of adrenaline course through me.

It is 2015, and last night, my boss Phumzile and I arrived in Reykjavík, Iceland, on a very important mission. Even at night, the capital looked to me like a child's model of a city: houses with bright doors and shuttered windows spaced perfectly apart; bells chiming from church belfries; cobblestone streets teeming with life even at the late hour, filled with people fashionably dressed in warm scarves tied just so under their jacket collars.

Phumzile, sitting next to me, looks calm and collected. I try to match her patience as we wait for the brown door to open and for the two of us to be called into the prime minister's office. Noticing my discomfort, she flashes me a confident smile, and I wonder: *Is she as nervous as I am?* There is so much at stake in this meeting. We are so close to the goals we've been working day and night to achieve, and the thought of losing it all now makes my stomach turn. I try to distract myself with thoughts about how hard we have worked and how far we have come.

At the first of the year, we engaged the world's most powerful men as *HeForShe* "Champions" to help create real and transformative change toward gender equality. This quest has proven to be incredibly difficult—negotiating with presidents and prime ministers, urging CEOs to rise to the challenge, encouraging university presidents to do their part—while encountering intense scrutiny from the media about the validity of the Champions' commitments to gender equality.

We also faced a major setback when several countries' presidents and prime ministers pushed back on reporting against their progress, despite having agreed to transparently track it as a prerequisite for joining the initiative. We persevered, visiting and lobbying each committed head of state and their government's ambassadors, offering reminders such as: "Your Excellency, as member states of the United Nations, you *are* the UN, and we can't ask others to abide by the highest level of transparency if we are unwilling to lead by example." I cited other leaders in their cohort—the CEOs of Fortune 500 companies and presidents of leading universities—who were publicly reporting progress against their gender equality commitments. Finally, they agreed, and they are already ushering in change at a pace and magnitude I had only dreamt about.

In Japan, over a million women are rejoining the workforce as part of the prime minister's gender commitment, which we are hopeful will change the day-to-day realities and future prospects of young women like Akiko, whose husband left her when she decided to pursue a career in medicine.

PricewaterhouseCoopers, a global professional services firm with 276,000 employees, is reaching parity in their global leadership team as part of their gender pledge, moving from having only 18 percent of their leadership positions held by women to 47 percent equal female representation, finally achieving a goal that had remained elusive for more than sixteen years.

So many stories tug at my heart and remind me of the stakes of this work, as well as the power of individuals to create change when given the opportunity. I met Lupita, born in Indonesia and the daughter of a military officer, when she bravely shared her story during one of our *HeForShe* events in New York City. In her midtwenties, she wore a flowy, bright pink top that precisely matched the color of her lipstick. She had a striking presence, even more so when she spoke: "My father always gave equal opportunities to my brother and me. He pushed and supported me to be brave and confident as a young woman. He is my role model; he is my first *HeForShe*." Then, at the age of ten, while walking from home to school, Lupita was sexually assaulted by a group of young men.

"Because of my father, I grew up believing that I could achieve everything, but when the assault happened, I learned that the outside world can be hard for women," she said. "I was terrified by the notion that men can be so malicious to girls and that they can treat us as undignified objects. The incident traumatized me, but it also gave me the courage to speak up and stand up against sexual violence." Resolve burned in her eyes.

After Lupita finished college, she began working for a leading French multinational company, Danone, in their Indonesia office. When she learned about the *HeForShe* movement, she immediately took action, creating an internal *HeForShe* program with four other female colleagues at her workplace, launching special empowerment initiatives for female employees—including cross-gender mentoring and leadership training with male coworkers who volunteered to participate. In the span of a single year, her brainchild had reached Danone's offices in Russia, the Netherlands, Singapore, China, and most importantly, the corporate headquarters in France. While this was unfolding, neither I nor my colleagues knew anything about Lupita's efforts or the success of the program she had started, until one day we received a surprising phone call from

Danone's CEO—*volunteering* to become a *HeForShe* Champion in the pilot initiative.

Because of Lupita's tenacious advocacy, Danone made an unprecedented gender commitment, becoming one of the first companies *in the world* to roll out a global, gender-neutral paid parental leave policy for all of its 120,000 employees. The policy provides mothers, fathers, and adoptive parents *eighteen weeks* of paid parental leave, no matter what country or territory they work in, including in the United States, which currently has no such law for new parents.

Just like that, a young woman in Indonesia, together with her four female colleagues, changed the lives of their fellow coworkers, positively impacting 120,000 lives.

"I have learned that we are never too young to create change, and that no action is ever too small," Lupita explained. "I believe that with passion and energy, we all can drive small things into big things. But even then, I never could have imagined that young Indonesian women could make as big an impact in a global corporation this fast," she said, choking up with pride.

Lupita was absolutely right. I witnessed the same level of passion myself when I spent months on a bus traveling across Europe and North America, determined to bring the message of gender equality directly to students at colleges and universities. Our goal was to help break the generational cycle of inequality, as research has shown that these formative years inform if and how much you care about issues of social inequality.

Engaging with students was invigorating, and I was routinely surprised by their input and the stories I heard. When I asked a young male student at Cambridge University in the UK what gender equality meant to him, his response was "Being able to drink my sparkling apple juice without judgment." His answer was quite unexpected, to say the very least, and so when I probed, he elaborated: "I was brought up in a very conservative family. No one in my family drinks alcohol and neither do I. But then last year I started university, and noticed that all my mates were always hanging out at the pub. One day I joined them and when one of my mates asked what I wanted to drink and I said a sparkling apple juice, everyone laughed and said 'Man up!' so I succumbed to peer pressure and drank beer. It was my first time drinking alcohol." He paused and his voice grew quiet; he would not meet my gaze. "I was so drunk when I left the pub that night that I ended up sexually harassing a fellow female student, a friend of mine. I still feel so ashamed for my behavior. Since that day I have vowed never to touch alcohol again and neither do I hang out with those mates." He hung his head in shame. It was quite a lot to take in. I remember thinking that if something as basic as a drink can be gendered and used to demean someone, then we still have a long way to go.

At one of the leading universities in the US, a female student confided in me about the unwelcome advances of her male professor. "I don't know what to do. I am afraid that if I turn down his advances, he will fail me, and I really can't afford for that to happen. My mom works four jobs so I can afford to be here." She looked and sounded utterly defeated.

These were some of the real issues and concerns of the students we encountered. In hallways and in campus student centers or common areas, we sat on dusty floors and in the damp grass, holding heated debates that challenged students' notions of gender biases and gender norms. We discussed how gender equality means liberation for all genders.

"Our gender should not impede our ability to be ambitious and career-driven *and* committed to family life," Valerie, a student at the Paris Institute of Political Studies, or Sciences Po, stated. We talked about the fact that there are fewer women in Engineering classes, while men remain under-represented in the Social Sciences; we lamented the fact that domestic and intimate partner violence impacts one in three women globally, but also how the UK has documented that one in eight men are also victims of domestic violence in Britain. We talked about how words like "bossy," "bitchy," and "emotional" are used to undermine women and girls, while men and boys are ridiculed for showing any emotion. "We don't want to be held back by outdated notions of masculinity. Our gender should not restrict us from showing our emotions. We can be strong and vulnerable and that's okay. It just makes us more human," added Darrel, a student from Stony Brook University on Long Island, in New York. He talked about his struggle to align his thoughts and actions with society's definition of what it means to be a man, including expectations that he should be a breadwinner and never show emotion. He was taught to believe that seeking any kind of mental health support—even when he needed it—would render him "weak," which made him less of a man.

Many of our dialogues dove into the intersectionality of gender, the way that multiple aspects of discrimination—involving gender, race, sexuality, class, disability, and more—converge in people's lived experiences. At the University of Leicester in the UK, a student named Amy had her own frustrations. "People need to stop talking about gender equality as if it is binary, because it is not, it is a spectrum," she said. As difficult as some of those discussions were, I always left feeling hopeful and inspired, and full of an even greater conviction that the only real way to create lasting change is for all genders to work together.

"How long?" Phumzile asks, jolting me out of my thoughts. I check my watch and say, "Ten more minutes," then refocus on the goals of our meeting with the prime minister. Although I have been working closely with the prime minister's office and the Icelandic ambassador to the United Nations in New York City on their gender commitment, this is my first time in Iceland.

Long before coming here, I learned to appreciate the country's history in the fight for women's rights through my friend Halla, a leading women's rights activist and former presidential candidate in Iceland. "I want to tell you when I realized that women matter to the economy and to society," she told me. "I was seven, and it happened to be my mother's birthday, October 24, 1975. On that historic day, women in Iceland went on strike and took the day entirely off work. They refused to work, cook, or care for children in order to create a new way to see women in Iceland; namely, as indispensable. On that day, nothing worked in Iceland; everything ground to a halt. The women marched into the city center and demanded that women's issues be added to all national policy agendas moving forward. Some say that this marked the genesis of a global movement. For me, it was the start of a long journey, and I decided to make that day matter," Halla explained, and the joy of this story made her brown eyes shine.

She went on to tell me how the efforts of the Icelandic women paid off. Five years after the strike, in 1980, Iceland elected its first female president, Vigdís Finnbogadóttir, who became *the world's first* democratically elected female president. This was a giant step for gender equality on a global scale, and this milestone event propelled Iceland to become the most gender-equal country in the world according to the World Economic Forum Gender Index. However, despite this unprecedented progress, women in Iceland were unable to attain one of the core rights they had been fighting for: legislation that would legally enforce equal pay for equal work.

Knowing Halla's story and this history, when the prime minister of Iceland expressed an interest in becoming a *HeForShe* Champion, I leapt at the opportunity to advocate for a policy that would deliver equal pay for Icelandic women. This was not an easy ask, considering that, at the time, no other country had come close to making such a commitment. It was one thing to ask a company to commit to equal pay for their workforce, as we had done with the CEOs of two French companies, AccorHotels and Schneider Electric—who both pledged to eliminate unequal pay for their one hundred thousand plus global employees—but it was an entirely different story to have such a law adopted and enforced at the national level for an entire country.

In my travels around the world, I've met hundreds of women who must work several jobs just to make ends meet, and I have seen the impact of pay inequity on many more. Women's work continues to be under-valued and underpaid; globally, women are still paid 23 percent less than men for doing exactly the same work. In the US, mothers in two out of every five households with children are either the sole or primary source of income for the family, meaning that nearly half of American families are robbed of over 20 percent of their annual income. This unfair reality is exacerbated by racial inequality, which has created an unjust hierarchy that sees African-American women making less than white women, and leaves Hispanic women to bear the biggest brunt of the pay gap, earning the very least among their counterparts. In my own home continent of Africa, the World Bank reports that nearly one in four households are now headed by a woman. Given that this is the reality for much of the world, it is difficult to understand why equal pay is still seen as a women's issue, when it is more accurately an issue of fairness that impacts the lives of many people in obvious, measurable ways.

With these factors in mind, Phumzile and I stuck to our conviction that Iceland was in the unique position to lead the world on this issue, knowing that the gender pay gap needed to be closed, forever and for good. Such a move would be historic and life-changing for the entire population of Iceland, establishing a beacon of hope and progress for women in the rest of the world.

When the door to the president's office finally opens, we are ushered into a long, narrow meeting room decorated with an elegant blond wood table and cabinetry, understated Scandinavian glam. Phumzile, a colleague from the UN Women's regional office, and I sit across the table from the prime minister and his three advisors, who look serious but receptive. I hope they understand how high the stakes of this conversation truly are.

A few months ago, the Icelandic government made a *HeForShe* commitment to close the gender pay gap in the country by mandating equal pay for equal work for *all companies* doing business in Iceland. This groundbreaking commitment means that every business in Iceland must ensure pay equality for their workers, and any company that has not implemented this standard by 2022 will be asked to cease doing business. To achieve this hugely ambitious goal, the government—working alongside Icelandic women's rights groups, UN Women, and other key stakeholders—has developed an auditing tool that will detect discrepancies in equal pay for any company in Iceland that employs more than twenty-five people. Once a company achieves equal pay for equal work, they will receive an equal pay accreditation from the government. However, due to the enormity of the undertaking, the tool has yet to be implemented, and we worry that progress has stalled, potentially jeopardizing the fulfillment of the pledge. This is why Phumzile and I have come to such a high-level meeting, and with such high expectations.

As soon as we are done exchanging formal greetings, Phumzile gets straight to the point. "Your Excellency, we need your extra efforts to push for the equal pay legislation. While our teams have made great strides, we need your support in expediting auditing so we can begin to make progress," she says.

The prime minister articulates the challenges in building internal consensus on the best approach to roll out the auditing tool, but he assures us that his office will hold a meeting with all relevant stakeholders to fast-track this important step of the tool's implementation. His commitment to keeping the process moving is a huge win, and we leave his office feeling elated and relieved.

As we depart Reykjavík, making our way to the airport through rolling hills carpeted in green moss and flora, I finally relax, roll down the car window, and fill my lungs with the crisp, clean air. I have never seen such terrain, which reminds me of something out of a science fiction movie. The land is treeless and barren, but beautiful in its own unique—almost lunar—way. As I take in this otherworldly landscape, reveling in this important step toward reaching our goals, my mind drifts to a student I recently met named Anya, who is studying Astrophysics with the dream of becoming an astronaut.

"Receiving the *HeForShe* scholarship was an absolute thrill," Anya told me at one of Canada's leading Engineering schools, the University of Waterloo, which launched the scholarships as part of their commitment to facilitate the admission of young women into Science, Technology, Engineering, and Math (STEM) classes, with the ultimate goal of eliminating the gender gap in this field. "It has of course been a financial help, but it was much more than that," Anya explained with excitement. "It gave me the confidence to run for vice president of the Physics club twice, and in that position I was able to make real change. I made sure that each newly elected Physics team is comprised of 50 percent women. A few of those women told me that they never would have had the courage to run had other women not run alongside them. It has completely broadened my own thinking about what I can do, and how I can be more involved in promoting gender equality in STEM." Her words fill me with joy; just like the women in Iceland, Anya has been empowered to make the most of her opportunity, while also creating an opportunity for others. Now women in Iceland will hopefully achieve equal pay for equal work, due in part to the tireless efforts of their fellow Icelandic women who decades earlier stood up for equality during the 1975 strike.

A few months after our visit, Iceland manages to complete the pilot phase of their pay parity commitment—certifying seven companies after each met the equal pay standard and reaching an important milestone.

What I don't know in this moment is that in 2018, the world will wake up to the breaking news that *Iceland is the first country to make it illegal to pay men more than women*. A huge weight having then lifted from my shoulders, I collapse onto my desk with relief and thank God for everything. All those years of hard work—all the travel and listening and diplomacy and determination—all of it will pay off, making me feel part of something very important. On January 2, 2018, the government publicly declares that Icelandic women are now guaranteed, by law, to receive equal pay for equal work, the legislation requiring that women be valued and treated as equal to their male colleagues. This historic milestone is literally world-changing, and I feel honored to be both a facilitator and a witness to this seismic shift.

As my colleagues and I pause to celebrate in New York City and around the world, I am overcome with gratitude. I think of all the communities and individuals who stood together to create a bold and unified force for gender equality as part of the *HeForShe* movement. I am humbled by the commitments and actions of so many that have created so much change. I think of Lupita, and what she said about the power of an individual to create impact, and how her father was her first role model, a man who instilled in her the belief that she had both the right and the ability to pursue her dreams and goals in order to build a life of meaning and purpose. Her story resonates so deeply because it reflects my own. When I began the *HeForShe* movement, I was inspired by the many men who had encouraged and supported me, but none did so as profoundly and powerfully as my uncle Sam.

✛

I am eighteen years old, chatting with Uncle Sam in his office. He has just returned after months of traveling across Africa for his work. Whenever I spend time with him, I'm reminded of how deeply he has shaped my life: he has modeled for me the integrity, perseverance, and kindness that I seek to emulate. He is just the kind of person I aspire to be, and I am excited to be here, with him, now that I live full-time in Epworth where I help take care of my siblings. His office is a cozy and familiar place; it feels like home, for him to be on one side of the desk and me on the other, talking about anything and everything.

Uncle Sam has been asking me about work. I'm embarrassed about the supermarket job I have held for almost a year now. Moments before, I apologized for letting him down and disappointing him, for wasting the *mukana* of a great education that he and Aunt Jane supported me with. He seems surprised by my reaction and reminds me that he and Aunt Jane are still very proud of me. Still, I know that they wanted me to go to university, even expected it. I have not and am not sure if I will ever be able to. When I tell him this, I cannot bear to look him in the eyes.

"Yes, that would have been lovely," Uncle Sam says. "But you should not let your situation get you down. You should still be proud of yourself for continuing to fight, even when things seem impossible."

I look up at Uncle Sam's kind face and nearly burst into tears. All this time, I have been carrying so much guilt for not going to university as I promised him, and this feeling of failing him has haunted me, tortured me with disappointment, keeping me up at night.

"Promise me something, Elizabeth. Never let your current circumstances limit your potential. Never let anything diminish your dreams. Okay?"

I look into his eyes, continuing to blink back tears. "Okay, Uncle Sam. I promise."

Uncle Sam stands up and walks around the desk to place his hand on my shoulder. I feel the weight of his love for me, and his confidence in my abilities. His absolute support is just the motivation I need. I leave his office feeling uplifted, committed to my new promise to him and reassured by his wise words of guidance, reminding me that I must keep working hard, that I must remain focused, and that I must never, ever give up on my dream.

A few months pass, and I am in the supermarket helping a customer when I hear my name over the intercom. Aunt Jane is on the phone for me, and not with good news.

"Your uncle has been admitted to Parirenyatwa Hospital." Her voice is spiked with panic, which is unlike her; she explains that Uncle Sam has been sick since he returned home from a business trip to Ghana several days ago.

I quickly leave work to meet Aunt Jane at the hospital and follow her down the narrow corridor toward the patients' ward. "He said he felt ill during the conference. He thinks a doctor accidentally gave him penicillin," Aunt Jane tells me in a rush. Uncle Sam is highly allergic to penicillin; ingesting it could kill him.

I say a quick prayer to God as I run ahead of Aunt Jane into his hospital room, but what I find there stops me in my tracks. Uncle Sam is lying on the bed, looking as helpless as a child, with a complicated network of tubes connected to different parts of his body. His eyes are closed, so I sit on the edge of his bed, place my hand on his cheek, and whisper, "Wake up, Uncle Sam. It's me. Can you hear me?"

"He is unconscious," Aunt Jane says, standing in the doorway. She looks terrified and refuses to enter the room. I have never seen her like this before, which only increases my worry. I say another fervent prayer, this time with my hand on Uncle Sam's shoulder.

I stay in the hospital while Aunt Jane returns to her patients, pulling a chair from the corner of the room so I can sit next to Uncle Sam and continue holding his shoulder, praying again to God for a miracle as terror sprints through my body.

I can't lose Uncle Sam! "*Shiri yakanaka unoendepi? Huya, huya, huya titambe,*" I sing softly, leaning closer to him, my grip tightening around his shoulder. I wait for Uncle Sam to sing back, "*Ndiri kuenda kumakore. Kuti ndifanane nemakore.*"

In my early days of living in Harare, Uncle Sam nicknamed me Pretty Bird, because I chirped to the birds anytime I saw them, just as I had done in the Good Forest. He then taught me to sing "Pretty Bird," a classic Shona lullaby, which immediately became our favorite song; I wanted it anytime I felt down or missed Gogo, and he sang along with me. I liked being called Pretty Bird; I imagined myself free, flying through fluffy white clouds, moving through time and space, making my way back home to Goromonzi, back to a simpler time when I was just Gogo's dear child. "*Shiri yakanaka unoendepi? Huya, huya, huya ti-tambe*—Pretty bird, where are you going? Come, come, come, let's play," Uncle Sam would sing. "*Ndiri kuenda kumakore. Kuti ndifanane nema-kore*—I am going to the clouds. So I too can be just like the clouds," I would respond.

When I was fifteen and contracted the mumps virus, Uncle Sam nursed me back to health, taking a week off from work so that he could be home with me. Since there is no treatment for mumps, apart from a preventative vaccination which I should have received when I was a baby but hadn't because Gogo couldn't afford to pay for one, Aunt Jane ordered bed rest until I recovered. My face and jaw puffed up like a balloon, which made it difficult to swallow or chew. Uncle Sam made me carrot soup and attended to me, making sure that I stayed hydrated. He decorated my bedroom with colorful blue, white, and orange balloons and bright yellow African daisies. He sat for hours by my bedside reading me novels from some of his favorite African authors—Chinua Achebe, Buchi Emecheta, Ngũgĩ wa Thiong'o—until my eyes became heavy with sleep. Then he would stop reading, place his hand on my shoulder. "Pretty bird, where are you going? Come, come, come, let's play," he whispered, his voice soothing and healing as I slowly drifted off. This was one of many times when Uncle Sam nursed me back to health or took care of me. And now I long for my voice to do the same for Uncle Sam, only he is unconscious and unable to hear me. Still I keep singing "Pretty Bird" quietly until visiting hours are over and I am asked to leave.

The next day, when I return to the hospital with Amai, I am shocked to find Uncle Sam sitting up in his bed, reading a newspaper as if nothing has happened. Amai is so startled when she sees him that she immediately begins to wail.

"Who died?" Uncle Sam says, smiling, teasing Amai.

"Eeee you, you scared us. Lizzy said you were unconscious," Amai says, and sits down next to the bed.

"Uncle Sam, don't ever scare us like that again," I say, light-headed with relief, wrapping my arms around him so tightly that I crumple his newspaper. He assures me that he is okay and set to be released the day after tomorrow. He tells us that it was indeed penicillin he was given that made him so sick. I tell him that I have to work the next day, but will arrange to pick him up the day after that.

"Deal," Uncle Sam says, getting out of bed and tightening his green hospital robe around his waist. He insists on walking with us to the top of the stairs, where I hug him goodbye.

Late afternoon the following day, I am in the back of the supermarket restocking the shelves when I look up and see Amai, which startles me.

"Is everything okay?"

"Eeee, Lizzy, me, I don't know," Amai says. "Your Uncle Sam is worse again."

"I will go after work," I say, knowing from experience that Amai has a tendency to overreact, and I cannot simply leave work in the middle of the day again. But when Amai reaches for my hand and says, "Lizzy, us, we have to go now," I understand that this is serious and we quickly leave.

When we arrive at the hospital, we immediately run to Uncle Sam's room, but he isn't there.

"Where did you move my uncle?" I ask the nurse.

"Follow me this way," she says. Amai and I follow her down a long corridor. I have a bad feeling. *Where is she taking us? Where is Uncle Sam?*

"Wait here," she says, opening a door and leading us into an empty room.

Amai and I sit next to each other on two chairs facing a doctor's desk. We sit in silence, lost in our thoughts, heavy with dread.

Finally, a male doctor in a white coat enters, sits down behind the desk, looks at us, and says, "I'm sorry."

I am completely confused. *What is he talking about?* "Where is Uncle Sam?"

"I am so sorry," he repeats. "Your uncle has just passed away. I am so sorry for your loss."

It feels as though my body is drifting slowly away from me, floating untethered through space like a tiny feather. *This cannot be happening. This cannot be true.* But there is the doctor in his white coat, telling us that Uncle Sam is gone. There is Amai, speechless and shocked. I collapse on the cold, hard floor of the hospital and curl myself into a ball; no sounds come, but I feel an utter and total despair unlike anything I have yet to experience in my life. It's as if the ground has fallen out beneath me and with it, all of my plans for the future. I am utterly bereft. My uncle Sam has just died. Nothing will ever be the same.

However long the night,
dawn always breaks.

◐

—Congolese proverb

15

"Shhh, shhh," I say softly. Kneeling next to the large orange metal basin, I gently lift one of the wailing babies from the soapy water, leaving the other baby in the safe hands of the woman next to me. I place the baby on my chest, wrap my hands around her tiny wet body, and feel my white shirt dampen and cling to me. "Shhh, shhh, *chinyarara*—don't cry. God is going to take care of you," I say, and then begin to cry myself. I bend my knees and lower my body to the dusty ground, tightening my arms to cradle the distressed baby; she feels so small and helpless in my arms.

"Shhh, Shhh, it is okay," the woman says, and I'm not sure if she is talking to me or to the baby, but both of us are crying now—the baby's loud sobs mixing with my softer weeping as I try to collect myself. "I am so sorry, Ambuya Rufa," I tell the woman, wiping my tears with the back of my hand. She nods, lifts the other baby out of the orange basin, wraps her in a colorful sarong, and hands me a matching one. I wrap the wet baby in the sarong; she whimpers, and I feel her warm breath against my chest.

It is late 2015, and I am back home in Goromonzi visiting my family. Even though Gogo is gone, I still return home as often as possible to see all the *ambuyas* and *sekurus* and their children. Yesterday, when I arrived in the village, Ambuya Chop-Chop told me the devastating news about a woman—Ambuya Rufa—whom she knows from church. Two weeks ago, Ambuya Rufa buried her daughter after she took her own life, leaving behind her two-week-old twin daughters. Ambuya Rufa's village is located past the Township Center where Gogo and I once sold our maize each harvest, and I have traveled here to extend my condolences.

Ambuya Rufa and I sit together in her yard, under a large tree with patchy leaves that do little to protect us from the sun, which is just now beginning to set. To our right is a round thatched hut with a small wooden door that looks exactly like Gogo's. To our left is a plastered rectangular sleeping house covered with weathered tin. Unlike Gogo, Ambuya Rufa does not have a storage hut for her crops; she doesn't have a goat shed or a chicken coop in her yard, she doesn't have much. Apart from the hut and the sleeping house, the yard looks barren, save for the tomatoes, pumpkins, and green beans that grow in a small garden patch behind the large tree. I calm myself down and force myself to smile at the woman who sits next to me, the baby resting in her arms. Ambuya Rufa, in her late fifties, has a long, slender face like Amai's, with a slim nose, small black eyes, and sharply defined cheekbones. She wears a brown cotton dress, with short sleeves, and matching brown canvas shoes. Her hair is styled in cornrows, accentuating her high forehead. I have just met Ambuya Rufa and this is the first time I have been to her home. I only wish my visit was taking place under different conditions and better circumstances.

"Ambuya Rufa, I am so sorry—again—for everything that has happened," I say and once more begin to cry.

"Eeee, it is tough, my grandchild. Me, I leave everything in God's hands," she says with conviction, her voice laced with sadness.

"What happened, Ambuya?" I speak softly so as to not disturb the babies resting peacefully in our arms, these sweet babies who will never know or remember their mother, and who will someday have to learn the story of how and why she died.

Ambuya responds in a hushed voice, "Huhhh, me, I blame myself. My daughter Tanaka would still be here if I had stood up to my husband." I nod, and she continues. "Tanaka wanted to go to school so she could become a teacher, but eeee, my husband refused and married Tanaka to an old man when she was just fourteen years old. Tanaka was very unhappy in the marriage; her husband was beating her up too-much-too-much. She tried to come back home so many times, but we kept sending her back to her husband because, us, we did not have enough food to feed her and her twin girls. We had to turn her away." Her eyes fill with tears, and she stops talking for a moment and swallows hard before continuing. "Three weeks ago, I woke up and found Tanaka, my sweet angel, right here, hanging from a thick rope from this tree. Huhhh, she had taken her own life to end her suffering. Sometimes I wish it is a nightmare and I will wake up," Ambuya Rufa says. She looks up at the tree branch and her face looks startled, as if she's just seen a ghost. I feel shivers run down my spine. Then Ambuya Rufa opens her mouth and wails with the kind of raw emotion that I have only heard from a woman who has lost her child and survived that ragged and bottomless grief. Her weeping frightens the babies and we all cry with her—wrenching, hopeless sobs that are the only response to such a devastating and unspeakable loss.

This time I don't say "I am so sorry for your loss" to Ambuya Rufa, because this time I am wildly upset. I am upset with Tanaka's father and husband for taking away her chance to live a life she wanted; for marrying her off when she was still a child; for condoning abuse; and for making this girl who had hopes and dreams feel as though death was preferable to living a life of such misery and sadness. I am heartbroken to know that the majority of child marriages happen in my home continent of Africa as a result of poverty. Every year, fifteen million girls are forced into child marriage before the age of eighteen: the equivalent of twenty-eight girls every minute, or one girl every two seconds. I have met some of those girls, and their stories weigh heavily on my heart as I think about Tanaka's death.

I recall meeting Nira, a fourteen-year-old child marriage survivor, in India. As the driver of the yellow *tuk-tuk* I was in navigated traffic in the crowded streets of New Delhi, a young girl leapt in front of him, as if out of nowhere, and was nearly hit and killed. A bright green chiffon scarf covered all of her hair and half of her face. The sleeves of her bright red dress flapped in the wind and were so long it looked as if she had no hands. She stumbled along in blue flip-flops, her dress billowing like a parachute behind her. I panicked, jumped out of the *tuk-tuk*, and ran to her. "Are you okay?" I asked, and pulled her out of the road and onto a dusty sidewalk. She said she was fine, and introduced herself as Nira. She was in a hurry, trying to get to the temple, and hadn't seen the *tuk-tuk* coming. I offered to drop her off, and when she sat next to me in the *tuk-tuk*, I noticed that half of her face was badly scarred and one eye was sealed shut.

Nira shared her story with me: she was from a rural community in India, and when she was only eleven years old, her parents forced her into child marriage. When Nira turned thirteen, she ran away to New Delhi to live with her aunt, but her husband tracked her down and then poured burning sulfuric acid all over her body. The acid melted Nira's face, leaving her with permanent blindness in one eye, and it melted some of her bones, disfiguring her hands. "When I was young, I had a dream, you know," Nira said. "I wanted to become a big movie star in Bollywood, just like my favorite actress, Madhubala. But now how can I act when I look like a monster with my face all melted by the acid?" A palpable sadness fell over us as we sped through the busy, crowded streets. Sadly, Nira's case is not unique, as every year more than fifteen hundred women and girls are attacked by acid globally, including in countries like the UK and Canada.

Child marriage doesn't just happen in India or Africa, as people often assume, but also in the developed world, even in the United States. In New Jersey, I visited a synagogue with a Jewish friend of mine who introduced me to Sarah, then seventeen years old, whose parents forced her into child marriage when she turned fifteen.

After the service, we sat in a local café drinking peppermint tea and eating bagels and cream cheese. Sarah wore a pair of trendy, blue-rimmed reading glasses, a long black dress, and a white head scarf. She explained that she had tried twice to run away from her abusive husband, but unlike Nira, none of her family agreed to take her in. When she sought refuge at the women's shelter, she was turned away because she was not yet eighteen, and as a legal minor, she required parental consent to stay. She decided to live on the streets rather than return to an unsafe home, but she was arrested both times by the police, who brought her back to her husband, because again, she was a minor and considered a child in the eyes of the law.

"Am I not supposed to be living in the greatest country in the world? So how come I feel trapped?" Sarah asks with intense frustration. "But I won't let them win. Next year I will be eighteen and I am going to run away for good this time. You wait and see, one day I will be a lawyer so I can change laws for girls like me," she said with determination. I felt the same frustration; on one hand the US law protected Sarah as a minor; yet on the other hand, the law failed to offer protection when that very same minor was being violated. The United States, despite being one of the world's most wealthy and powerful countries, has never passed a law at the national level banning child marriage, meaning that according to federal law it is permissible to marry a child as young as twelve years old. Even worse: child marriage is still legal in forty-six out of the fifty states.

I share none of this with Ambuya Rufa, for these are not her burdens or stories to bear. I can feel my heart breaking as I rock the little baby against my chest. It breaks for these two motherless babies, and for Ambuya Rufa who must live with her grief while struggling to feed two extra children. My heart breaks for my community, having lost one of our *sisis*, and for Tanaka herself, who was driven to take her own life. Ambuya Rufa is still wailing; I throw my arm around her shoulder and say, "One day, change will come, Ambuya. One day change will come." I make a promise to myself that I will find a way to put an end to the unjust practice of child marriage, wherever I find it.

When I return to my office in New York City and learn that the president of Malawi has expressed interest in joining the initiative as a *HeForShe* Champion, I immediately jump at the opportunity to push for a commitment to enact legislation that will end child marriage. Despite more than five years of UN Women's tireless efforts working alongside the government, civil society organizations, and female chiefs in Malawi, advocating for and investing in anti–child marriage initiatives, nearly half of the girls in Malawi continue to be married before the age of eighteen. Here is my chance to make good on my promise: for Tanaka and Nira and Ambuya Rufa and Sarah, and for so many others that I have never met but know are out there, suffering.

I meet with the Malawian ambassador to the United Nations in his office in New York, and waste no time in making my case. "Your Excellency, Malawi has an unprecedented opportunity to be a beacon of light on the African continent," I say, channeling the same calm and authority I watched Julia exude that first time I saw her in full diplomatic action, at the beginning of my career. I sit across from the ambassador, who sits behind a cherrywood desk. I look directly at him, taking in his dignified face and proper, coiffured jet-black hair. He looks back through square reading glasses that frame his serious eyes.

I take a breath and continue. "We know that child marriage has been a part of our African culture, but it is also one of the main causes of perpetuating poverty on our continent. As you know, Your Excellency, when girls are married young, we not only rob them of their childhood, we rob them of their dreams. The loss of those dreams—to get an education, to make life better for themselves and their families, to broaden their possibilities—is also a loss for our communities and countries. When a girl loses her dreams, none of us achieve the prosperity that we would otherwise enjoy." I hear the conviction in my voice, and I can tell that the ambassador feels it as well.

My proposal is initially received as too ambitious, which is something I've grown accustomed to hearing. However, after months of relentless diplomatic negotiations with the ambassador and the president's office, with the support of our UN Women colleagues in Malawi, we successfully secure the president's personal pledge, as part of his gender equality commitment, to end child marriage in Malawi.

To our joy and surprise, within just fifteen months of making this commitment the government of Malawi in a determined and unprecedented manner passes Malawi's first ever "Marriage, Divorce and Family Relations Act on child marriage," making it illegal to marry a child under the age of eighteen. Because the *HeForShe* movement, in the spirit of *ubuntu*, engages everyone to work together toward gender equality, thousands of girls will have better and more meaningful lives.

Phumzile and I meet with the Malawian president at a formal dinner of *HeForShe* Champions in New York City, the evening before the start of the annual 2016 United Nations General Assembly, which brings together all world leaders to discuss issues of global cooperation and peace. In a cozy restaurant in midtown Manhattan, we are served beautifully plated dishes of wild salmon with steamed vegetables and potatoes. Phumzile and I sit alongside impeccably dressed global CEOs, university presidents, and the president of Malawi. I am almost too anxious to eat. Tomorrow our *HeForShe* Champions will stand in front of international media and share the progress that they have made as part of their gender commitments. Tonight's event is a rehearsal dinner to provide Phumzile with a first look at the remarkable results.

When the Malawian president speaks, he not only highlights the passing of the anti–child marriage law, but he also specifically acknowledges the remarkable efforts of communities in Malawi that are actively supporting anti–child marriage efforts. "I am happy to announce that in the past twelve months alone, our communities have annulled more than 1,455 child marriages and those girls are now back in school," he says in an authoritative voice laced with pride. These developments are truly groundbreaking, and provide a strong foundation for lasting change. I feel my heart swell with pride, and my eyes sting with tears of joy.

A year ago, in Goromonzi, I told Ambuya Rufa that one day things would change. I made a promise to myself to play a part in creating that change, even though at the time I didn't know how I would do it, or what shape my plan would take. And now things are actively changing for girls and communities in Malawi, due in part to the *HeForShe* movement. So many unsung heroes—youth activists, nonprofit organizations, and communities—have worked alongside us and their government to collectively make child marriage a thing of the past in Malawi. One of those people is Memory Banda, a fearless, nineteen-year-old anti–child marriage youth activist.

I met Memory the year before when I was invited to give a TED Talk during the annual TEDWomen Conference in San Francisco. A fellow speaker, I found Memory pacing up and down in the green room, polishing her speech for the packed theater of people waiting to hear her story. Her lacy yellow dress reminded me of the beautiful African sun and was paired with bright blue pointed shoes. She was both the sun and the sky. Her hair, braided and pulled back into an elegant bun, highlighted her round face and big brown eyes. I knew that Memory had led many of the community efforts that made the anti–child marriage bill possible. She even stood outside the parliament house for months with fellow youth activists, tirelessly lobbying members of parliament to support the bill.

"My little sister was only eleven years old when she got pregnant," Memory told me. "As is the custom in my culture, she was sent to an initiation camp, where young girls are taught how to sexually please a man once they reach puberty. There is a special day, which they call 'Very Special Day,' where a man who is hired by the community comes to the camp and sleeps with the little girls. Some girls end up contracting HIV/AIDS and other sexually transmitted diseases. My little sister ended up pregnant. Now she has three children even though she is only sixteen years old."

There was so much pain on Memory's face as she shared her sister's experiences. But that's not how the story ended. After having refused to go to the initiation camp herself, Memory was ostracized for disrespecting traditions. She turned her pain into action and started advocating with both female and male village elders to end harmful practices in their village. This wasn't an easy task, but Memory persevered until, one day, the elders relented and agreed to end child marriage.

"I had a lot of dreams as a young girl," Memory explained to me. "But every day I refused to go to the initiation camps, the older women in my community badgered me. 'Look at you, you are all grown up, your little sister has a baby, what about you?' But I wanted to get educated to find a decent job in the future. I imagined myself as a lawyer seated on that big chair. I knew that one day I would contribute something, a little something, to my community. So I refused to give up." When she looks at me, with pride and passion in her eyes, I am reminded of all the struggles on the winding path to achieve my own dreams—and the moments I feared those dreams would never come true.

✛

Uncle Sam is lying on his back inside a shiny wooden coffin padded with white fabric. His eyes and lips are closed, his short hair nicely combed back from his familiar face. He is dressed in his favorite gray suit, paired with a crisp white shirt and a patterned blue tie. He looks peaceful, like he is having a nice, long sleep. I lean in closer to his face and whisper, "Wake up, Uncle Sam," and for a moment I truly believe that he will rise.

"Wake up. Please, Uncle Sam," I repeat, louder this time, just to be sure he heard me, and then I keep my eyes trained on his face, waiting for his brown eyes to open. When they don't, I wail at the top of my lungs, throw myself onto the wooden floor, and bellow like a bull.

"Eeee, Lizzy, stop! You, you will hurt yourself," Amai shouts as she yanks me off the floor and drags me away from the coffin, through Aunt Jane's crowded living room, then down the corridor into my old bedroom. We both collapse onto the bed, throw our arms around each other, and wail at the top of our lungs. Uncle Sam is dead, and he is never coming back. It feels too horrible to be true.

When I have no more tears left to cry and my throat feels dry and raw, I realize that Amai has left the room and I am alone. I sit up with my back against the wall and stare into empty space. I haven't eaten anything in days. A part of me wants to die, because the pain feels too unbearable, so final, so unfair, so impossible and unfamiliar. At least hunger pains I can understand, but not this loss. *If I don't eat*, I think, *then perhaps I too can disappear from this world and I will be free of the devastating weight of grief.*

"*Shiri yakanaka unoendepi? Huya, huya, huya titambe*—Pretty bird, where are you going? Come, come, come, let's play," I sing to myself, but Uncle Sam has gone to the clouds, just like the bird in the song. From now on, I will never hear his response apart from the memory of his singing voice in my head.

From the living room, I can hear the loud chatter and occasional screams from grieving *ambuyas* and *sekurus* from Goromonzi, as well as some of Uncle Sam's relatives. As is the custom in our Shona culture, Uncle Sam's body will remain in the living room in an open coffin for three days, allowing everyone to say goodbye to him and see his face one final time before he is buried. Over these next three days, the *ambuyas* and *sekurus* will create a fire in the yard, and make drums full of *sadza* and cow and goat stew to feed the hundreds of relatives and neighbors who will come by to pay their respects. We will sing songs of praise and pray to God for the safe return of Uncle Sam's soul back to the heavenly father.

There is only one problem with this plan: Aunt Jane and I don't want Uncle Sam in the house for three days. What is the point of tormenting ourselves, being forced to see him every day, when he is never going to wake up, when he is never going to come back to us?

Aunt Jane is angry and wants him buried right away. Her face is a mask of fury and her eyes are bright with rage. She wants him gone from the house and from our lives for breaking his promise. When God refused to bless Aunt Jane and Uncle Sam with a child of their own, they made a promise to each other that they would never be separated, that they would live for each other, and therefore have no choice but to die together. Now Uncle Sam is dead, and Aunt Jane is alone. As soon as Amai brought Uncle Sam's coffin into the house with the men from the morgue, Aunt Jane rose from the green couch and went into her bedroom, and a few minutes later, she emerged dressed in black, to say, "I am going to work." A few of the *ambuyas* gasped with horror and then whispered, "Eeee, Germany made her forget our customs." Aunt Jane left, only to return home the following morning.

I also want to run away, but I feel weak and numb from my pain, without focus or purpose or drive. I keep walking to Uncle Sam's coffin and whispering for him to wake up, hoping each time that he will come back to me. Each time I ask and nothing happens, it's like losing him all over again, and I become more and more distressed. Amai finally locks me in the bedroom until it is time to bury Uncle Sam.

After Uncle Sam's funeral, everything changes. I move from Epworth to Harare to live again with Aunt Jane, who insists that she is fine, even though everyone can see that she is falling apart. Now that Uncle Sam is gone, Aunt Jane is afraid to sleep alone or be alone in the dark. She is no longer sleeping well or eating properly, and she vacillates between extreme anger and gutting sadness.

One night, when I go to bed, I have the same dream that I've had many times before. I am standing in the middle of the living room and Uncle Sam is leaning against the front door, still wearing his green hospital robe. "Elizabeth," he says, calling me to him.

I have begun to walk toward him when I hear Aunt Jane's voice behind me. "Elizabeth, don't go."

I turn around and see Aunt Jane sitting on the sofa, wearing her white nightdress and reaching out to me. I change course and walk in her direction until I hear Uncle Sam call to me again. When I look at him, he lowers his gaze and opens the door, flooding the living room with bright white light. He turns around, walks out the door, and disappears into the light.

"Uncle Sam!" I scream, but the door closes before I can follow him. I scream again, jolting myself out of sleep, and bolt upright. I gasp for air, wipe fresh sweat from my forehead, and allow my eyes to adjust to the light in the room. I am now fully awake, sitting in Aunt Jane and Uncle Sam's bedroom, in their bed. Aunt Jane is still sleeping soundly on the pillow next to me.

I settle back into bed, burying my face in Uncle Sam's pillow to smell his familiar musky scent, and wait anxiously for dawn to break. Gogo always said, "However long the night, dawn always breaks . . . bringing with it a new beginning." I think Gogo was wrong, because it feels like Aunt Jane and I are stuck in perpetual darkness, waiting for our sadness to lift, for the cracks in our hearts to mend, for the scars to heal. I shut my eyes, waiting for morning, and allow the darkness to consume me.

Now that Uncle Sam is gone, this is our new normal: our nights are filled with nightmares and painful memories, our days feel too long and seem completely pointless, and even our food has lost its taste. Aunt Jane and I refuse to eat until our clothes are hanging off our bodies. Aunt Jane throws herself into her work and refuses to talk about Uncle Sam, and when I say, "I miss him too, Aunt Jane. I think it will do us good to talk about him," I feel a wall go up between us. I feel hopeless and defeated. I can see that Aunt Jane is in immense pain and feels all alone now that Uncle Sam is gone. Time moves painfully slowly, and suddenly Uncle Sam has been gone for three years. All at once, I wake up from what feels like a coma and remember my dream to become the girl in the blue uniform, wondering if it is forever lost to me, or even worth pursuing.

My dream seems farther away than ever, and it seems too late to pursue it now. I am still responsible for helping Amai search for money for Chio's school fees. Even though Osi and Memo have both completed secondary school, they are unemployed because of a job shortage. They both live with Amai and Baba, who need money for their food. Now that Uncle Sam is gone, I have a new responsibility to take care of Aunt Jane, who is lost in her grief and depression, even as she refuses to acknowledge it. I need to be there for her just like she has always been there for me. How can I chase a dream to uplift others without first uplifting my own family? I am saddened and burdened by this reality, but I also know that supporting my family is the right thing to do.

✛

When the president of Malawi shares his country's success story the next morning to a room packed to the brim with journalists, activists, and UN officials and staff, I am immediately inundated with questions: *How were the communities able to annul 1,455 child marriages? How did they manage to convince the young girls' husbands to end the marriage with no retribution as is often the case? Did the husbands demand a reimbursement of their dowry? If so, who paid it back to them? What about the girls? Where are they living now that their marriages have ended? If their parents couldn't feed and clothe them or send them to school the last time, how are they now able to suddenly be expected to provide for them, in addition to possible new babies from their marriages? If the families accepted the girls back, how are they dealing with the shame and stigma of having a child that is now considered "damaged goods"? Also, what is going to stop the parents from remarrying the girls when they realize that they still can't take care of them due to poverty? How do the girls feel about being back at school, and who is paying for their school fees?* These are all real questions and concerns shared by our partners and the media.

Within a few weeks I send our UN Women team to communities in Malawi to search for answers. Our goal is to learn lessons from Malawi's significant progress over the past year, gaining insight directly from the communities that will help create a template for ending such marriages in other African countries and worldwide, a plan that can be adapted and used to accelerate global progress on the issue.

In the Karonga District in the northern region of Malawi, an eight-hour drive from the country's capital city of Lilongwe, our team is met with a warm welcome from the whole community: religious leaders in nicely pressed cassock robes and tailored suits with ties; traditional leaders in colorful African print attire with animal fur headgear; parents and children, including child-marriage survivors; and a strikingly powerful female chief whose neck and waist are adorned in layers of colorful beads and who is regal in a burnt orange dress with a large front bib and sleeves made of leopard skin and fur. Her fur headgear features long ostrich feathers that stretch out beyond her round face, infectious smile, and eyes as bright as the African sun. This is Senior Chief Kachindamoto, and she is the woman in charge.

Dusk falls as everyone gathers in a wide yard, the sun casting delicate patterns on the ground through the tree branches. Among the child marriage survivors is a fifteen-year-old girl named Frazia, who has a perfectly shaped round head, short black hair, a calm demeanor, and highly alert eyes. She wears a blue skirt and a loose blue shirt over an orange T-shirt.

Frazia is one of the 1,455 girls whose marriages have just been annulled, and she happily shares her story. "One day when I was home, I saw a man and his parents. At the time I was going to school. Then the man came with his parents again. This time they came for me. When I heard I was about to get married, I got very upset, but my parents told me that if I refused, I would have to move out of the house. I knew that I couldn't stay alone. My parents insisted that I should marry the man because they could not afford to support me. And so by force I was married at the age of fourteen. Nothing good came out of getting married." She pauses, pain blanketing her face. "My life changed after my marriage was annulled. I went back to school. To me it was a big opportunity. When I get educated, I think . . . no, I shouldn't say I think, I *know* that I will become an international journalist," she says, and now her face is beaming with joy.

When Frazia finishes telling her story, the community members all chime in with their personal contributions toward ending child marriages within the community. Their stories reveal a sophisticated system, developed by the community for the community, where everyone's input is valued and where everyone is able to make a difference, men and women alike. Working on the front lines are the "Mother Groups," which consist of mothers who volunteer their time to search for cases of child marriage that have gone undetected or undocumented. As one member of a Mother Group shares, "Our job is to assist and patrol the community. Us, we call ourselves secret mothers and we operate in open areas—for instance, at boreholes where everyone collects water. Much of our information is sourced from there. When I learn a child has been married, I borrow a phone and report the case to the Village Head."

On the second line of defense are "Village Heads," also known as community leaders, who oversee all activities at the village level. Once the Mother Groups notify the Village Heads about a child marriage, the Village Heads act as first-line responders, visiting both the girl's family and her husband to negotiate an amicable termination of the marriage. If they are not successful, they bring the matter to a "Group Village Head," who is the person in charge of overseeing all activities at the district level, who returns to the girl's family and husband for serious negotiations. "Yes, we try our best to make sure that parents and husbands understand that our children need to go to school, so we encourage them to end their child marriage. And if they refuse to listen to us, we take them to Senior Chief Kachindamoto," the Group Village Head explains.

And that's when Senior Chief Kachindamoto gets involved, but she doesn't act alone. She has a whole network behind her, which she happily describes to our team. "In the beginning, I didn't know that things were that bad. When I walked around in the community, I noticed that many young girls aged thirteen and fourteen were carrying babies on their backs. When I asked them, they answered that the children were theirs. Then I sat down and thought, *I cannot be a chief that rules over young children living their lives like this*. So I created a committee which includes child protection officers, community police, Village Heads, and Group Village Heads, and together when we hear that a child has been married, we visit the girl's family and we also visit her husband. At this moment, whether one likes it or not, this marriage has ended," Senior Chief Kachindamoto says with fortitude.

As the sun sets and community members share their experiences, it is clear to see that this is truly a collective effort to uplift the community in the spirit of *ubuntu*, just like Apio's village in Uganda. We hear from male chiefs who have begun to educate other male chiefs about the importance of girls' education, all as part of their own personal *HeForShe* commitment, while continuing to work with Chief Kachindamoto and other female chiefs to prevent and end child marriages. We speak to religious leaders who now demand to see birth certificates before agreeing to any marriage. We witness the power of *ubuntu* as husbands who would have otherwise demanded their dowry back accept the annulment of their marriages with no retribution toward the girls and their families. Families welcome their girls back home, supporting them and their babies with feeding, clothing, and schooling. Members of the Mother Groups help raise the girls' babies while they are in school, providing essential child-care free of cost. We hear about development partners and the United Nations itself treating communities with more dignity by ensuring that the people themselves lead and inform change; partners provide support when it is needed and asked for, including a provision for the girls' school fees. "Our children are now going back to school and we are happy about that, because the future of our children and our nation depends on education," the chief continues. "When you educate a girl, you educate a nation."

And just like that, so many girls' lives are changed for the better. That's what happens when everyone comes together in the spirit of *ubuntu*: the burden is shared; the load is lessened; the investment is total. Members of the community make a firm commitment to stand behind the initiative regardless of the challenges they may face. And by the end of 2018, the results are outstanding, with more than twenty thousand child marriages annulled across Malawi. The community's incredible efforts inspire us to publish the story of Malawi's historic anti–child marriage law in an official United Nations publication for distribution in 196 countries around the world. This example of communities rising up to create a world that is safer and happier and healthier for young girls—this story *out of Africa*—sets an example for other governments around the world.

Once again, I feel immense pride to know that *ubuntu*, when fully embraced, elevates everyone, not only in Iceland, where unequal pay has now been outlawed, but also here in Malawi, where child marriage is no longer legal. Similar to Iceland, these changes were only possible because of the efforts of entire communities coming together to create real and lasting change. Now girls in Malawi have regained their potential; they are holding hands and laughing as they run to school; they are dreaming about the future, offering advice and support to other young girls, and believing in their worth and their options. This is *ubuntu*, a recognition that when we uplift each other, everyone wins.

If you think you are too small to make a difference,
try sleeping in a room with a mosquito.

☾☽

—African proverb

16

I fumble in the dark, moving toward a light that flickers inside a small building with dusty, steel-barred windows. My feet sink in and out of the sandy ground and dust covers my shins. The chirping of crickets in the nearby shrubs fills the night with joyous sound, brightening what would otherwise feel like an ominous darkness. The air is warm and thick and clings to my skin like a loving, invisible hug. I look up to the heavens, at the twinkling stars, take a deep breath, and chuckle gleefully as the familiar earthy scent fills my lungs. *I am back on the African continent.*

A dimly lit sign hangs on the wooden door of the building; it reads *HeForShe Tavern*. It's 2018, four years since the launch of *HeForShe*. I am as curious as I am apprehensive. I know that I shouldn't have come here. My work, in fact, forbids me to be here, but I have traveled too far to go back now: from New York City to Johannesburg, South Africa, followed by a two-hour drive to Klerksdorp, a city located in the North West Province of the country. I cannot just walk away. I must go inside and see for myself what is actually happening in this place.

I gently push the door open and enter the room, coming face-to-face with a group of thirty or so casually dressed women and men of varying ages. The room is full; almost every seat is taken. I quickly introduce myself, find one of the last remaining seats next to my local colleague, and take my place in the open circle of men and women facing one another.

I am unfamiliar with the Klerksdorp community and have never been to a *HeForShe* tavern before. In fact, I learned of their existence only recently, and they are somewhat controversial. The community did not seek permission from the United Nations to establish the tavern which bears the *HeForShe* name. In any case, such a request would have been denied on the basis of a UN policy that forbids association with individuals or organizations involved in the alcohol business. This is due in part to the fact that excessive drinking has often been closely linked with acts of gender-based violence and domestic abuse, not to mention its negative effects on overall health and wellness.

I look around the room, notice open beer bottles beneath the chairs, and feel my nerves twitch with anxiety before promptly reminding myself not to worry about UN protocol. Right now, I need to be focused on what is happening inside this tavern. I need to remember the bigger purpose behind this gathering and cannot forget the devastating story that brought the *HeForShe* taverns to our attention.

One year ago, a young girl from the Klerksdorp community was abducted, brutally gang-raped, and then burned to death. This was a heartbreaking story, but sadly not unique. One in three women in South Africa will experience some form of violence during their lifetime, and tragic stories of young girls being raped and murdered often go unreported. But this time something incredible happened. A group of self-proclaimed *HeForShe* men from *HeForShe* taverns rallied alongside the women in Klerksdorp. The community worked together to identify the main perpetrator, reported him to the police, and got the rapist placed behind bars. Then they helped raise money to cover legal costs for the girl's family, and for months they picketed outside the courthouse demanding justice for the victim's family.

When I heard the story from my colleagues in South Africa, I felt encouraged by the community's actions, but also saddened by the girl's death. I recalled many more stories of suffering that remained largely unknown. During my first months working with Phumzile, we visited Safe Horizon—one of the largest women's shelters in the United States—

to advocate for more support and essential services for survivors. We stood on a street corner shivering in the bitter New York City winter cold, waiting to be escorted to an undisclosed location to meet the survivors. For the safety of the women, the organization wouldn't disclose the exact address to us, as often the abusers track down the survivors to cause more harm.

"I needed a place where somebody would listen to me and where I could just cry," one of the survivors, Lisa, who had fled a violent relationship with her two children, told us. "It is not an easy step to leave, but I didn't want my kids to ever think that violence should be part of a relationship," she said, recalling her trauma, and the incredible support she and her children had subsequently received from the shelter. Two months after she left her partner, Lisa was able to finish her doctorate to become a reverend.

As Lisa and the other women recounted their painful experiences with raw emotion, I felt my heart ache with sadness: "I am exhausted, but I am afraid to sleep. Every time I close my eyes, I see him charging toward me with clenched fists"; "I feel as though my life is over. I had a job I loved and now I am homeless and unemployed as I can't leave the shelter for fear that he will find me. Many times, I think of ending my life, but then I think about my kids and know that I have to live for them"; "I had to cut all ties with my family so that even they don't know where I am. I am afraid that he will threaten them for my address and find me and take away my children"; "I am ashamed to face my friends and colleagues. My partner and I were supposed to be this role-model couple for what a successful marriage should be. I had a big job, I was a powerful woman, and now I fear that everyone will judge me."

As Phumzile and I said our goodbyes and stepped back into the freezing cold, I knew that these stories would leave an indelible imprint on my mind. It felt entirely unjust that these strong and hardworking women now lived in perpetual fear, hiding away from society and putting their lives on hold. Sadly, these singular stories formed pieces of a much large mosaic of equally devastating violations. In shelters, homes, and hospitals the world over, in Asia, Africa, Europe, and the Americas, I met more survivors and their children as part of my work with UN Women. In Helsinki, Finland, Hanna, a survivor of domestic violence, shared her story. "They say that our country is one of the leading countries in the world when it comes to gender equality, but look at me, I have two broken ribs and four embarrassing stitches across my chin. How is this fair?" Hanna was right. It wasn't fair, and neither was it fair for Neza, another domestic violence survivor, in Rwanda's capital city, Kigali, whose husband dislocated her jaw far too many times; or for the one in three women in every single country *in the world* who suffer from physical and emotional violence.

I found the opportunity to bring in men as part of the solution in addressing gender-based violence, with the launch of the *HeForShe* pilot initiative three years ago, which engaged the president of Rwanda and the president of Finland as two of the Champions committed to combating gender-based violence in their respective countries. I had come to understand that gender-based violence is a terrible loss to women, but also a loss for families and societies. When women are hurt, societies hurt. And the impact to the children involved often perpetuates this cycle of abuse. Gender-based violence is as much a men's issue as it is a women's issue; the impact of such violence is not just detrimental to women, but to all of us. Thus, given the rallying call of *HeForShe* to men, we decided to make gender-based violence core to the movement, and a tangible issue that men could play a role in combating. Now, in 2018, we are witnessing two world leaders creating concrete change.

Rwanda put in place substantive, targeted care for survivors of domestic violence, establishing a network of centers across the country called the Isange One Stop Centres (IOSC). At these forty-four facilities, victims and survivors receive appropriate and comprehensive medical, psychosocial, and legal services, all free of charge.

In Finland, the government is addressing the issue at its source, rolling out a course on gender-based violence and how to manage aggression across the entire Finnish army—which is mandatory for all Finnish men. As a result, incidents of domestic violence are on the decline as men get better at managing aggression and take responsibility for their actions.

In other countries, I have also encountered countless men whose perception of male responsibility in ending gender-based violence is starting to change. Men like Paul, from a rural community in Uganda; a father of four daughters, two of his girls had been raped while going to fetch water from the river in the forest. Pain was seared into his face as he told me this story. Often after an incident of violence, or in the face of consistent violence, women and girls are given the advice to avoid going out when it is dark. But instead, this father explained, "Us, we decide to create a team of *HeForShe* bodyguards. I invited other men and boys in our community to join me so we could go to the river with the women and girls to fetch water together. Now we carry more buckets and share the load. Now our wives and daughters don't have to go back to the river too often or feel afraid to go because now we all walk together," Paul explained. I felt myself choke up with emotion at this visible action of solidarity.

And now, thanks in part to the *HeForShe* movement, men in Klerksdorp have stood up against rape and gender-based violence, taking concrete steps to ensure that the perpetrator of that terrible crime was brought to justice. As I look around the tavern, watching women and men sip their beers, my mind floods with questions: *What exactly is a* HeForShe *Tavern? What further impact are they creating here?*

"Good evening, my dear friends," says a short, smiling man dressed in a green-and-black striped sweater, blue jeans, and a white *HeForShe* ball cap. "Tonight, me, I am your facilitator. Tonight, as always, we will talk about domestic violence and respect." He continues, "But first we start with the reminder of our rules," and he begins reading out loud from the list written on the poster on the wall. I lean in closer, following along, feeling pleasantly surprised and impressed—even astounded—by the words. This isn't a poster I have seen before or ever expected to see. The rules are certainly not verified or approved by the United Nations, and this is what is so notable: these are rules made by the community for the community, rules that surpass anything that I could have hoped for when we launched the initiative four years ago.

I Am a *HeForShe* Tavern:

- *NO selling alcohol to underage and pregnant women*
- *NO harassment of women in the Tavern*
- *NO form of violence will be tolerated in the Tavern*
- *Weekly community dialogues on gender-based violence will take place in the Tavern*
- *Organize at least five community actions per year as part of awareness raising against women and girls abuse*
- *Organize at least three health testing sessions in a year for clients*

Over the next three hours I watch men and women of all ages share perspectives as they try to find common ground on difficult, complex, and often deep-rooted issues; debate ways to address rape and other gender-based violence, which some time ago felt like intractable or even impossible problems; build consensus on how to put an end to domestic abuse; and find creative solutions to foster respect and encourage positive masculinity.

I keep listening and asking questions, determined to learn more: "What are you most proud of?" "What challenges did you initially face in setting up *HeForShe* taverns?" "How have you been successful in getting tavern owners engaged in the initiative?" "What can other communities in South Africa and other countries learn from your experience in Klerksdorp?" "What support, if any, do you need to accelerate the positive impact of your work?"

As community members explain, I begin to understand. After witnessing high levels of domestic violence in the community, a few men got together and decided to change things.

"When we heard about *HeForShe* on the radio a year ago, talking about what it means to be good husbands and fathers, us, we decided that this one is for us. We decided to become *HeForShe*," the smiling tavern facilitator wearing the green-and-black striped sweater says. "We looked at ourselves as men and said, us, we are the problem here. If it is us who are beating up our wives and children, then it is us who need to stop their suffering." He pauses, and then continues. "So we said, okay, how can we do this, not just for ourselves but also for all the men in our community? We had to think of a clever-clever plan to engage the other men in a way that was easy for them. At first, we thought of organizing a community gathering, so we could talk to them about stopping domestic violence, but then we worried they would not show up. So we came up with a new plan and decided to go to the place where the men were already socializing. We decided to go to taverns and speak to them," he says, pleased with their plan.

"Yes, us, we liked the tavern plan very much, because taverns were creating a lot of problems for our community. Men would spend all day drinking and then go back home drunk and beat up their wives and children. Us, we decided to turn taverns into places where both women and men can come together and find ways to end domestic violence in our community," a tall, older gentleman explains.

"So, we started visiting tavern by tavern, telling tavern owners about our *HeForShe* plans, asking them to join us in turning their taverns into *HeForShe* taverns. When they agreed, we all came together as a community and created our own *HeForShe* tavern rules, the ones you see on this poster," the facilitator chimes in, pointing to the poster on the wall.

"And if a tavern owner does not respect the rules, then they must stop being a *HeForShe* tavern. And no one wants to stop because less people will visit their tavern. So being a *HeForShe* tavern is also good for tavern owners," another man chimes in, chuckling softly.

One of the women joins the conversation. "Aaaa, now, us we thank God for the *HeForShe* taverns. Now we can discuss issues that affect us women with our husbands without fear, knowing that they will listen to us. Now less men are beating up their wives, and when they do, we confront them as a community and tell them to stop. There is more peace in our community, and we are proud of what we did for ourselves," she says with the same pride communities in Malawi showed as they joined together—women and men—to end child marriage. A solution by the community, for the community—and it worked.

"Us, we started with just one *HeForShe* tavern in the beginning, but now, aaaa, we are more than one hundred forty-four taverns here in Klerksdorp, reaching four thousand men every week. But we are just getting started, we won't stop until all the men in our country become *HeForShe*," the facilitator explains with passion and conviction in his voice. This is what I always envisioned could be possible, and here is solid proof that my belief was not unfounded. The girl in the blue uniform had told me "as Africans we must uplift each other," and this is the embodiment of her words in action, the words that had inspired my dream and fueled my fierce determination to pursue it, even when the odds seemed insurmountable.

✛

I am twenty-five years old, sitting in the living room and sorting through Uncle Sam's old boxes from his office, trying to organize his papers, which Aunt Jane, in her grief, refuses to touch. In one box I find Uncle

Sam's old diary, and beneath it a glossy plastic folder. Inside is my "dream essay" from Roosevelt Girls High School—though it was written not so long ago, so much has happened in the interim that it feels like a lifetime.

I am surprised and also moved. I didn't know that Uncle Sam had kept it. I quickly glance over the pages and remember my dream to become the girl in the blue uniform. A dream which I have now given up on so that I can support my family.

Light spills through the windows and falls over the papers spread out on the floor, covered with Uncle Sam's familiar handwriting. I am overwhelmed with emotion, light-headed, as I hear Uncle Sam's words ring in my head: *Promise me something, Elizabeth. Never let your current circumstances limit your potential. Never let anything diminish your dreams.*

What have I done? I have to find a way to pursue my dream again. I cannot just give up. I made a promise to God under the tree in Gogo's field. I made a promise to Uncle Sam that I would do more with my life. And I haven't. Yes, I have helped Amai search for money, and I have supported Aunt Jane in her grief, but at the cost of losing sight of my own dream. I was supposed to be the girl in the blue uniform. I was supposed to uplift not just the lives of my own family, but the lives of others in my entire community, country, and hopefully the African continent. This was my purpose and the only reason why God had saved my life during the drought—of this I was certain.

I clutch the essay, the pages rustling between my trembling hands. I ferociously scan the words and, then and there, renew my promise. "Thank you, Uncle Sam, thank you," I say out loud. "I promise never to give up on my dream. I promise to make you proud." I turn my head up to the heavens and cry.

When I wake up the next morning, I know that I will do anything and everything it takes to chase my dream. So, nothing has gone as planned: things rarely do. But I will no longer let my circumstances limit my potential. I will not let anything diminish my dream. I will leave my country and get myself a Commonwealth visa and go to

London and find a job with the United Nations. If I do not go now, I may never go.

Amai and Aunt Jane are not impressed by my plan when I break the news to them at the clinic. Amai says, "Eeee, Lizzy, London is far-far. How will you get there?" I say I have a plan, which Aunt Jane quickly interrogates: "Sure you can get a visa, but do you think the United Nations is going to give you a job just like that without a degree?" I explain that I will ask the United Nations for the most junior job that doesn't require a degree, then save money and go to university.

Aunt Jane responds, with quick German precision, "That's not a plan, Elizabeth. Take it from someone who has lived abroad, alone, away from family. It can be very lonely and scary. This kind of haphazard planning that you are proposing won't work. If you want to go to London, then fine, you have our full support. But we need to put in place a proper plan. We need to figure out how you will get there, where you will stay, and how you will find a job. Right now, all my savings have gone into the clinics, so we need time to help raise money for your ticket and accommodations in London, in case you are unable to find a job right away." She is right. I need a better plan, especially given that I don't have enough money to buy a plane ticket or pay for rent in London. Besides, I don't know anyone in the UK who can take me in while I look for a job. Still, I decide that I must go now. I will find a way. "I will figure it out, Aunt Jane. Don't you worry about me," I say, and shut down the conversation.

I apply for a standard UK Commonwealth visa that will permit me to live and work in the UK for two years. When I get the visa, I go back to Goromonzi to visit Gogo. I am ashamed that I still haven't saved enough money for my plane ticket, but when I share my plans with Gogo she quickly says, "I can help."

"But Gogo, you, you don't have money," I say, knowing that Gogo will need to keep the little she has in case there is another drought.

"But I have cows and goats, my dear child. What use are our possessions, if not to serve the ones we love?" We are sitting on the stoop in front of the hut, our shins soaking up the afternoon sun. I look around Gogo's yard, then at Gogo, and feel sadness consume me. I am excited about going to London, but I now feel the weight of my decision. I will miss Gogo terribly. I will miss my home in Goromonzi, and all that it has given me.

Gogo senses my sorrow. She takes my hand, places it on my heart, and says, "I will always be with you, right here, inside your heart, my dear child. Never forget that, never forget." Her eyes mist with tears and I feel a lump rise in my throat. I throw my arms around Gogo, snuggle my nose into her neck, and fill my lungs with her earthy scent. As her heart beats against mine, I know that no matter the distance between us, I will always be one with Gogo. My heart will remain right here in Goromonzi, and here in Africa is where I will always belong.

Two months later, Gogo makes an incredible sacrifice: she sells a few of her cows and goats to raise money for me to go to London. Soon after, I'm on the long plane journey from Harare to London to start my new beginning. I'm on my way to chase my dream, to become the girl in the blue uniform and work for the United Nations. *I will not fail.*

✤

Now in Klerksdorp, almost two decades later, I am grateful and proud that I didn't give up on my dream, even when life got in the way, as it always will. And now I am witnessing another powerful reaffirmation. As the night wears on and the laughter from the now very merry community members grows louder and more exuberant, I lean back in my chair and try to take it all in. Indeed, there is a palpable peace in this gathering; even as people debate and challenge one another, they also sing and laugh and smile and converse. Perhaps many of them have known each other all their lives; perhaps some of them are new friends, but they are all committed to uplifting one another. Here, in front of my eyes, is real dialogue and exchange about the issues that impact so many women and girls globally, and in particular in this part of the African continent. Here is *ubuntu* in beautiful, complicated, colorful, joyous, and hardworking action. I am so buoyed by hope that I feel as if I might float out of the room. What I am seeing is a new Africa, but one founded on our most fundamental and ancient philosophy.

I am so happy that I made the long journey from New York to witness such a milestone moment in the history of this movement, as I witness my own people, my own community, redefine what a tavern space can provide; not just a place to drink, but a place to be seen and heard; a place to change the lives of more than four thousand women and many more, whose husbands have begun to evaluate their own behaviors, thriving to be the best possible *HeForShe* versions of themselves. I quickly become choked up with emotion.

I am grateful to the people of Klerksdorp for showing me once again what communities are capable of achieving for themselves: real change from within. After all the hard work and self-doubt and setbacks and sadness; after the long days and even longer nights, worried that I had lost my way; after all the doubts and triumphs and tears and laughter; after all the people I have met and their stories of struggle and pain and joy that I hold within my mind and heart, here before me is an example of all that I had hoped and wished and worked for; here is all that I have longed to do since my dream of becoming the girl in the blue uniform became my life's purpose. I am grateful for every step of the journey, every opportunity, every person, every story, every moment.

It takes a village to raise a child.

⊗

—African proverb

17

My pulse quickens the moment I answer the phone in my office at the United Nations. I pray that I will have sufficient time to tell the whole story, in all of its nuance and texture and complexity. My mind spins with thoughts and ideas, barely keeping pace with my racing heart, when I hear a serious voice greet me on the other end of the line.

Alexandra, a journalist at the *New York Times*, is writing an article about gender equality that examines the dismal representation of women at the World Economic Forum, an annual event that convenes the world's most powerful leaders in Davos, Switzerland, to discuss global issues. Infamously dubbed the "Boys Club," the forum has experienced intense scrutiny and criticism for failing to increase the number of female delegates. Since I am one of only a few women attending in a few weeks, Alexandra is curious to learn about the groundbreaking work of the *HeForShe* movement and how it reflects my views and ideas about gender equality.

"First, tell me about you!" she says, without missing a beat.

As I clear my throat to speak, I realize how complicated my answer must be, and how rich and triumphant and harrowing and remarkable the path has been. I have experienced and witnessed so much to arrive at this place in my life: from my humble upbringing in a small village in Zimbabwe, where I was a small girl with big dreams, to my unlikely and often turbulent path to the United Nations. Along this journey that is my story, I have been uplifted and championed by the support of my loving family, mentors, and communities: without their belief in me and the great personal sacrifices they made to enable me to pursue my dream, I would not be here. Without their stories, my singular story would not exist. Although some of these beloved people are no longer living, if I close my eyes, I can still hear their voices of encouragement, challenge, and love.

I think of my Gogo, with her indomitable spirit and her gifts of wisdom, which form the core of who I am; I remember Amai's resilience and how she bore the heartbreak of sending me away—not to abandon me, but to give me a chance for a better life. I think of Baba's incredible sacrifices and of my siblings' unconditional love. I remember Aunt Jane's mentorship, which instilled in me the desire to always do more and showed me what it takes to be of service to others; I think of Uncle Sam's unwavering belief in me, and his wholehearted support each step of the way, even when the path sometimes became bumpy or unclear.

In all of these communities, in Goromonzi and Epworth and Harare, I was raised to live in keeping with the central, definitive African value and philosophy of *ubuntu*: that when we uplift others, we are ourselves uplifted. This has guided and sustained me, literally and figuratively. I have such a powerful mosaic of memory to call upon that shows *ubuntu* in action: in Goromonzi, *ambuyas* fed me and Gogo, even if they didn't have food to spare; *ambuyas* and *sekurus* taught me the valuable lessons of kindness and forgiveness; *sisis* and *hanzwadzis* lightened my load as a child carrying water, or tying up goats, or tending crops; and the girl in the blue uniform, an African *sisi* from a different village, working for the United Nations, saved my life.

So how shall I answer Alexandra's question? What shall I tell her about myself?

My story, their stories, and all of our stories stitched together are part of a colorful and beautifully woven African tapestry. I am humbled to know, unequivocally, that I am living proof of the power of *ubuntu*—that "*I am* because *we are*." I think of all the powerful Africans I know and have known and will come to know, and how proud I am to be *Mwana Wevhu*, a child of the African soil. I know that without each and every one of these people and so many others along the way, I would not be the person I am today.

What shall I tell Alexandra about myself?

I take a deep breath, and say, "I will tell you everything."

I am a girl from Africa. This is my story.

APPENDIX I

My story is a testament that we all have the ability to uplift one another and create positive change in our communities, no matter our current circumstances. Creating change starts with informing ourselves about the issues, from those impacting our local communities, to the global challenges affecting communities around the world. Below are some of the issues covered in this book that you might consider championing.

HUNGER

Every day, too many families across the globe struggle to feed their children a nutritious meal. In a world where we produce enough food to feed everyone, 821 million people—one in nine—still go to bed on an empty stomach each night. Even more—one in three—suffer from some form of malnutrition. Eradicating hunger and malnutrition, as well as food insecurity, is one of the great challenges of our time. Not only do the consequences of not enough—or the wrong—food cause suffering and poor health, they also slow progress in many other areas of development, like education and employment.

Take Action at: World Food Programme (WFP); wfp.org

POVERTY

Poverty entails the lack of income and productive resources to ensure sustainable livelihoods. While global poverty rates have been cut by more than half since 2000, one in ten people in developing regions still live on less than US$1.90 a day—the internationally agreed poverty line—and millions of others live on only slightly more than this daily amount. Significant progress has been made in many countries within Eastern and Southeastern Asia, but up to 42 percent of the population in Sub-Saharan Africa continues to live below the poverty line.

Take Action at: ONE.org

EDUCATION

Education is an empowering right and one of the most powerful tools by which economically and socially marginalized children and adults can uplift themselves out of poverty and participate fully in society. Yet millions of children and adults remain deprived of educational opportunities, and despite progress, more girls than boys still remain out of school—16 million girls will never set foot in a classroom (UNESCO Institute for Statistics)—and women account for two-thirds of the 750 million adults without basic literacy skills.

Take Action at: United Nations Educational, Scientific, and Cultural Organization; UNESCO.org

HIV/AIDS

Since the start of the epidemic in 1981, around 75 million people have become infected with HIV and around 32 million people have died of AIDS-related illnesses. In 2018, there were 37.9 million people living with HIV. Found in the bodily fluids of a person who has been infected—blood, semen, vaginal fluids, and breast milk—HIV can be transmitted through unprotected sexual contact. It is also spread among people who inject drugs with nonsterile needles, as well as through unscreened blood products. It can spread from mother to child during pregnancy, childbirth, or breast-feeding when the mother is HIV-positive.

Take Action at: UNAIDS.org

RIVER BLINDNESS

Onchocerciasis—or "river blindness"—is a parasitic disease caused by the filarial worm *Onchocerca volvulus* and is transmitted by repeated bites of infected blackflies (*Simulium*). These blackflies breed along fast-flowing rivers and streams, close to remote villages located near fertile land, where people rely on agriculture for their survival. In the human body, the adult worms produce embryonic larvae (microfilariae) that migrate to the skin and eyes and can lead to visual impairment and permanent blindness. River blindness occurs mainly in tropical areas, with more than 99 percent of infected people living in thirty-one countries in Sub-Saharan Africa.

Take Action at: World Health Organization (WHO); who.int

HEALTHCARE

Ensuring that all people can access the health services they need—without facing financial hardship—is key to improving the well-being of a country's population. However, currently at least half of the world's people cannot obtain essential health services, and eight hundred million people spend at least 10 percent of their household budget on health expenses for themselves, a sick child, or other family member. For almost one hundred million people, these out-of-pocket health expenses are high enough to push them into extreme poverty, forcing them to survive on just $1.90 or less a day (UN 2017 data).

Take Action at: World Health Organization (WHO); who.int

MATERNAL MORTALITY

According to the most recent United Nations data (2019), about one woman in the world dies every two minutes from preventable causes related to pregnancy and childbirth. A majority of them die from severe bleeding, sepsis, eclampsia, obstructed labor, and the consequences of unsafe abortions—all causes for which there are highly effective interventions. For every woman who dies, an estimated twenty or thirty encounter injuries, infections, or disabilities. Most of these deaths and injuries are entirely preventable. And the tragedy does not stop there: when mothers die, their families are much more vulnerable, and their infants are more likely to die before reaching their second birthday.

Take Action at: United Nations Population Fund; UNFPA.org

CHILD MORTALITY

Remarkable progress has been made in child survival over the past few decades, meaning that millions of children have better survival chances than in the early nineties. Despite significant progress, however, in 2018 an estimated 5.3 million children under age five died due to preventable or treatable causes such as complications during birth, pneumonia, diarrhea, neonatal sepsis, and malaria (UNICEF 2018 data). Half of all deaths took place in Sub-Saharan Africa, and another 30 percent in Southern Asia. In Sub-Saharan Africa, 1 in 13 children died before their fifth birthday. In high-income countries, that number was 1 in 185.

Take Action at: United Nations Children's Fund; UNICEF.org

GENDER EQUALITY

Gender equality is not only a fundamental human right, but a necessary foundation for a peaceful, prosperous, and sustainable world. While there has been progress over the last decades—more girls are going to school; fewer girls are forced into early marriage; more women are serving in parliament and positions of leadership—many challenges remain: discriminatory laws and social norms remain pervasive, and women continue to be underrepresented at all levels of society—socially, economically, and politically.

Take Action at: UNWomen.org

CHILD MARRIAGE

Child marriage is a human rights violation. Despite laws against it, the practice remains widespread: globally, one in every five girls is married before reaching age eighteen. In the least developed countries, that number doubles—40 percent of girls are married before age eighteen, and 12 percent of girls are married before age fifteen. Child marriage threatens girls' lives and health, and limits their future prospects. Girls pressed into child marriage often become pregnant while still adolescents, increasing the risk of complications in pregnancy or childbirth. These complications are the leading cause of death worldwide among older adolescent girls.

Take Action at: GirlsNotBrides.org

GENDER-BASED VIOLENCE

Violence against women and girls is one of the most prevalent human rights violations in the world. It knows no social, economic, or national boundaries, occurring in every region, country, and culture and cutting across income, class, race, and ethnicity. Worldwide, an estimated one in three women will experience physical or sexual abuse in their lifetime. Gender-based violence takes many forms and may be physical, sexual, psychological, and economic, and it undermines the health, dignity, security, and autonomy of its victims— yet it remains shrouded in a culture of silence.

Take Action at: SpotlightInitiative.org

* All content and data about the issues above is cited from the United Nations.

APPENDIX II

To celebrate the use of symbols, which are an important aspect of African culture and its languages, the book incorporates two Adinkra symbols from Ghana. African symbols are used extensively in fabrics, pottery, and architectural features to convey concepts or aphorisms.

✤

Nyame Nwu Na Mawu
(If God dies, so shall I)

This symbol, used as a visual cue in the book to move between the adult and young narratives, represents the immortality of the human soul. Its meaning is interpreted as "as God never dies, so my soul never dies."

◍

Nyame Biribi Wo Soro
(God is in the heavens)

This symbol, used to anchor the African proverbs at the opening of each chapter, represents hope.

ACKNOWLEDGMENTS

To my fellow Africans, thank you for constantly reminding me what it means to be part of *ubuntu*. I am immensely proud to truly know that "I am because we are." It is in this context that I titled this book *I Am a Girl from Africa*, as a love letter to our beloved continent. The title celebrates the spirit of Pan-Africanism and affirms the values that my Gogo taught me about the importance of African unity and solidarity. As "*a* girl from Africa" I am one of many, and my experiences do not reflect or represent the lived experiences of the millions of other girls from the fifty-five culturally vibrant and diverse countries that make up our beautiful African continent.

To the love of my life, my husband, Jay, thank you for your endless love and for being my rock and partner. It is truly a blessing to spend my life with you and to walk this journey together.

To my irreplaceable manager, Suzan Bymel, knowing you is one of the greatest gifts of my life. Thank you for your love and guidance and for inspiring me to dream bigger. You were the first to make me believe that this book was even possible.

Thank you to my formidable agent, Nancy Josephson, a fearless champion for diversity and inclusion. What a privilege it is to work with you, and to be a witness to the trail you blaze for women like me.

Erin Malone, you are not only a brilliant book agent, but an awesome human being. Thank you for your unrivaled energy and enthusiasm in shepherding this project from its inception.

ACKNOWLEDGMENTS

There is no way this book would be what it is without the amazing Emily Rapp Black. E, you rule, and I am eternally grateful for your passion and invaluable guidance in making this book possible.

My Gogo always used to tell me, time and time again, "You, you ask too many questions for a child." Now, as an adult, I still ask too many questions. To my incredible editor, Sally Howe, who is likely the most patient person in the world, thank you for your unflappable attitude as you've steered me patiently through this process, and of course for your faith in me.

And then there is my incomparable publisher, Nan Graham. Dearest Nan, there simply aren't words enough to fully express my gratitude. I hope you know that the magnitude of this *mukana* will never be lost on me. Telling my story in a way that challenges traditional misperceptions of my beloved African continent and its people was always going to be an ambitious undertaking. I feel truly humbled for your very hands-on approach, pushing and challenging me to tell the story in its most compelling form. I am proud of what we have been able to accomplish and hope that the message of *ubuntu* in this book will inspire and motivate all of us to show compassion to each other and see ourselves as part of a collective human community. I am forever indebted to you and the entire team at Scribner.

To my role model and mentor, Phumzile Mlambo-Ngcuka, they say "you can't be it unless you see it." I see you, and working with you and colleagues at UN Women to advance gender equality around the world is without a doubt one of the most meaningful things I will ever do with my life. Thank you for the opportunity to serve and for your endless love and support.

To my brilliant advisors, thank you for your wisdom and unwavering support: Amina J. Mohammed, Pat Mitchell, Gail Heimann, Bob Moritz, Isabelle Magyar, Cuong Do, Tina Brown, John West, Vanessa Bouquillion-Coqueret, Ronda Carnegie, Musimbi Kanyoro, David Honigmann, Susanna Schrobsdorff, and Margaret Nienaber.

I am beyond grateful to all of my former and current colleagues without whose support none of the projects would have achieved the same impact. A special thank-you to the small and mighty *HeForShe* team: Lauren, Sarah, Dinal, Nick, Aamina, Charlotte, Raymond, Marine, Kerry, and Edward.

My story, like so many others, is only what it is because of the unconditional love and support of my family. You each are a continuous reminder of what matters most in this world. I love you all dearly. Betty, Libby, and Ron, I bask in the glory of your love—thank you for giving me a second home and for showing me what it means to be truly loved.

And to my outstanding friends, thank you for always being there for me: Dario, Belinda, Edgar, Barbara, Brendan, Ritu, Alex, Anna, Alison, Annie, Adam, James, Miriam, Ru, Craig, Nnenna, Lillian, Stephanie, Kelly, Tessy, Luisella, Loveness, Charity.

To all of the communities around the world who opened up their doors and hearts to me, thank you for sharing your stories, joy, and sorrow with me. Your words continue to inspire me to search for more ways to create greater positive impact in this world.

Finally, I wouldn't be here without the love of God. Thank you, Lord, for the air that I breathe and for giving meaningful purpose to my life.

ABOUT THE AUTHOR

Elizabeth Nyamayaro is an award-winning humanitarian and former United Nations senior advisor on gender equality. Born in Zimbabwe, Elizabeth has worked at the forefront of global development for over two decades, improving the lives of underserved populations, and has held leadership roles at the World Bank, the World Health Organization, UNAIDS, and UN Women. Elizabeth is a political scientist by training and holds a master's degree in politics from the London School of Economics and Political Science. *I Am a Girl from Africa* is her first book.

ElizabethNyamayaro.com
Twitter: @e_nyamayaro
Instagram: @enyamayaro